John Smith
SPELLING BOOK

O

CASSELL

Cassell
Wellington House
125 Strand
London WC2R 0BB

© Cassell plc 1961, 1986, 1998

ISBN 0-304-70374-5

Original edition first published 1961
Revised 1986
This new edition first published 1998

Typeset by Digital Imaging,
          Formby, L37 7AU

Printed and bound in Great Britain by
The Guernsey Press Co. Ltd., Guernsey, Channel Isles

Books in this series:

John Smith Spelling Books series:

Book 0	0-304-70374-5
Book 1	0-304-70375-3
Book 2	0-304-70376-1
Book 3	0-304-70377-X
Book 4	0-304-70378-8
Book 5	0-304-70379-6
Book 6	0-304-70380-X
Book 7	0-304-70381-8
Book 8	0-304-70382-6

The Spelling Quiz Books series:

Book 1	0-304-30050-0
Book 2	0-304-30051-9
Book 3	0-304-30052-7

Spelling Quiz Books 1/2/3
Bumper edition:
          0-304-32911-8

For Spellers

1. Number your page 1 to 12.
2. Read the clue; choose the word from the 'frame' which best fits the clue, and write it against the proper number.
3. Where two 'frame' words appear to fit the same clue, careful thought will show you that one of them is better than the other.
4. Only correctly spelt answers will be counted.

For Teachers and Parents

1. These books are designed to give children practice in spelling once or twice a day – when they come in from play, for instance.
2. Using this book only once a day, a child will go through it five times and write more than 2000 spellings in 'families' in the course of a school year.
3. Each page is a challenge to a child, as a crossword puzzle is to an adult, and should be presented in that light.
4. Correct spelling is all-important. The accurate writing of the answers is the main reason for doing the page; the solving of the clues is of secondary importance.

   An answer which is incorrectly spelt should be marked wrong.
5. If this book is used in the few minutes after play, scarcely any teaching time is taken up, and lessons begin quickly, quietly and purposefully.

Contents

a

bat

tap

hat

bag

rat

gas

e

ten

peg

hen

leg

bed

pen

1. It has four legs and a long tail

2. It is used for hitting a ball

3. You may use this for cooking

4. We turn this to get water

5. This is worn on the head

6. We put things in a —

7. A bird

8. We sleep in a —

9. 10

10. To hang your coat on

11. We use this to write with

12. A part of the body

1

1. A part of the mouth

2. This has a sharp point

3. Some foods come in a —

4. Chairs are used to — on

5. A piece

6. We — a nail with a hammer

i

pin

hit

sit

tin

lip

bit

7. A baby's bed

8. A pet

9. Mist

10. The girl tried to — on one leg

11. A piece of wood

12. Mandy had icing on the — of her cake

o

hop

cot

log

top

dog

fog

1. We can pour milk from this

2. We eat this at teatime

3. It shines in the sky

4. A small wooden shed

5. A mat for the floor

6. If you — your finger it bleeds

7. We wipe our feet on this

8. A pet

9. The children — out to play

10. This has wheels

11. A man

12. He was a very — man

U

sun

hut

rug

bun

jug

cut

a

cat

Dad

fat

mat

ran

van

3

e

beg
net
bell
wet
pet
red

1. A colour

2. It makes a ringing sound

3. Not dry

4. A rabbit makes a lovely —

5. Fish are caught in this

6. Some dogs can — for titbits

i

bin
sip
fit
chin
win
pip

7. A seed inside an apple

8. Rubbish is put into a —

9. A part of the face

10. People go jogging to keep —

11. A very small drink

12. If we come first we shall — the race

4

1. Not cold

2. A small mark like a full stop

3. We eat a — of fruit

4. A fish

5. Move the head up and down

6. A bar of wood or metal

7. It carries people

8. For drinking out of

9. Pull

10. Part of a plant

11. Ryan took a spade and — the garden

12. To move quickly

O

lot

rod

hot

dot

cod

nod

U

bud

dug

cup

bus

tug

run

a

1. Dad is a —

2. Not good

3. Ali — down on a chair

4. Not happy

5. Crazy

6. James opened a new jar of —

bad

man

jam

sad

sat

mad

e

7. A lion lives in this

8. A spider lives in this

9. A fast plane

10. Listen and I will — you a story

11. I am trying to save a — of football cards

12. Mum told me to — ready for school

web

set

den

get

jet

tell

i

1. I began to — with my spade

2. Large

3. A little mountain

4. A baby wears one

5. 6

6. A loud noise

i
six
bib
din
dig
big
hill

o

7. To steal

8. We grow a plant in this

9. The — wore smart red trousers

10. To throw

11. Used for cleaning the floor

12. Daniel did — go to the party

o
mop
not
pot
rob
doll
toss

1. We can drink out of this

2. Throw your arms around a person

3. It grows on a tree

4. A farm animal

5. We do this when we polish some-thing

6. A baby fox

7. Gemma is always happy and full of —

8. Not wet

9. I do not know — you are sad

10. We — to write neatly

11. We must — the eggs first

12. Tears came into his eyes and he began to —

U

fun

bull

mug

nut

hug

rub

cub

y

why

try

cry

dry

fry

1. Ian can run very —

2. A bird lays its eggs in a —

3. A part of the hand

4. Sit down and have a —

5. It was hot so he took off his —

6. She said she had — her dinner money

7. We have to — rooms to keep them clean

fist

lost

fast

dust

rest

vest

nest

8. Does not bend easily

9. It holds up the flower

10. We can stand on this

11. Quiet and peaceful

12. Cars must — when traffic lights are on red

stop

step

stiff

stem

still

er

her

jerk

fern

term

1. Holidays come at the end of —

2. A plant

3. Holly ate — dinner

4. Pull sharply

or

horn

born

worn

corn

short

torn

ports

storm

5. A nail had — his trousers

6. Rain and strong winds make a —

7. It grows in the farmer's fields

8. She was — in 1978

9. Ships sail out of these

10. The car sounded its —

11. Susan has — this dress for a long time

12. It's only a — walk to school

10

ar

1. For putting jam in

2. Do not play too — from the house

3. It twinkles in the sky

4. It has four wheels

5. A part of the body

6. A metal rod

___

car

arm

bar

far

jar

star

___

7. A person who paints pictures

8. It was a very — night

9. Begin

10. Pigs and cows are found on a —

11. A piece

12. Something we eat

part

tart

start

dark

farm

artist

11

1. A sparrow is a —

   stir

2. Not clean

   shirt

3. When we make a cake we — it

   bird

4. The — wore a pretty dress

   dirty

5. Jason came — in the race

   girl

6. He put on a clean —

   first

ur

7. Lisa had — in her hair

   burn

8. Move round

   hurt

9. To set fire to something

   hurl

10. Michael fell and — his knee

    curls

11. A large bird

    turn

12. A word meaning to throw

    turkey

sh

1. We buy sweets from the —

2. For putting things on

3. Worn on the feet

4. It sails across the sea

5. A snail has one on its back

6. A pin has a — point

shell

shoes

ship

shop

shelf

sharp

---

7. Money

8. Hurry

9. In stories a fairy can grant you a —

10. This lives in water

11. To go red in the face

12. Eye—

lash

fish

cash

wish

blush

rush

13

ch

1. A part of the face

2. A building

3. A friendly talk

4. Part of the body

5. You — wood with an axe

6. Often eaten with fish

---

7. We use it to see in the dark

8. Soldiers — from place to place

9. We play on this at the seaside

10. Having lots of money

11. Part of a building

12. Adam did not know — way to go

chat

chop

chin

chips

chest

church

---

rich

beach

which

march

torch

porch

14

ee

1. An animal with big horns

2. A strong metal

3. A car went past at high —

4. The skin of an orange or lemon

5. It makes honey for us

6. We — with our eyes

ee
speed
bee
see
steel
deer
peel

oo

7. The — is in the sky

8. To bend forward

9. Knife, fork and —

10. To fire a gun

11. We all eat this

12. Daniel's glove fell into a muddy —

oo
pool
moon
stoop
food
spoon
shoot

15

1. Water from the clouds

2. You have a broken finger—

3. I will — for my Mum to come back

4. A dog wags its —

5. Water runs into a —

6. We sometimes have a — when we are ill

ai
nail
tail
rain
wait
pain
drain

7. We have a good football —

8. We — with our ears

9. We pour this from a pot

10. These come when we cry

11. Ships sail across the —

12. Not hard

ea
sea
tea
team
easy
hear
tears

oa

1. Footballers try to score —

2. Motor cars travel on the —

3. Something we wear

4. Used for washing our hands

5. A small ship

6. At breakfast I like a slice of —

boat

soap

road

toast

goals

coat

oi

7. A kettle is used to — water

8. Money

9. A needle has a sharp —

10. Fasten together

11. Put — on your bicycle to make it go better

12. Plants grow in the —

soil

oil

boil

coins

join

point

1. One hundred pennies make a —

2. To speak in a very loud voice

3. Joshua — a present near his bed

4. Not in

5. Sixty minutes are the same as one —

6. The shape of a ring

ou

out

hour

round

shout

found

pound

7. A hen — eggs

8. Horses eat —

9. After lessons we go out to —

10. To say prayers

11. The fifth month of the year

12. There are seven — in a week

ay

days

pray

May

lays

hay

play

oy

1. To tease someone

2. We — good food

3. Most children like — trains

4. Most schools have girls and —

oy
toy
boys
annoy
enjoy

ack

5. Uncle bought Emma a — of sweets

6. Father Christmas carries a —

7. You lean — in your seat

8. A man's name

9. To put things in a suitcase

10. A colour

11. A very small meal

12. There was a — in the wall

ack
back
Jack
snack
packet
black
sack
pack
crack

19

1. A bird does this

2. A part of the body

3. A sailor walks on the —

eck

deck

pecks

neck

4. Do you know — way to go?

5. A lion tamer may carry a —

6. A bicycle has two —

7. I wonder — tea will be ready

wh

whip

wheels

which

when

8. We like to — pictures

9. A part of the head

10. Tea can — a tablecloth

11. Frozen rain

12. Mum — for the petrol

ai

brain

stain

paint

paid

hail

ick

1. We went slowly as there was a — fog

2. The sound made by a clock

3. The boy was — and stayed in bed

4. You — a football

5. Adam was told to — up the suitcase

6. On hot days it is fun to — an ice-cream

pick

kick

lick

thick

tick

sick

- - - e

7. A narrow road

8. A strong wind

9. You — this in your money-box

10. Things are cheaper in a —

11. Used to tighten a shoe

12. We'll — a cake

make

lace

sale

lane

gale

save

1. A key fits into this

2. Worn on the foot

3. A father bird

4. A big stone

5. Ships sail into a —

6. A fright

ock

rock

lock

dock

sock

cock

shock

7. To dry with a cloth

8. To go headfirst into water

9. What — will tea be ready, Mum?

10. Jill can — a horse

11. A heap

12. The edge

- - - e

dive

pile

side

wipe

ride

time

uck

1. It travels on wheels

2. The baby began to — his bottle

3. I wish you good —

4. The name of a bird

5. John — the stamp on the letter

6. Mum told Judy to — in her blouse

luck
truck
duck
tuck
suck
stuck

- - - e

7. An animal which lives underground

8. A long, thin piece of wood or metal

9. A flower

10. A mouse lives in a —

11. To push your finger into something

12. A dog likes a —

hole
rose
mole
bone
pole
poke

23

1. Used to stick things

2. Ben hummed a little — to himself

3. I like — stories best

4. We squeeze toothpaste from a —

5. Very big

6. A colour

- - - e

tube

true

tune

blue

glue

huge

7. A road in a town

8. Horses and cows sleep on —

9. Cats purr when we — them

10. A thin piece of leather

11. A small river

12. A long step with our feet

str

stream

strap

straw

street

stride

stroke

ang

1. A group of children

2. The blackbird — sweetly

3. The bell — loudly

4. Let's — the picture on this wall

5. A loud noise

bang
rang
hang
gang
sang

all

6. Round and used in many games

7. Drop down

8. High

9. A shop in a market

10. My friend is — Asim

11. Tell me — about it

12. All buildings have —

fall
stall
all
ball
walls
tall
called

25

age

page
stage
age
cage
passage
rage

1. Wild birds should not be kept in a —

2. I am seven years of —

3. The dancers came on to the —

4. My book has a torn —

5. A word meaning anger

6. The old house has a secret —

ing

ring
king
sting
fling
string
wings

7. Wasps and bees can do this

8. Tie it with a piece of —

9. It is worn on a finger

10. He wears a crown

11. For flying

12. Now — your arms into the air

ong

1. Cut — the dotted line

2. A — wind blew the tent down

3. Shall we sing a — ?

4. A rabbit has — ears

5. She sat — the other girls

6. Does this hat — to you?

ong
long
song
belong
along
strong
among

ice

7. Two times

8. They were skating on the —

9. Seeds we can eat

10. The sun is shining and it is a — day

11. I ate the last — of cake

12. Small animals with long tails

ice
nice
rice
twice
ice
mice
slice

Numbers

1. How many days in a week?

2. 5–4

3. How many toes on one foot?

4. We each have — eyes

5. 2+2

6. How many months in a year?

7. 8+3

8. On two feet we have — toes

9. What are three threes?

10. Half a dozen

11. 4x2

12. 5–2

ten
three
nine
twelve
eleven
one
four
six
two
eight
five
seven

ung

sung

hung

rung

stung

1. Gail was — by a wasp

2. The bell was — at four o'clock

3. The wet shirt — on the line

4. The children have — their song

ied

dried

cried

tried

died

5. The pilot — in the crash

6. I — hard with my writing

7. We — our hands under the hand-drier

8. She — because she was so unhappy

qu

queen

quiz

quick

quack

9. The sound a duck makes

10. Fast

11. This lady sometimes wears a crown

12. Puzzle questions

ight

1. Not wrong

2. If shoes are too — they hurt our feet

3. The moon shines at —

4. This plane made a — to New York

5. A battle

6. Switch on the —, please

ight
night
light
fight
right
tight
flight

k

7. Seven days

8. A bird has one

9. We read this

10. Shall we — lunch today?

11. For hanging things on

12. Side of the face

k
cook
book
week
cheek
beak
hook

kn

1. You can tie one with string

2. Used for cutting

3. Part of the leg

4. In olden days he would ride a horse

5. The postman gave a — on the door

6. I — that two and two make four

kn
knee
knock
knight
know
knot
knife

ow

7. It has a stem and petals

8. A high building

9. To bend forward

10. A bird

11. We can — in deep water

12. Dogs and wolves do this

ow
owl
howl
flower
tower
bow
drown

31

1. A game

2. To push hard

3. The princess was wearing her new —

4. Which — are you in at school?

5. To bring

6. She makes magic spells

7. When struck it makes a flame

8. I can — a ball with one hand

9. Made with a needle and thread

10. Having lots of money

11. Sarah is — happier now

12. Paul is — a tall boy

ss

dress

press

chess

class

tch

match

catch

fetch

stitch

witch

ch

much

rich

such

wa

was

wasp

water

swan

wash

want

watch

1. The name of a big bird

2. It is cool to drink

3. It tells the time

4. An insect with a sting

5. I — Sally to come to my party

6. Callum — seven last birthday

7. We should — our hands before meals

y

daisy

funny

baby

penny

fairy

8. The clown has a — face

9. I have a book of — tales

10. A coin

11. A yellow and white flower

12. When I was a — I slept in a cot

1. A person who steals

2. Made with soap and water

3. Used to rub out mistakes

4. It is put in the dustbin

5. May I have an ice —, please?

6. To go after someone

7. It has green leaves and red berries

8. A horse does this

9. A soft shoe

10. Not sad

11. A baby dog

12. A late meal

bb

rubber

rubbish

bubbles

robber

ll

holly

follow

gallops

lolly

pp

supper

puppy

happy

slipper

34

1. Small

2. It goes through the eye of a needle

3. The colours in your dress are very —

4. Eaten with bread

5. A part of the body

6. Another name for Mum

7. A tool for knocking in nails

8. Spring, —, Autumn, Winter

9. A hot drink

10. His — leg made him limp

11. Sweets

12. These are steep and rocky

tt

pretty

little

butter

cotton

mm

Summer

hammer

Mummy

tummy

ff

cliffs

toffees

coffee

stiff

1. Not alive

2. Eaten in slices

3. Part of the body

ea

bread

head

dead

4. For keeping sheep and cows in

5. A leader

6. A part

ie

chief

piece

field

7. A very big animal with a trunk

8. We ride this at the seaside

9. It swings from tree to tree

10. These are used for racing

11. Known as the 'King of the Jungle'

12. A very tall animal with a long neck

Animals

lion

giraffe

horses

monkey

donkey

elephant

36

1. One hundred of these make £1

2. Another name for Grandmother

3. He fell down as he was —

4. The morning was warm and —

5. It is fun to — in the sea

6. A — is put on a horse's back

7. The robin's nest was — in the hedge

8. Another name for Dad

9. The dog — its tail

10. A short knife

11. Larger

12. Misty

nn

running

Granny

sunny

pennies

dd

Daddy

hidden

paddle

saddle

gg

dagger

foggy

wagged

bigger

1. Speak

2. Used for writing on a blackboard

3. To move along on foot

alk

walk

talk

chalk

4. Grows our food

5. Someone who looks after sick people

6. Another name for Mum

7. Another name for Dad

8. He works on ships

9. This man is in the army

10. The son of a king and queen

11. The daughter of a king and queen

12. Someone who teaches in a school

People

soldier

farmer

teacher

nurse

princess

prince

sailor

Mother

Father

Days

1. The last day of the weekend

2. We start school on M—

3. The day before Wednesday

4. The day before Thursday

5. The day after Wednesday

6. The day before the weekend

7. A holiday at most schools

Days
Monday
Wednesday
Saturday
Friday
Sunday
Thursday
Tuesday

Fruits

8. Small green or black fruits sold in bunches

9. A long yellow fruit

10. A big round fruit with a thick skin

11. A bright red fruit

12. Very good for putting in pies

Fruits
orange
apples
banana
grapes
tomato

Months

1. What is the first month of the year?

2. second

3. third

4. fourth

5. fifth

6. sixth

7. seventh

8. eighth

9. ninth

10. tenth

11. eleventh

12. twelfth

March

May

December

November

October

January

September

February

June

August

July

April

The Body

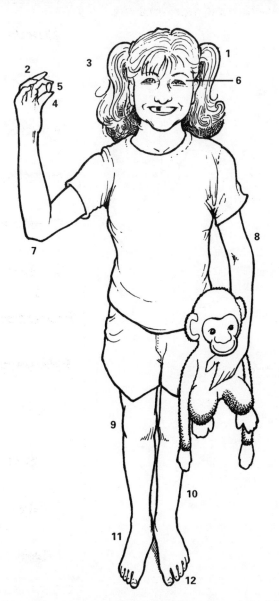

leg

arm

eye

fingers

toes

ear

thumb

tooth

hair

foot

knee

elbow

41

Nature

cat

dog

cow

sheep

pony

hen

fox

crab

fish

bird

pig

snake

42

Kite Strings

OF THE SOUTHERN CROSS

Kite Strings

OF THE SOUTHERN CROSS

A WOMAN'S
TRAVEL
ODYSSEY

Laurie Gough

TRAVELERS' TALES
San Francisco

Kite Strings of the Southern Cross: A Woman's Travel Odyssey
By Laurie Gough

Originally published in Canada under the title *Island of the Human Heart* (Turnstone Press, 1998).

Travelers' Tales and *Travelers' Tales Guides* are trademarks of Travelers' Tales, Inc., P.O. Box 610160, Redwood City, CA 94061.

Art Direction: Kathryn Heflin
Jacket and Interior Design: Susan Bailey
Calligraphy: Georgia Deaver
Cover Illustration: Michael Surles
Page Layout: Cynthia Lamb, using the fonts Bembo and Lithos

Distributed by: O'Reilly and Associates, 101 Morris Street, Sebastopol, California 95472

Library of Congress Cataloging-in-Publication Data
Gough, Laurie.
  Kite strings of the southern cross: a woman's travel odyssey / Laurie Gough.
  p. cm.
    1. Gough, Laurie—Journeys—South Pacific Ocean Region. 2. Gough, Laurie—Journeys—Asia. 3. Gough, Laurie—Diaries. 4. Travelers—Canada—Biography.
  I. Title.
  G155.C3G68   1999   98-55502   910.4—dc21
  ISBN 1-885211-30-9

For my loving parents,
Tena and Patrick

CONTENTS

WHEN I RETURNED TO CANADA after a year and a half in the South Pacific and Asia I found myself at a loss as to what to do next with my life. Travelers often find it strange to come home after a long journey, to try to make sense out of all those days spent on the road. A traveler has collided with new aspects of the world she never imagined, encountered sounds, sights, smells, and skins of other lands that have left her breathless. It's too vast a universe to leave smoldering in a skull. She might explode. So what's to be done with travel when it's over? I did the only thing that made sense at the time: I told my travel stories to friends and family, to those interested and kind enough to listen.

People kept telling me the Canadian economy was in a shambles in that fall of 1992. You won't find a job if you don't have one already, certainly not a teaching job, they warned me. Since nobody was hiring in southern Ontario, I took off for my old stomping ground up north, back to my cabin in the woods outside of Bancroft, Ontario, near Algonquin Park. Of course there would be no jobs there either—the economy is always depressed in those Ozarks of the North—but at least there I'd be like everyone else, jobless, and I was back in the woods. Luckily, I found enough substitute teaching in country schools to get me through the fall. Winter came heavily that year with twelve-foot drifts of snow. Sleeping one night in my cabin warmed by the wood stove, I awoke with a terrifying electric jolt. My God, I thought, I'm all alone in the woods, thousands of miles from the South Pacific, from those sultry Fijian nights. Where has it all gone? I could feel my travels dissolving as each cold minute passed, as if my trip were a dream I'd invented to keep sane in the solitary woods. Running over to my desk in the dark, I fumbled to find a pen and paper and the light. I was panic stricken that if I waited another minute to write about my travels they would melt away entirely or, worse, become hazy anecdotes. So as the snow fell outside my window and the fire crackled, I began to write. I wrote about another dark night, the night I returned to the island of Taveuni off the boat. That first writing was sappy, too melancholy, I think now when I look back at its original form. Yet it captured something of that night on "the road" I never want to forget, and it captured me. I was lost to the world of writing for the next four years. That story marked the beginning of *Kite Strings of the Southern Cross*, although I didn't know it at the time. After writing it I became obsessed with my time in Fiji and the people I had known there. Poring over my Fiji travel journal and all the journals from my other trips, I was shocked to find the wealth of impressions, reflections, joys, traumas, and revelations hidden in their pages. From the passionate writings of a spirited twenty-year-old hitchhiker with a copy of Kerouac's *On the Road* in her backpack, to the wiser and more worldly narratives of insight from a twenty-seven-year-old still struck with wanderlust, I had much to read, and much to remember.

Why I felt compelled to write the story of returning to Taveuni in particular, I don't know. Far more adventurous stories of my travels awaited my pen and paper (and very soon, my computer) in the months and years to come. But writing that night in my cabin set me on the road to writing my travel stories rather than telling them, just as years earlier I set myself on the road of travel itself.

All the stories in *Kite Strings of the Southern Cross* are true, more or less. The names of most people have been changed and a few blank spots in my memory have been filled in with details. From my travel journals I chose what intrigued and absorbed me most and tried to bring these things back to life.

Writing, like traveling, deepens my life, and writing about my travels gives them new meaning. Sometimes, it even allows me to live those journeys over again, minus the mosquitoes and sunstroke.

I wanted to set down on paper all that I had seen out there, all my encounters with the world and its people. I didn't want my travels to evaporate.

INTRODUCTION

ANYONE WHO HAS EVER BEEN to the Southern Hemisphere will know that the Southern Cross, that distant constellation of stars so fabled in song and myth, is not all it's cracked up to be. In fact, once you finally spot it or, more likely, have it pointed out to you, you may say, "That's it? That's no cross. Sure ain't the Big Dipper. Looks like a little kite up there in the sky."

That's what I said.

Paradises aren't all they're cracked up to be either. From the outside they may appear heavenly in their mango-treed, smelly-blossomed kind of way. But I've become suspicious of places that are all smiles and show scant little of themselves on the surface. You know, places where people never talk about sex but you just know it has to go on there. And places where people never say what they're really thinking from behind their shiny teeth and glazed eyes.

Every place, like each of us, has its dark side. It just takes a while to see it.

But as a traveler and dreamer, I like to cling to the notion of paradise, just as I cling to my travel stories as if they'll hold me up and define me. I like to yank the kite strings of fancy, the kite strings that should be dangling underneath the Southern Cross. Now that would be an impressive constellation.

All stories, like rainstorms and revolutions, must begin somewhere. So let my story begin on the night of my re-arrival at a little island in the South Pacific which I then believed to be a place cut out from the peach pie of paradise.

———

The beauty of the world has two edges, one of laughter, one of anguish, cutting the heart asunder.

—Virginia Woolf

The universe is made of stories, not of atoms.

—Muriel Rukeyser

LIGHT ON A MOONLESS NIGHT

I LIKE TO REMEMBER THE NIGHT of my return to the remote Fijian island called Taveuni. Remembering it makes me smile. Warm winds dried off the saltwater slapped in my face during their earlier tantrum as I beached myself ashore after a thirty-six-hour boat ride on high South Pacific seas. My balance was as off as a tone-deaf minstrel after a night of medieval merriment. I didn't care. I was back in Taveuni.

TAV-EE-UUN-EE. I loved the feel of the word in my mouth, full and rich and ripe like the island itself, about to burst with ancient lava and laughter and secrets from the past. It made me think of jumping from a place up high, like a rock, a tree or a cliff, into someplace unfamiliar and alive. The mere speaking of the island's name carried its own magic for me, was a way of entering and leaving the world. When spoken during the day, Taveuni was an expansive name for a place containing mirth and light and possibly mischief, but at night the name held its own dark sort of

grace. And if whispered at night, or, even worse, whispered
in just the right tone, the name caused shivers. Taveuni
whispered. Think of it.

Eight months had fallen from the earth since I'd left
Taveuni. Eight months of exploring other places: New
Zealand, Australia, Malaysia, Thailand, Indonesia. It didn't
feel real, standing on that old Fiji dock again in the hot
night, everything familiar in a dreamy kind of way. Even the
taxi drivers came on like old friends. They sauntered towards
us boat escapees looking as if they'd just heard the world's
best joke. Or seen it. Our faces had to be green. One man
was puking his boiled-fish dinner into the sea while his wife
patted his back. That's true love. New visitors aren't hassled
here as in parts of the world where a traveler can be
swarmed by a sea of faceless strangers speaking the few
words of English they know to conjure up business: "Room,
room, taxi, hotel cheap, Miss, Miss, good food, cheap, speak
English, please Miss, come, cheap."

Life's gentler on Taveuni.

Like salty fermenting pickles crammed in a jar, six of us
shared a taxi ride along Taveuni's one road. The driver sang
us a ditty. He was a happy man. As the taxi jerked its way
along the bumpy road over hills and too fast around curves
into the blackness of the night, I could imagine exactly where
we were, what we'd see if it were daylight. Memories spilled
over each other like ocean waves: of the two months I'd spent
here, of the Fijians and their children I'd taught at the school,

of the village that clings to the tropical mountainside, of the other travelers I'd met at the campground by the sea. And Laudi. Of course Laudi. I wondered if anyone would be awake at this hour. Would the quiet Fijian men and their children with immense eyes still be on the beach, circled around the kava bowl singing South Pacific harmonies? They'd be surprised to see me, of that I was sure.

I was surprised myself. Rarely do travelers return to such remote destinations even if they had the best of intentions when leaving them. I was seventeen when I visited the island of Madeira on a school-sponsored holiday and I vowed to return one day. Over ten years have passed, many of them spent traveling, and my list of secret spots on Earth to come back to is ever growing, with Madeira so far recessed that I don't know when I'll find my way back there.

But Taveuni called me back and I'd listened. I had day-dreamed of this countless times over the past sweltering months, lost and bone-weary on noisy diesel-hazed streets, caught in crushes of human traffic in jammed Asian markets, or waiting for trains, buses or cars with only a series of mangled straw hats between me and the unkind blaze of the equatorial sun. Ideas of returning to Taveuni—hidden so far and so secretly from the rest of the world that I often wondered if it really was of this world—had been growing steadily in my scorched mind.

I asked the taxi driver to stop half a mile or so before arriving where I thought, in the dark, Buvu Beach Campground lay. I wanted to walk the last part of the road as I imagined it. In my daydreams it had always been broad daylight, but I wasn't fussy. The driver didn't even question dumping me in the middle of nowhere at two o'clock in the morning. The other passengers eyed my tent sceptically. They were off to Taveuni's resort. An elderly English woman warned me, oblivious to our native driver, "They were cannibals here, dear, right in this jungle. Whatever are you thinking?"

"That you shouldn't knock eating people until you try it yourself."

Okay, I said that after the taxi roared off and left me standing in the mud. I set off with my backpack through the darkness, hoping I wouldn't veer off the dirt road into the bush. I suppose it was possible that ghosts of cannibals might still be hanging around, suspended in the confusion of trees. Or perhaps underneath the tender ground lay mute bones of half-eaten men carved up for special occasions. If I stepped in the wrong place, the bones would crumble into powder and release terrible secrets. So I looked up instead, into the soft center of the universe. The sky is ancient and the ghosts there don't remember cannibals. The storm had passed back out to sea and a great white sweep of Pacific stars poured down. I tried to find the Southern Cross but couldn't see it. As usual. Instead I spotted Orion directly over me and its familiarity reassured me that I was doing the right thing to return here. It's a consistent constellation.

No light of the moon floated down into the world that

night. Into an awkward blackness I walked for what seemed like hours, gradually losing confidence that I knew where I was. Not only disoriented, I was dizzy. Landsickness. I wavered back and forth along the dirt road, giddy and excited. No lights shone anywhere since Taveuni (only twenty-five miles long and six miles wide) has no electricity except for the occasional house with a generator. Most people use oil lamps, all that is needed by islanders who live naturally with the sun, sea, and land.

I finally came to a hill so I knew I'd passed Buvu Beach just behind me. Exhilaration lifted my load of clothes, books, and gifts as I found my way back to the campground's entrance. I walked barefoot—the only way to walk on a muddy road. The earth is softer in Taveuni than in other places, and darker. It's how the earth must have been millions of years ago, in the world's warm beginnings. My hands remembered their way up a giant tree marking the pathway leading into the wooded beach. I'd arrived.

Heaven owns real estate on Buvu Beach. An extended Fijian family owns it also. They live up a hill across the road. The campground is shaded by towering and twisted trees which drop down leaves large enough to hide overfed cats. Coconut palms, mango trees, ferns, and bamboo shoots jump up everywhere to join the lush green picnic of it all. But it's the flower blossoms that lure people inside. The smells they emit refuse to be shunned. Scent-drenched, the blossoms fill your nostrils, swarm the cracks of your memory until you're inhaling more than flowers. You're inhaling echoes of how the world once was. Three or four little bamboo huts, known in Fiji as *bures,* lie hidden among the voluptuous vegetation. A few tents are always edged away somewhere too. I like to believe that travelers are blown this way by ancient sea winds. We fall inside the soft air and sleep to the pounding waves of the ocean's heart which beats in time to our own. Only the occasional annoying rooster or thud of a wayward coconut interrupts one's sleep.

Pitch black. The hand extended in front of my face was invisible. This was the kind of utter darkness that falls only in remote places, inconceivable to city dwellers. Nothing but an eight-month-old memory of the place could get me over the preposterous tree roots erupting out of the sand. They were like mutant flora. Last time here I'd broken a toe, twice, on one of these roots. The Fijians made such a big deal about it and laughed at me so much that if I did it again I'd be forced to hop back out to the boat unseen. There's only so much jocularity about my feet I'll tolerate.

I walked in slow motion toward the grass-roofed hut and heard it creaking in the wind. The little hut always reminded me of *Gilligan's Island,* being so makeshift, crafted out of whatever grew on the beach. The hut was our refuge, our hangout, our sheltering haven. Here campers and Fijians would cook, talk and laugh for hours into the night. It had a sand floor and no walls, a stove and cupboards, a few benches and a little table that mangoes, coconuts, and pineapples always lay on. We called the little hut our kitchen. Sometimes when the moon was full, the tide was high enough that the sea would slip right up and wet our kitchen floor. We didn't mind.

Beside the kitchen, we would gather on the beach at the end of each day and watch the sun setting over the Pacific. It would spread over us like a mauve shadow. When it grew dark we would sit around a fire, drinking the Fijian elixir of life, kava, out of coconut bowls. Kava isn't alcoholic, but it's something. It slows down time. The Fijian men would sit with us and sing and play their guitars. After a while we'd all be singing. Then we'd tell stories. We'd tell travel stories mainly, since we were all travelers of some sort. The Fijians would tell stories too, stories of their lives growing up on Taveuni. Storytelling is important in television-free places like Taveuni. It's important anywhere. I remembered all the stories told around those campfires. And now I stood in the kitchen again, remembering these things as if I'd never left.

But I had left. I left because I couldn't stop moving. I couldn't stop searching for the perfect place. That's the thing about travelers. We always have to see what's over the next hill. But someone once wrote that to leave is to die a little. So I came back to the place I left. And immediately I found my heart beating alive inside this strange island's quiet grace, stirred to see into the life of things here. I stood still and listened as moist night air invaded my hair like seaweed. What I heard was a kind of song coming out of the sea, like a drum

banging in the waves, but singing too. All that time over in
Asia, I'd only remembered the adventures I'd had here—the
hiking, the snorkelling, the music, the family, the kids in the
school. But now I understood it was the waves that had
pulled me back. They'd been here all along like a steady
pulse, patiently keeping time for the world. Waves like this
never stop rolling inside a person, just beneath one's awareness. The sea has a way of slipping us back to our beginnings,
soothing a rusty place inside us, to remind us of something.
Like a secret trance, a forgotten calling.

I stood in water as warm as my blood and exhaled a
tremendous unconditional breath like the wind itself. The
sea washed something out of me, freed me in its imper-
ceptible way of what lay smoldering within: eight months
of traveling alone on a road full of startling faces and
unfamiliar tongues. I'd been traipsing through too many days
and nights of dog-ridden streets and climbing over shaky
mountaintops, not always liking what I found on the other
side. But traveling is a journey to the center of the soul, a
crazy Irishman once shouted at me. One forges through
dark mountains and unnamed streets until there's nothing
left to see but chiselled pieces of light.

As I walked along the shoreline I thought about how
nature overwhelms everything with the sea's pastel painted
fish and purple coral, the island's extravagant trees of sweet
unrecognizable fruit growing amidst waterfalls and volcanic
mountains, rugged and wet. It would be difficult not to be

delirious in such a place, a place where nature overpowers people, where people give themselves over to the land and sea. Little bits of phosphorescence, colored dots of fluorescent green, washed up at my feet. Laughter came in on the waves. I was home, as close to home as a traveler can get, and I felt like staying for good.

Eventually I turned and felt my way back in the dark to the woods and the little wooden shower house behind the kitchen. Two days on a dirty boat had left me with a film of dust and salt I didn't want to experience Taveuni through. Showering in blackness isn't as bad as it sounds. The cold water jolted me awake. The familiarity of the shower and the same old creaking of the bamboo door latch made me think of Laudi. Laudi was part of the Fijian family who owned the campground and lived across the road. The first time we met he'd just returned from university in Suva, Fiji's capital on the main island. He'd missed Taveuni and wanted to take care of his family campground. Laudi was raised on this island, under a canopy of enchanted trees and the enormous breasts of his aunts. When we saw each other the first time we flashed identical sideswiping grins, the truest kind. It made us laugh that he and I were the same age exactly but had led such different lives. We'd written letters back and forth while I'd been away. Gushy love letters.

Laudi and his cousins would come down to the beach after sunset every night to sing and play their guitars for the campers. Almost always, an astonishing little group of

travelers from around the world would collect, none knowing each other initially, stay for days sliding into weeks, and
become lifelong friends. It was easy here. The music brought
us together. The high-voiced harmonies of such big men
singing Fijian love songs touched a chord in us that could
reverberate anywhere in the world if listened for under the
stars or beside the ocean. It was the unexpectedness of it all.

At this hour, though, no guitars strummed, no fires
burned, no kava slid down throats and lulled minds, and no
stories were born into the night. I couldn't possibly sleep.
I'd look for Laudi, or his teasing cousin, Kalisi. I knew if I
waited until morning to see the family, they'd ask me why I
hadn't woken them immediately. But it was so late. Maybe I'd
just find Laudi.

I walked back out to the road again, still dizzy and
wavering, needing a flashlight. The rain had muddied the
hill up to the family houses and I now slipped as well as
staggered. Anyone who saw me would have wondered who
the drunken white person was and where she would be
going at this hour. Fortunately only a dog saw me.

A dim light shone in Laudi's old room. Fijians often sleep
with their lanterns dimmed low so it didn't mean he'd be
awake. I felt like a kid as I stood on a stump beneath the
window, looked in and whispered, "Laudi, Laudi." I could
barely make out someone sleeping on the bed. "Laudi, it's
me, Laurie." A head jolted up. Then another body on the
floor rustled and mumbled something in Fijian. I tried to

remember what Fijian I knew and whispered, "*Bula, keri keri, Laudi e vei?*" hoping that meant "Hi, please, where's Laudi?" Clearly, neither of these two people was turning out to be Laudi and being awoken in the middle of a dark night by a foreign stranger in your window who's screwing up the language would confuse anybody. The boy who had been asleep on the floor turned the oil lamp up bright and held it toward my face. All I could see was a set of perfect piano-key teeth. I was surprised I didn't recognize the boy or the man on the bed.

"*Bula*, please who are you?" the boy asked in his lovely polite mix of a Fijian English accent.

"I'm Laurie, Laudi's friend, Laurie from Canada."

"Oh, Laurie! *Bula, bula,* Laurie! I'm Pita, Laudi's cousin."

"*Bula,* Laurie. I'm Salote," spoke up the man on the bed. "Laudi sleeps down the beach tonight in his tent. I'm his uncle."

While never taking their eyes off me they whispered to each other in Fijian. I felt silly standing there. I said thank you, apologized for waking them, and accepted a lantern. By now it was probably close to four in the morning. I was still wandering around, still not in straight lines, but at least I knew where Laudi was and with the lamp I wouldn't crash into anything.

Back on the beach I began my search of tents. How many could there be? I whispered outside four different tents and disturbed at least six more strangers that night before I spotted a tent with a broken zipper. It didn't look like the other tents. It wasn't igloo-shaped nor was it the fancy multicolored variety. It was more like a gypsy tent, a large canvas triangle with several tarps cleverly tied to trees to keep out rain. No dangerous coconut trees hovered above this tent. I figured only a Fijian could be staying there. The tent was cradled inside the massive crawling roots of a gnarled tree that drooped white blossoms.

I set the lantern down on the sand outside the tent. A guitar, a flashlight and a mosquito coil lay in the tent's corner. I looked inside and saw Laudi sleeping. It was one of those moments that catch a person off guard, that come from a place unknown and rarely suspected. A moment that if frozen and preserved for future generations to thaw out and contemplate, would make them think life had ripped them off because happiness doesn't come like that anymore. I started to call Laudi but hesitated. Everything would change after this. Here and now, as I crouched on the sand in the warm dark night, were all the things I wanted to feel or see or hear and I didn't want it to end. In the precious space of time just before drinking water in a desert, before a child opens a present, before calling out Laudi's name, the world tells us a secret. It's a quiet message that whispers life can be what we want it to be. Any sudden movement could destroy it—a voice, a shudder of wind, a dog barking in the distance.

A fruit bat whooshed its wings just over my head.

"Laudi," I finally called out, "Laudi, it's me, Laurie." Laudi jumped up and yelled—Fijians are very superstitious.

"What? Laurie! Is it really you? I thought you were a ghost! Is it you? Am I dreaming?"

"I think we are," I said. He held out his arms to me as the day's first light was just breaking. We hadn't seen each other in eight months. I'd been traveling alone a long time and had almost forgotten what human touch felt like. When his sleepy warm skin pressed against mine, I nearly melted into dark eternity.

Somewhere there exists on the horizon an invisible line between dream and reality. That night I think I crossed over that line and found that all of us, all of life, in love and beauty, can, if we choose, lie out there in the hazy glow of the pink dawn where no lines exist. For a little while anyway. We must cherish the little whiles. They're all that really matter in the end.

CHAPTER ONE

*Of course that didn't last. Bliss seldom does. I found my jour-
nal the other day, the journal of my return to Fiji, and it brings to
mind many things. As I read it, even smells come back to me. Like
the salty fish smell from the sea cucumbers the women would collect
on the reef every morning and sell for export after cleaning them.
Apparently they're a delicacy in Japan. Or the heavy lamp oil and
kerosene smells of the evening mingled with the sickly sweet smell
of draping orchids. The sultry scent of coconut oil on skin could
almost overpower the smoky burning smell of food roasting over
fires. Smells of the tropics. I'd like to recall more of the smells so more
things would come back to me, things I didn't write down. But I'd
have to go back there to do that, to smell those things again, and I
know I can never go back. Not while he's alive.*

FIRST MORNING

I'm ecstatic! I'm whirling and raving and softly exploding.
Here on this small but significant island I've returned to seek

out Life. Here I'll dust off my heart. I'll touch passion like music touches chords, moves spirits, sets sails and love free to roam. This is the place for everything, where all of life can occur. This is the original garden, the island the sailors forgot to leave, the mythic utopia, the chosen land. Lying under corralled pieces of only the most velvet of skies, this island rises out of the deepest part of the ocean onto moist sunwarmed earth, giving off a smell of bruised freshness and notions of buried treasure. This island is a collection of memories from a thousand sultry summers.

I'm not dreaming this up. I've returned.

Nothing has changed. The water is still dizzying, crinkled blue and aqua green. Everything is either alive or in a state of delicate awakening. I feel the heat beginning to burst out of the sky. Birds and butterflies swirl on currents of wind. Laudi has gone off somewhere. Fijians are always going off somewhere. I remember that from before. They get up far too early in the morning. I don't know what to do first. I feel like running straight into the ocean.

I've been swimming all morning and playing with Kalisi's little sisters, Ivy and Kura, in the water. I've just spent the last hour laughing with Kalisi and her mother, Uma. This morning Uma is gathering sea cucumbers. Thigh-deep in water and clutching a handful of slime, she shouts at me, "Laurie, you're back! We missed you. There's been nobody to laugh at with you gone."

I love Uma. She has a fiercely passionate nature and a deep tender heart. From the shore I can see the familiar friendly gap between her teeth as she smiles at me. Her black hair bushes out to the sky and when she laughs the world shakes and is happier for it. It's laughter that hums, warm and true and uncompromising. Uma is supremely solid, with abundant flesh, generous hips, breasts that are entities unto themselves, and thighs that are in charge of the entire operation of her body. "You stay here in Taveuni, marry Laudi. Then I'll show you how to clean these things," she says as she throws a sea cucumber at me. It misses, lands near my feet, and I watch its black squishy flesh coil into itself. Disgusting.

Uma is trying to earn extra money from the sea cucumbers. It makes me wonder how they usually earn money. I know Laudi and his cousins earn money by spear-fishing at night and selling the monstrous parrot fish they catch, but they only do that occasionally. All they ever need to buy here is tea, kerosene, pasty white bread sometimes, kava, and a few household things. Almost everything they eat is free, collected the day it's eaten: seafood that's so sweet and fresh it puts anything caught the day before to shame, root vegetables like cassava and taro, yams and sweet potatoes torn out of the ground, fruit that swells up overnight in the most shockingly fecund place—mangoes, papayas, pineapples, avocados, passion fruit, mandarins, guavas, coconut, bananas, plantain, breadfruit, and soursop.

I remember my last time here the family amazed me

when they took me on a boat to a little island for a picnic. Nobody lived on the island; it was completely wild. I wondered why we hadn't brought anything with us to eat for the picnic but I didn't know them well then so didn't ask. Even though we hadn't brought any food, we left completely stuffed at sunset. We ate all kinds of fish and seafood they'd caught in a net, nuts off trees called *tavewas,* cassava pulled out of the ground and roasted in the fire, breadfruit picked by the kids and fried in oil like french fries, green leaves resembling spinach cooked in coconut cream, and armfuls of fruit, like miniature bananas. We even had dessert—sweet coconut cream with ginger over mangoes, and nuts on top. I think they did that for my benefit, to be like a sundae that they must have heard about somewhere, from a foreigner. It tasted better than any sundae I'd ever eaten. They laughed when I told them that, as if they didn't believe me. Maybe they did. Thank God television hasn't made its way here yet to put them down, make them want western things. The kids even sing on the school bus, play outside all day, and tell each other stories.

When I wander out of the campground I see Laudi coming down the road. He waves and calls *"Bula"* (hello) out to me. What a kind and gentle face he has. His smile bends my heart and fills me with love. I hadn't realized how much I've missed him. He's been at the little shop a mile away, the only shop in the vicinity, the shop almost everyone visits daily whether they're shopping or not. Laudi is carrying a basket loaded with kava for tonight's campfire. We run towards each other with our arms extended as if we're in a long distance telephone commercial. Although Laudi has never seen television, he's laughing as hard as I am at how corny we're acting. We hug and kiss. We can't get enough of each other.

"Come up and see my family. They're waiting for you."

I walk up the hill to visit the family—much easier in the daylight. I give them gifts bought in Bali and New Zealand and hope I don't cause a minor upheaval or perform a cultural faux pas. Levels of communication run deep here, deceptively. They smile at me and say thank you—*vinaka*—over and over but then I see them snatch alarmed little glances at each other and mumble things in Fijian. Maybe they don't like what I brought. Maybe they're all the wrong things. Maybe I present them in the wrong order. I give Laudi's grandparents, Nana and Papa, the best gifts. They run the show here, being the oldest, the most respected. And they're my favorites. Laudi's grandfather has suffered a stroke and can no longer speak. This explains why so many extra family members are here. He may die soon. I hold his hand, kiss him on the cheek as he lies on his bed, and he remembers me. Although he can't speak, his eyes still hold the knowledge of his life. They still cast light.

"We thought you were a spirit coming to haunt us at the window last night," laughs young Pita. "When I turned the lantern up and saw you had long red hair, I was scared, but

only for a minute." The family has been laughing all morning at how afraid Salote and Pita apparently were when they
gave me the lantern in the dark.

"Afraid of a white ghost woman," they tease. Salote laughs
too, in an embarrassed kind of way. Men aren't supposed to
be afraid here, especially of women.

Vix, Laudi's uncle who claims he owns the campground
although everyone else says he doesn't, hasn't been here yet
today, thank God. He scares me. He scares everyone as far as
I can tell. Not that anyone says this. Something is chilling
about Vix, disturbed, slightly dented. People feel it when he
walks into a room, like cold cave air. I remember how he
watches people. He smiles but his smile always seems to grip
his face as if it doesn't belong there, like a stain. My instinct
is to stay out of his way. Kalisi says he's down at his cousin's
drinking kava for the day. She says that will lead to beer
which will lead to one of his drunken rages. But I love the
rest of them. They laugh all the time.

AFTER SUNSET

I'm stuffed. I feel as if I have lead in my stomach.

Ten of us sit cross-legged on the floor, as is the custom, in
front of a long hand-woven mat covered with dishes of food.
Mountains of food. Enough food to feed the planet. Fijians
love to eat until they can't move and they assume everyone
else does too. Whenever my plate is no longer heaped high in
food, someone immediately picks up a piece of fish or cassava

and plunks it down on my plate as if in some kind of automatic replenishing response. I can neither make any headway nor see an end to it all when they do this. Priggy, one of Laudi's numerous cousins, sneaks an entire fish onto my plate when I'm not looking. He thinks this is hilarious. Priggy is short and round and very dark, much darker than the others. His smile always stretches the width of his face before erupting into deep-bellied laughter. Priggy loves to eat. The women love feeding him. They stuff him with inconceivable quantities of food all day and he, in turn, loves the women for it.

I love the food here but I've forgotten how heavy and rich it is. Coconut is the culprit. Coconut invades almost everything in one form or another. We eat sweet fish boiled in coconut cream with roast-your-tongue red chilies, *lolo* (spinach cooked in coconut cream), curried cow meat, cassava and taro both fried in coconut oil, and fried breadfruit. Only the yams managed to escape the coconut tonight. Food isn't processed, refined, or packaged. The only sugar they eat comes from sucking on sugar cane and what is added to tea. I've never seen children eating candy in Fiji. I don't think candy exists here. This explains their perfect teeth—always strong, white, and straight. They love looking in foreigners' mouths to study our silver fillings. But their diet is heavy in oil, meat, and starch. They're big people, especially the women. Some of them are gigantic.

I feel almost like part of the family again even though I barely understand a word of what they say at dinner, except when they speak English for the first three minutes. I listen, let the strange words fill my head, try to break through into their world by seeing it through their speech, by their faces. Their language is simpler than English, closer to the earth. And what expressions. Their faces must tell each other more than words ever could. The words I've learned from them are basic and raw, connecting them to the unity of all life. But trying to break in through language feels impossible and I am aware of a profound separateness created from this barrier of unfamiliar human sounds. I know they talk about me for most of the meal because everybody looks my way when asking Laudi questions and says "Ooooh" and "Isa" while staring at me. But I don't care if they stare. They smile and laugh and are kind. I know I'm as much an oddity to these people as they are to me.

I've met the seven other campers staying here—a lively couple in their twenties from San Francisco who have brought a guitar and mandolin, a woman and her fourteen-year-old son from Australia, an eccentric guy from Romania, and two Swiss women that the eccentric Romanian is hitting on.

A curious human linkage is forged amongst travelers, making it possible to understand one another almost immediately because we recognize something of ourselves in each other. We're the sort that doesn't need a home. The desire to see the world is what matters. Traveling is like being in love; it has that kind of strength. The love some people give to another person, to a home, to a career, we give to the road, to the mountains and villages, to children running in the streets, to the women at the well, to the trees, the moon. We throw ourselves into the world and become creatures of chance, of the stars. Traveling alone can be hell, in its utter solitude and in its panic, panic not from rain or cold or sickness but from the sense of displacement, and the question Why am I here? But something compels us and it's this: when we travel we absorb fresh life around every corner. For years the urge to travel might refuse to identify itself, as if it's a dormant seed inside us. But one day we find it somewhere else, furrowed in the body of another person we may meet on a train or at a bus stop, and suddenly this yearning is happily, instantly recognizable. We understand each other's need to travel. We understand this without question.

We're about to make a campfire, just like old times.

Laudi and his cousins are pounding the kava and will play music tonight. Drinking kava or grog is the national pastime, no longer reserved for special celebrations. Every day and every event are now reason enough for celebration, for getting grogged. After pounding the dried root called *yaquona* into a powder, they wrap it in cloth and infuse it with cold water into a big wooden shallow bowl which sits in the center of their circle. Almost always a circle of men. They serve it to each other from a shared coconut-shell cup. All visiting heads of state are greeted with the *yaquona* ceremony. They even fobbed some off on the Queen of England. It tastes exactly like it looks, like murky brown water. You get used to it. Kava has a tranquilizing narcotic effect after you've lost count of how many bowls you've had. Before accepting a bowl of it, the drinker is supposed to clap once. After the kava is swallowed—no sipping allowed—everyone in the circle claps twice and says "*Bula*," which means life, health, happy days, happy greetings. It's a sacramental age-honored ritual that ensures friendships, even if it does taste like dirty dishwater.

We sit on the sand around the fire beside the shy lapping of the great slack sea. Beside us, Laudi and his cousins play and sing Fijian songs for hours in soft voices that melt the night, melt it like dripping chocolate. Their guitars and ukuleles are old, beat-up and loved. Laudi is the lead singer of their little band. What a sweet voice. His great-grandfather was an Irishman who married a beautiful woman from Taveuni and they say he lulled their children to sleep with sad Irish ballads and took a shine to the new and strange kind of grog. Fijian songs can be almost as tragic as those of the Irish. When we ask them to translate songs, they tell us they're about lost love. They're old-fashioned lovesick heart-achy songs, played almost like cowboy music with a reggae beat. The South Pacific breathes through every refrain. The word *isalei*, which means longing and sorrow, sad farewell, dripping hearts and I'll remember you forever, is in almost all Fijian songs. One word can mean all that. The language, like the people, is gentle. Besides, gushiness and sentimentality are allowed this far out in the ocean. And I admit it: I can't take my eyes off these men. They put flowers behind their ears. They don't wear pants. Fijian men, like the women, wear a length of cloth called a *sulu* around their waists. It's like a sarong or wraparound skirt and is always made of vibrantly colored material splashed with prints of giant red hibiscus flowers. The men look good in them. Fetching, say the women.

In relation to the rest of the world's men, Fijian men are huge. They have big bones, big lips, even big teeth. Their hands are wide and strong and full of scars and frighteningly intricate tattoos. Down their backs and chests are rippled accordion muscles. They have throbbing runners' legs.

Laudi, however, isn't huge at all. He's the average size of a western man, but compared to his cousins, he's almost small. His body is lean and muscular, athletic. He has short black hair and a high forehead, a smile that warms his brown eyes, and a contemplative face. Set at just the right angle in the sunlight, his face is a thing of uncanny beauty: dreamy, intense, and hopeful.

I watch Laudi sing in the circle around the fire with his cousins. He closes his eyes and the music escapes from his lips as if it has been stored inside him for centuries. I could listen to him sing all night. Laudi's Uncle Adi, Uma's husband, plays a wicked rhythm guitar. Adi makes everyone laugh. Priggy looks like a contented Buddha under a tree. On his perfectly rounded belly rests his banjo, which he strums lazily. Priggy often sets the banjo down on the sand mid-song, so he can drink extra kava. Next to food, kava is what Priggy lives for.

Vix, the uncle spoken of only in whispers, appears out of the dark. He falls into our night like a bad habit, piss drunk. Kalisi predicted he would be drunk and he is, staggeringly so. Flopping his body down beside Laudi, Vix casts his eyes around the circle. His eyes are black and glazed, emptied of life. I look at his large angular body, the flesh of his face sagging in hound-dog folds. I can smell the alcohol leaking out of his skin. Whenever he looks at me, he directs his eyes at mine and holds them there for too long. His smile is full of criminal reflections. I look into the fire instead, where it's safe.

Hours pass, until only Laudi, Vix and I are left on the beach. I can't relax until Vix leaves. When he finally does, he disappears without saying good night.

Laudi and I stay up half an hour later, even though we're exhausted. Perhaps we have to clear the tarnished night air of Vix, restore its purity, rub his vile presence from our souls. Laudi doesn't mention Vix and neither do I. Instead, we sing songs he's been learning from Lee, the musician from San Francisco, and two Judy Garland songs I taught him tonight: "Over the Rainbow" and "Dear Mister Gable." I'm glad he likes the lyrics; I love singing Judy Garland songs.

I dreamt of a night like this one many times when I was away, of lying back into this sun-warmed sand with pieces of the night sky scattering down, Laudi singing quietly with the ocean surf. I watch Laudi in the dim lantern light as he sings and see his strong lithe build, his skillful hands strumming the guitar, and his deep-set eyes. It's his face that stirs

me most, a face so completely content it seems to demand
nothing more for the rest of its days, as if desiring anything
beyond a night like this one isn't even a consideration.
After the music, Laudi and I run out to the water to dive
into the rising tide. I love warm and moist night air. It's like
a blanket to my skin against the evening breeze. Laudi finds
his guitar again and we sit on the sand while he sings a Fijian
love song. The stars fall into the ocean and sand crabs bolt
across the beach sideways like alien creatures who have
beached themselves here from another planet. The music,
like the kava, makes me dreamy, and I think of how this one
starry night can carry me far into my life.

"I'm so happy you're back," says Laudi, suddenly stopping
mid-song. "I knew you'd come back. I knew you wouldn't
find a better place than here. I read all your letters thirty
times over. My cousins read them too."

"Your cousins read them! Your cousins read my letters? I
hardly know your cousins."

Laudi laughs. "They know you."

Laudi has a soft English accent which always surprises me
out here, so far from the Western world. I often wonder
what the English explorers thought of this place when they
first arrived. The English poet Rupert Brooke wrote about
the South Pacific in the nineteenth century: "Tonight we
will put scarlet flowers in our hair and sing strange, slum-
berous South Sea songs...bathe in a soft lagoon by moonlight, and eat great squelchy tropical fruits...."

CHAPTER TWO

WHEN I WAKE TODAY THE SKY is a bright aching blue, blue enough to stab through light. Clouds collect in wisps but don't mean anything. They swirl through the sky like thoughts through the mind, leaving nothing in their wake but memories of childhood days at the beach with sand castles and suntan lotion. (That's what they called it back then, suntan lotion, back when we thought the world was innocent and the sun friendly. As if the soft white cream and the sun could together make you as brown as the bottle it poured from, the bottle your mother kept in the picnic basket with your *Archie* comics and the sandwiches, carefully wrapped, for those Sunday afternoons at the beach with the blue skies.)

This morning, Laudi and I climb into the hills to what they call the plantation to collect the day's fruit for the family. Fruit falls all over the place. I trip over what I pay a lot of money for at home. The soil is rich; it's a volcanic island. By the time we get up to the plantation we're so baked by the heat we drink the water inside three whole green coconuts. Laudi chops the top off the coconut with his machete and we guzzle the liquid almost desperately. It slides down my throat like sweet wine until it spreads through every vein. After we're surging with liquid, Laudi carves a spoon from the coconut's top to be used for eating the soft white flesh inside. Eating the flesh is like biting into the solid life of the coconut water, slippery and sweet and sure of itself. This feast wouldn't be the same anywhere else. Only on a green island this saturated, in a forest where sweet decadence is deeply hidden, could this occur, this delicate ancient feast.

Laudi climbs the tallest coconut tree like a monkey. Every Fijian man can do this. Even Fijians with Ph.D.'s who dress in business suits and live in Suva can climb coconut trees. I can't think of a North American equivalent. Not every man in North America can fix an engine, nor can every woman make chocolate brownies. In Fiji, as in most of the non-Western world, gender roles are clearly defined. A man wouldn't be caught dead washing clothes, or chopping an onion, nor would a woman hunt wild boar or pound kava.

In the hills we collect basketfuls of juicy mandarins the size of grapefruit by climbing the trees to get them. Half of them we eat right there. To collect avocados we throw rocks at the tree until they fall down. We gather mini bananas, guavas, jackfruit, and cassava and find a luscious vine of passion fruit. It's too early for mango season. Inside this forest of fruit I start to feel like a ripe melon on a vine, gushing and dripping heavy with sun. Laudi walks ahead of me. I love watching his calves, strong and warm brown in the sunlight. He's bushwhacking our way through this thick rain forest with his razor-edged long machete. All Fijians, even children, can swing a machete as if it were an extension of their arms. They walk barefoot almost everywhere, especially in the bush. Every day in countless ways they make use of the bush's virtues. We run out of baskets to carry the food back, so Laudi hacks off long reeds from a plant and weaves a new basket in two minutes. I feel so useless and ignorant of everything here. Too cerebral. They have control over their immediate world, know it intimately. When we walk back down to the beach, he asks about finding food in Canada. Where do I begin?

After the bush, I swim at least two miles over the glowing green reefs. Swimming is one of my passions. I have to remember this and swim every day to keep the coconut fat off me. Two Giant Aunts (Laudi's aunts are exceedingly large and impressive) have told me already they intend to fatten me up. That's what they do to the wild pigs they hunt. They keep them in wooden crates and stuff them with food so they'll taste better at special feasts.

I also snorkeled today with Ana from San Francisco and Deseree from Australia. We've become instant friends and talk continually about how much we love it here. Paradise, we've taken to calling it. We fantasize about staying forever. To them it's a whim; to me it's more than that.

When I'm floating face down in the water with the mask, I'm spying on a whole other world that's untouched by this one. The private lives of fish. My scouting could be compared to aliens flying over the earth, gazing down at us, trying to make sense of it all. I can't get over how many brilliant colors light up this underwater world. I've never seen so many natural colors all at once. Every color that exists is down there, ten times brighter than anywhere else. Metallic blue angelfish shoot off together in privately arranged formation. Fat royal blue starfish stretch out on vibrant purple coral. Parrot fish are the colors of the rainbow. The fish and sea creatures live amidst an intricately designed coral reef that's green, pink, but mostly violet. It looks as if they have their own castles and roads, little houses and apartment buildings, and they swim around to visit each other. Some of them look purposeful, fish with intent; they know what to do with their day. Others seem to have no intent at all. Leaving this world and falling into theirs looks easy and delightful at first glance. But then I see a school of particularly luminescent little fish with sequins and jewels on their skin who are out for their daily little joy ride when, in a gulp, some hideous larger fish nabs a couple. You're someone's picnic lunch in one crack of a jaw.

What is animal life and what is plant life become confused in the sea, almost joined. The Fijians know the sea world well. They know what tastes good and what doesn't, what stings, poisons, infects the skin, and what makes pretty decorations in their homes.

We swim over to what we think may be jellyfish, the non-poisonous kind, we hope. Angelic translucent bodies form a gently swaying cathedral near the sea's surface, quivering stained glass enraptured by the filtered sun. Some fish glow, as if they have colored lights turned on inside them. We wonder where all the color comes from.

We swim back towards the shore and watch ugly sea cucumbers, the things that Uma collects for Japan, looking lazy and pudgy. Skinny little pearl fish hide right inside sea cucumbers' bums. It's shelter for the pearl fish but we wonder what's in it for the sea cucumber.

But we don't wonder about it too much. We're in paradise.

The bottom of the sea is void of color, completely black. The sun's light can't cut through the watery miles to reach down there, just as some stars are too far away in outer space for their light ever to reach earth. When I close my eyes to sleep at night, the backs of my eyelids flash me all the vivid colors of the sea, and no darkness at all.

Laudi and I walk up the hill tonight to visit Uma's family. Uma is Laudi's aunt and Adi is his uncle. Adi is the uncle who plays the rhythm guitar. Like Uma, Adi makes people laugh merely by his presence. Adi is one of those people who are allowed to get away with so much more than the rest of us by the sheer virtue of their entertainment value. Make the world laugh and you get a free ride on its Ferris wheel. Make the world sing and it will take care of you forever.

Adi breaks into some sort of absurd soliloquy as he tunes his guitar: "Hey you hippie freaks, quit your damned drumming and leave me alone, screamed the mooooon...this ain't no tuuuune...don't wake me till nooooon...nuthing interesting to sing about Juuuune..."

He's hilarious. I don't know where he comes up with this stuff. Adi and Uma's children, Kalisi, Kura, Ivy and Luna, laugh too, except they're laughing at me laugh at their father. These are Laudi's teasing cousins. Kinship patterns are complicated here. Teasing cousins are cousins on the maternal side as opposed to the cousins on the paternal side who are supposed to respect each other and never tease. Teasing cousins only joke with each other and never say a serious thing. The two types of cousins even address each other differently, with different names for each other, such as "Hey bro, hey sister" as opposed to "How do you do, cousin?" This is just the beginning. It goes much deeper. The people of every individual island in Fiji—and there are three hundred islands—relate to the people of every other island, or group of islands, either respectfully or in a teasing manner, all depending on tradition, on historical ties with the islands involved. For instance, if someone from Taveuni were to meet someone from the island of Koro, the two strangers would immediately joke with each other and call each other specific names, like "Hey you crazy sister islander." But if a Taveunian were to meet someone from the island of Kadavu, the two must show respect, no joking allowed. These rules apply even if they meet each other in a grocery store in the capital city, even if years and miles separate them from their island homes. When I ask people how this came to be they shrug and say it's always been this way.

Eight months ago I loved visiting Uma's family and I still do. They don't gossip like the rest; they laugh and joke with me and are open-minded. Adi lived in Australia for a while, and although he found it strangely isolating, crude and unfunny, he learned a lot about the world. Kalisi wants to travel to New Zealand next year when she turns nineteen before returning to start university. They're poor. Their house would be called a shack back home. They're also the people I feel closest to here. Uma is a comic. Her facial expressions crack me up. I think it's been months since I've laughed as hard as I do around them. I believe Uma possesses a kind of purity because she obeys her own private standards. Her feelings and opinions are her own. This is rare in Fiji. While Laudi and Adi and a few cousins play music and drink kava, Uma, Kalisi, and the little girls and I laugh, massage each other, and tell stories for hours in this lantern-lit night. Already I'm falling back into the male-female segregation of their world. It's impossible not to.

"Come, Laurie, come lie here," says Uma. "I massage

you." Uma spreads a woven mat on the floor in front of her and opens a bottle of coconut oil. Fijian women make their own coconut oil and they all know how to massage. Massage is one of the things women do here, have always done. She holds the open bottle to my nose and I breathe it in to fill my lungs. Little Kura and Ivy do the same thing and then giggle, as if they've never thought to sniff it before. It smells so good I think I should carry a bottle with me and inhale it all day. Uma pours coconut oil over my stomach. I watch her eyes. I'd almost forgotten her eyes. They grow immense as she hovers above me, staring and massaging as if I'm bread and she's concentrating on kneading me. It's important I rise properly, like dough. She's in a trance.

After a long time she says, "You need to eat more. Not enough fat, not enough skin to massage." Kalisi and I laugh at this. Little Kura tickles my feet. In the background in the adjoining room, the men sing Fijian love songs in the dark.

I could get used to this.

I'm writing in the tent on the beach and I can hear one of the Giant Aunts calling me to eat lunch. I don't want to eat lunch. I'm still trying to get over the oil-filled pancakes we ate at breakfast. What they call pancakes are big doughy balls of white flour and water mixed to a paste and then submerged in coconut oil and fried. Ugh.

This afternoon I'm going back to visit the school. I hope to be able to teach here again. Teaching in Fiji is a dream. It's how I imagined teaching school in Canada could be but isn't. The school here has no fluorescent lights, which I detest; it has no electric lights at all. They aren't needed when sunlight pours through the open windows along both sides of the rooms. Cool breezes drift in with the sun. In this school, which sits high on a hill, to look out the open window on one side is to see a diamond-dancing green ocean stretching out as far as the next island, and to look out the other side is to see rain forest stretching into coconut groves. They're happy children. They even sing. How could they not?

S C H O O L

Okay, what did they do with all the real children? This can't be right. When I walk into what they call the library, which is a big old-fashioned breezy wooden room painted white with hardly any books in it, the kids are all sitting straight up in their chairs with their hands folded on their desks. They beam me radiant smiles. Their classroom is teacher-less. The teacher has left the room and these children are sitting there—forty of them—joviality bursting through their eyes and skin, but quiet, pretending to be non-children. A class left teacher-less where I come from is a class where chaos outdoes itself. It leaves chaos behind in the dirt with sand in its eyes. Things are different here. I'm in shock.

"Good morning," they call out to me in unison, in chorus, in perfect harmony. A little boy raises his hand. "Please, Miss Laurie, please can we sing for you like before?"

And they do. They sing for me. After I recover from hearing angels sing for me, a little girl stands up by her desk and says far too politely, "Please, Miss, tell us about the snow in Canada." Maybe I pass through a time warp when I enter this school. They ask me every question they can think of about North America and then about the rest of the world. They want to know it all and they don't know a lot. Since there's no television, their concept of the rest of the world comes only from outdated books and people like me. Being so out of the way, Taveuni gets few foreigners. I find a musty old book called *North American Indians* at the back of the library classroom so I show them pictures of people living in Canada's far north and tell them about the time I taught on a native reserve up there. They laugh at my stories and ask questions about what they call the Red Indians. Most of the children are confused about the word *Indian*. Since half of Fiji's population is descended from indentured servants from India, their concept of Indians ends there. They ask ingenious questions about snow: "Can you walk inside it? Does it hurt?" and they giggle wildly when I try to explain ways of playing in it.

British colonization still casts a long shadow. They begin studying English during their first year of school. The children still wear school uniforms as if they've just stepped off the train from Paddington Station.

The new principal of the little school told me they can't afford to hire any more teachers this year, but I'm welcome to come and volunteer teach in the library anytime I want. I like the library. I like the whole school. But it could use some books, especially books published since 1950, especially books without Dick, Jane, and Spot.

ON THE BEACH

Tonight a sheared slice of moon has us mad to talk and watch as it makes its way over the great hill of the sky. The Fijian men are pounding kava and we've made a roaring fire. After the pounding, the men will tune their guitars, an activity that always takes them at least half an hour. It's worth the wait. None of the campers, nor I, have heard voices like these elsewhere in our travels, voices this high and sweet and pure. When I drink the kava and listen to the men sing, something happens inside me that uproots me from this island and spirals me back in time to other lands, distant, almost forgotten. Suddenly I see starkly clear images of places and people and things I thought were lost. I see them in their smallest detail, images I had no idea were etched so precisely on my mind. The others seem to be affected this way too. Drinking kava makes us want to tell stories. I knew we would tell stories eventually.

As we tell our stories, the beach fills with life, with passing shapes lost in mist, and with color. The sand underneath us becomes the vast and timeless desert of North Africa. The trees above us creak and moan like the trees on the coast of India. A wind blows up from New Zealand. Wind chimes in

Burmese villages whisper through the woods. Puffs of clouds off in the distance and over the ocean become the Himalayas, the Andes, the Urals, the Italian Alps. The people we describe in our stories come to life and sit here with us at the fire. Tales are spun and woven deep into our souls. We listen spellbound, anticipating and dreaming of these places far away, these beautiful mysterious places.

Up in the sky, stars swim through the night, following their ancient routes. Down on the earth, I sway back onto the sand, catch the falling stars in nets and dream of a thousand more nights like this one.

CHAPTER THREE

THE ROAD

A week has flown by since I last wrote. I'm on the bus to the village to buy groceries and kava this morning. Having kava on hand is always a good idea because kava is an expected gift when I visit somewhere and I seem to do a lot of visiting. Fijian lives are completely social.

I love bus rides on shady country roads when I can stick my arms out the window and feel the breeze. I watch children chase alongside the bus and see their smiles stretch the width of their faces. Their hands are just inches away from mine as they run and I can almost touch their laughter. The bus stops for at least five minutes in front of a little house. I become impatient to feel the breeze again and wonder what we're waiting for. Eventually a woman appears at the door and calls out to us that she's almost ready. I notice when she boards the bus what a sturdy, firmly made woman she is. She's of unusually enhanced proportions, with football-playing shoulders and impressively vast dangling hands. The woman sits down across from me and smiles. She's wearing a dainty baby blue dress. I try not to stare but can't help noticing that aside from her colossal dimensions jutting out in all directions, she has a lot of facial hair. Sideburns, actually. Her muscular legs are a jungle of hair all the way down to her ankles, which barely squeeze into her white, heeled shoes. She sits with her legs apart, like a man would. Then I realize she is a man, has to be. Fijians have a custom whereby if a mother hasn't had a daughter by her fourth child, she'll raise the fifth child as a daughter, even if it's a boy. She needs someone around the house to help her do the women's work. So if a boy happens to be the fifth son in a family with no girls, he'll grow up a little confused. The Fijians call these people *pooftas*. I wouldn't choose it as a lifestyle myself, although the woman/man across from me on the bus appears perfectly content, anticipating an exciting day of shopping. The dress doesn't suit him, though. Some men look good in a dress; some men don't. Baby blue isn't his color.

The first person I notice in the village is an old woman sitting on a bench, a woman of distinction who is impossibly crinkly, as if the sun has etched an antique carving into her face. A green scarf is wrapped around her head and a faded *sulu* hangs on her sunken-in waist. With arthritic fingers, she is eating fish and fried breadfruit from a wooden bowl. She's staring at empty space. When she sees me her eyes focus, then soften.

"*Bula,*" she shouts.

"*Bula,*" I say, fanning myself, "*katakata*" (hot day).

My two words of her language are a cue for the woman to embark on a ranting monologue in Fijian that lasts for at least five minutes, which surprises me coming from such a slight figure who takes up so little space in the world. I nod my head and smile, not understanding a word. At first she seems not to notice that I don't understand her, or if she does, she doesn't care, but then she becomes excited, even angry the longer she speaks, more animated as she gestures with her hands about something horribly unfair that must have happened to her. A storm of strange sounds floods from her mouth. I nod again and smile. I want to get away from her. As I leave, I remember nodding my head means "no" here, the opposite of what I'm used to. Perhaps I confused her when I nodded my head; perhaps she thought I was disagreeing with her. Getting used to these differences is difficult, so firmly embedded are our customs in our culturally conditioned brains. I walk down the road, training my head to shake as it says "yes," and to nod as it says "no." Ouch. It's almost painful.

A group of Indian schoolgirls politely calls out hello to me when I pass. They're dressed in blue school uniforms and all of them have long black shiny hair in ponytails, straight thin limbs and gleaming smiles. They're eating homemade frozen popsicles of sweetened condensed milk. I ask for the recipe and they gather around me in excitement to write it in a notebook.

The sun beats into the village far too strongly for me, so after shopping I decide to walk back to Buvu Beach along the road under the trees instead of waiting two hours for the bus. I think I might be able to hitch a ride. The narrow road follows the undulating glitter of the sea and sometimes the spray from the waves breaks on the rocks and splashes close enough for the mist to cool me. I pass corrugated-iron roofs of *copra* sheds and gaze up at groves of coconut plantations that stretch from the road high into the hills. Sweet starchy smells of husked and drying coconut flesh hang on the morning air. Prince Charles Beach lies somewhere between the village and Buvu Beach. Prince Charles once visited here, in his days before Diana, and actually laid his royal skin down on the sand and frolicked in the waves, so say the Fijians. People from Taveuni constructed a special outhouse on this beach just for him. I always intend to walk into this outhouse, to see if Charles left any interesting graffiti, but I always forget.

A walk along the road is even more an adventure than riding the bus. Everyone I pass smiles and lights up his or her face, says "*Bula,*" and asks me where I'm going. It's a Fijian custom to ask this. They never say "How's it going?" or "Nice day." They also expect me to ask them where they're going, and if I forget to ask, they tell me anyway. When I first arrived here I was flattered that complete strangers I passed on the road stopped to tell me they were going to the shop, or to visit an uncle, or to find watermelon, or to cut cassava, or to drink kava and watch while their second cousin's wife's younger sister made pancakes in her friend's kitchen. I thought they were trying to be my friends by letting me in on the personal details of their lives. But then I realized that people tell everyone they pass where they're going. Not telling each other is impolite.

Another impoliteness is for people who live along the road not to invite a passer-by in for tea or to eat. At each house I pass, someone opens the door or calls out the window to wave me in and say "Come, come, *cana, cana*" (eat, eat). This makes walking along the road a fattening experience. I must have gained five pounds on my first couple of walks here. Now I've learned they don't mind if I decline the invitation and simply say "*Vinaka*" (thank you) and walk on. Since they all invite me in I'd like to be able to ask them what they're eating and then decide if I should take the invitation, but I've also learned that everyone eats exactly the same things anyway. They also seem to talk about the same things and I find myself having the same conversations with everyone I meet.

I see three women on the road ahead. One of them is chasing the other two in circles, making a hooting noise while the women being chased are laughing so hard they can barely run. Their shrieks sing into my chest like a band of bagpipes. When they see me they stop chasing each other and continue walking with sunny smiles spreading their faces as if they know they've been caught and don't care. They walk like African royalty. In an instant they have

transformed themselves from giggling girls into regal women capable of deep-bellied laughter. Cascades of colored
cloth hug their enormous bodies, enshrine their rippled
thighs. Bigness isn't shameful here, not something to hide
and beat down. Big is magnificent. I watch them, entranced,
as they parade themselves down the road like queens with
their heads held high enough to smell every passing scent.

I love walking along this road. I especially love a section
beyond a particular curve where walking down the hill I
catch sight of the emerald in the ocean overtaking the
waves. The emerald consumes the entire surface of the sea,
but only here, just past this curve high up on the road, does
it become clear to me that the ocean has a deep black heart.
A little further down the hill on the other side of the road,
a thick wild place always stops me in my tracks and tries to
pull me in. Everything drips green and wet and cold, and the
sun can never find its way down into the primal dampness
of the place. I always smell roses in there, although I never
see any. As I walk by, the whole universe swells up inside me
and I have to walk slowly, as slowly as Fijians walk, to keep
that part of the road from evaporating behind me. At the
bottom of the hill are a few houses, small thatched houses
made out of the surrounding woods, like almost everything
here is made, and I envy the people living there. In one of
the houses a family with many children invites me in to sing
and play guitars with them. I can't refuse, especially since the
one little girl puts her soft small hand around mine to tug

me inside and her eyes are never-ending wells, the source of
the world's happiness.

I can never get over how immediately loving and welcoming Fijian families are. I'm amazed that they're all related; their lives wrap around each other and they seem to
know each other as well as they know themselves. I love
how their day slides along like the sun over the earth, how
they awaken to roosters, how they nap on mats after lunch
to sleep away the heat of the day, how they pound kava at
dusk, and how they fall asleep to their own music. I love
their shining chocolate skin that they rub daily with coconut
oil. I love their throaty voices when they laugh. A natural
hedonist, I'm taking to this place like a moth to light. Fijians
take things as they come, simply, from the surface of life, and
I know they're happy, in one of the easiest ways possible for
humans to be happy.

I drink kava, eat fried plantain, and sing with the family,
and they don't seem to care at all that I'm tone deaf. As I
continue my walk along the road back to Buvu Beach,
singing to myself, a big pickup truck rambles by carrying at
least twenty people in the back, who all wave and call "*Bula*"
out to me. Their smiling faces radiate the day's warmth and
in this brief instant I know why we're alive. Everything
occurs here, the essential impact of life's rapture sweeps
through us and we smile back.

I've just been told by two of Laudi's aunts that I shouldn't have gone into the house of the family with the musical kids today. Apparently Laudi's family and that lovely family at the bottom of the hill don't get along. I'm glad to hear Laudi thinks this is silly and I shouldn't worry about it. Of course he told me this in private, after the aunts left.

How did the news that I visited there travel so fast anyway? I didn't mention it to anyone.

Laudi and I are planning a *lovo* on the beach tonight for his family and the campers. To make a *lovo* oven, Fijians dig a hole in the ground, fill the hole with wood and rocks, and light a fire until the wood is gone and the rocks are red-hot. They wrap food in gigantic banana leaves which they place in the hole and cover with earth. The food is left for a couple of hours to cook underground. Tonight we're going to cook cassava, sweet potato, taro, and fresh parrot fish this way. I'm hungry already just thinking of it and I'm never hungry here because everywhere I go people want to stuff me with food. I'm going swimming.

Every time I snorkel I find more passageways and deep secrets to the coral reef. The coral reef is an underworld galaxy entirely separated from the world of sound. I'm soaking wet but must write about how the reef itself has eyes that open and close. I'm sure it spied on me today, so if I disappear and someone finds this journal, look for me in the ocean. But be careful; the ocean is suspicious of aliens and

frighteningly intelligent. Before today I swam over a few of
the mauve-colored figures of coral that look like big brains
and was impressed. But today I passed over the Mother Brain
of the Sea. The Mother Brain of the Sea has to be as big as
a Volkswagen Bug. As I swam over it, I felt impelled to pay
my respects. Like giant mutated cauliflower, it thrusts up out
of nowhere like a megalomaniac's shrine to his head. A
colossal monument to the underworld, this bulging brain of
water knowledge and all things wet sends sea creatures circling round and round its girth because they must. Fish
Mecca. The Mother Brain keeps order in the ocean, thinks
for its purple-gilled followers. It knows things we don't.

I've always felt the need to record the events of my life. I trap
and collect my days into words. I want to know what life on
earth looked like, felt like, smelled like, as I walked through
it. I want to know I lived. It scares me to look at old calen-
dars filled with unmarked days, or empty pages for months
at a time in a diary. These are days lost. They were only lived
once. When I read about days I've written about, I remember things that make me smile, and although I can't go back,
something of them lives again inside me. It's like opening up
a magic that's always been there, but buried. Even as a child
I kept a diary. *Went tobogganing today with Julie. Got thorns in
our hair. Had to cut it off—our hair—half of it anyway.*
    I'm exhausted but I have to scratch down what I can, even
if I miss things. If I don't write things down, how will I know

in years to come this wasn't a dream? This place feels like a dream now even as I lie here on this sand, under this banyan tree with frangipani and jasmine in the air, scribbling words to prove to my fifty-year-old future self that life here, on this tiny South Pacific island, passed before me. But I can't catch everything that goes on around me into a net of words. Too much occurs in a day. Perhaps everything that happens here will be stored in that big brain out there on the ocean floor to keep safe all the things I don't write down. One day the brain will be smashed open and all the stories will come gushing out.

We've all gathered on the beach to watch the sunset. Except for Yurgen the Eccentric Romanian. Yurgen doesn't watch the sunset. He's not communal that way. He told us he has already seen the sunset once. He saw the sunset off the coast of Africa and that was enough. All other sunsets would be disappointments, cheap reproductions. He has seen the only sunset worthy of commenting on, and he was alone at the time.

When I eat this food that has been wrested only hours ago from the ocean and off the trees and vines, then cooked inside the ground, I'm convinced it's the best food I've ever tasted. I've always loved eating with my fingers, have always thought food tastes better this way, and finally, I've found a place where this is allowed. Like many people in the world, Fijians don't use forks. They don't like metal in their mouths. My mother would be appalled if she saw me now.

Vix sits directly across from me. Unlike his nephew
Priggy, who loves eating, or his brother, Adi, who is inces-
santly jolly, Vix isn't interested in food, or laughter. He
watches me and mumbles something to Priggy out of the
side of his mouth. Priggy smiles at me. I have no idea what
Vix could be saying, but I'd like to poke the insolence out
of his eyes.

After the *lovo* we lie on our backs on the sand, stuffed and
happy, looking like beached whales. A milky metallic moon
spreads its shine on the water and we watch the ocean's tide
come closer, bounding up to greet us like an enormous
friend. In a circle beside me and the travelers sit Laudi and
his cousins, drinking kava and singing to their guitars, laughing and speaking quietly in Fijian between songs. I always
wonder what they're saying and occasionally I catch things.
They laugh at us a lot. I can't blame them.

Shastri, a new camper, and a human specimen of particularly captivating interest, tells us a story. Shastri is a young
anthropologist, brought up in Europe, whose father is from
India and whose mother is from Spain. At eighteen, when
Shastri had to serve his two years in the Spanish army, he
pretended he was a Sikh so he wouldn't have to cut his silky
long hair. With his dark skin he managed to fool all of them
for the entire two years and he even invented his own prayers
and elaborate customs every week, just to see if he could get
away with it. And to keep his long hair. He's a little vain, but
smart. He's doing his Ph.D. on perceptions of paradise. The

idea of living in a paradise absorbs my days, especially since I've returned here to Taveuni. I want to know how close it comes. I'm looking for flaws. I see very few.

We talk about paradise for hours. I tell the campers and Fijians about Bali, that mystical island in Indonesia that I visited two months ago. When the moon shimmers through the trees in Bali, it speaks its own language. If you listen hard enough, you understand its loneliness.

BALI MOON

THE THING I LOVE MOST ABOUT BALI is that everything is connected to the spirits. Every morning, Balinese women place sweet-smelling offerings at doorways to greet friendly spirits. Offerings are prepared with sprinkles of rice, burning incense, flower petals, and jasmine. Even nasty demons are treated with concoctions of blossoms and delicious things to eat. All villages, including those no larger than a crossroads, are adorned with elaborate shrines and temples. Above dangerous curves on the roads and at busy intersections sit sacred shrines to watch over passers-by. In the countryside, stone-carved deities hide in the bushes to ward off evil demons. One is always protected by the spirits in Bali.

Almost every day of the year is celebrated with a ceremony or ritual. Once I was awakened in the middle of the night by a dreadful squealing noise. The next morning I discovered the neighbors had sacrificed a pig outside my window in some sort of pork-chop-offering-to-the-gods ceremony. Not a day went by when I didn't see a procession of colorfully dressed women balancing pyramids of tropical fruit, cakes, and flowers on their heads as offerings to the fertility goddess, or whoever the deity of the day happened to be.

Not only are the Balinese intimately connected to the spirit world; they're in touch with the animal world too. One morning I walked out of the artists' village of Ubud, past the Monkey Forest Road and into the Monkey Forest. In front of me walked an older man, a European tourist carrying a camera. Without warning, a monkey swooped down out of a banyan tree, ran over to the man, made off with his camera, and clambered back up the tree. The man stopped and shook his fist at the animal, as if that would mean anything to the monkey. Just then an old woman came along, singing to herself. Dressed in the traditional batik sarong of her village, she was carrying an armload of bananas.

"Bananas, you want to buy? Feed the monkey," she said to the old man. She didn't offer to sell bananas to me.

"No, thank you. I want my camera back."

"Buy bananas. Feed monkey bananas. Monkey give you camera back."

She was right. When the man bought bananas from the woman and offered one to the monkey in the tree, the monkey jumped down, dropped the camera at the man's feet as it grabbed the banana, and tore back up the tree to eat it. Brilliant. I wondered how many people a day the old woman and monkey tricked in the same way.

Bali is a country of sweet swaying bodies on buses and exquisite women who spit. My flight arrived in Bali so late one night that I decided to sleep just outside the airport on a bench in a little wooden pavilion surrounded by tall grass. The next morning, I caught a bus for a mountain village. The bus was hot, sticky, and crowded. Some of the people had to stand and I noticed how easily they melded with a roving bus that flew over curves, as if they were raised on rolling waves. Next to me on the bus sat a woman with such a serene smile and quietly delicate features, I thought she must have soaked herself in the juices of roses and must have been sung to all her life. She had the kind of gentle grace of a Gauguin Tahitian painting. I watched her gather her long black hair into a perfectly smooth collection of silk and then twist it into an ingenious knot on top of her head. I watched her, amazed, then tried the same maneuver with my hair. No matter how many times I tried, my hair refused to stay in place on my head. She had made it look easy. I was hot, and I wanted my hair out of the way. The woman turned to me, closed her eyes and bowed her head, and took my hair in her hands without speaking. She ran her fingers in a stream down my scalp to the very ends of my hair, then pulled it behind my ears. I felt her nimble hands whisk my hair around and around until it was secured tightly on top, just like hers.

The woman got off the bus when I did. I followed her, not meaning to follow her, but I found myself walking behind her along the dirt road of the village. I was looking for a guest house, but was in no particular hurry. The woman carried on her back a basket of vegetables with green shoots that stuck out of the top and rubbed against her neck. Around her waist hung a well-worn gold-and-red batik sarong that reached just below her calves. Her blouse was an unmatching floral design, and on her tiny feet were flip-flops. She took small steps. She waved and called out to another woman as she kept walking. I continued to walk behind her, vaguely watching for the guest house, or a place to eat, but really I wanted to know where the woman would go, to discover what her house, her family, might look like. She swayed her small hips back and forth, kicked little stones out of her way, and hummed to herself.

Then she spat. Right there on the road she spat without any grace whatsoever. She spat as if she had spat every day of her life, as if it was something that did not interrupt her stride, or even her thoughts, in the least. It shocked the hell out of me.

I continued to follow her. Not long after the spit, she strayed over to the side of the road and stopped at a volup-tuous bush, a bush intoxicated with creamy yellow flowers. She bent down to breathe in the blossoms. I slowed down and watched. I heard the inhalation, the ecstatic cry of the flowers as their scent rushed down her lungs. With her head in the bush, she turned to look at me as if she knew I would be there. I walked over to where she stood bent over the blossoms. When I stood next to her, I noticed how small she was. I hadn't noticed before. Tiny bones, tiny hands, like a little girl. Yet her hands were lined and weathered as if she had used them for many years. She picked one of the flowers off the branch, made another bowing gesture towards me, and put the flower behind my ear. She picked another flower and put it behind her own ear. We stood facing each other like two comets colliding, reeling from flashes of light, falling into the flames of each other. Then her face, so serene and still, broke into a smile. She turned and walked away. I remained standing by the tree, with the blossom behind my ear and my hair still in a knot. I wanted to watch her walk away until she disappeared down the dirt road, until I couldn't see her anymore. I didn't follow her. I didn't want to see her spit again.

I can still tie my hair in a knot that special way, and whenever I do, I think of her.

I love the Balinese because they love the moon as much as I do. Late one afternoon I was walking down a country road outside a village. The moon was to be full that evening and I wanted to be out in the open country when the moon rose, to watch it rise over a rice paddy. I came across a young Balinese man sitting on the steps outside a shop. He flashed a smile far too beautiful for me to ignore.

"Hello, what are you doing?" I asked him, surprised at my forwardness.

"Waiting for the moon to rise."

"So am I."

"Come watch with me. It won't come up until the sun goes down."

I joined him on the steps. He was wearing cut-off short pants and a white t-shirt, bare feet. His hair fell naturally into one eye and he kept tossing his head back to flick it out of his way. His forearms were muscular and darkly tanned. "What's your name?" he asked.

"Laurie."

"Lowee."

"Yes, and you?"

"Nyoman Bagus."

His name intrigued me. The Balinese have only four first names, regardless of their gender. The first child is Wayan, the second child is Made, the third child is Nyoman, and the fourth is Ketut. If a mother has a fifth and sixth child, she starts all over again, calling the children Wayan, Made, and so on. So Nyoman Bagus was the third child (or else the seventh) but his last name, Bagus, I had learned meant "good." The woman I rented my guest house from had explained that the Balinese say "bagus" with varying emphasis, depending on how "good" something actually is. If someone were to ask you how you are feeling and you're just okay, you would say "bagus," flatly. If you happened to be exceptionally happy that day, you would say "bagus!" with great emphasis, practically shout the word.

Nyoman Bagus was an artist, a painter. This explained his

well-developed forearms. He offered to show me his latest works of art. Inside his dark and cluttered shop, I saw massive canvases of jungles and dark forests filled with mythological beasts, freakish ghouls and demons, winged maidens, sleeping princes, and golden mountain people. Other paintings were of bizarre hairy animals entwined with powerful goddesses, ocean birds, and sorcerers. One painting was of the moon. I got lost inside Nyoman Bagus's paintings. Only when he suggested we go for a ride on his motorbike to watch the moonrise did I find my way back to earth.

"I'd love to go."

Nyoman Bagus put on some shoes. They were leather sandals and would not be considered safe, or even legal, to wear on a motorbike where I come from. He owned no helmets either, which was fine by me. I watched him swing his leg over the bike and rev the engine. He tossed the unruly flop of hair out of his eye as he turned to smile at me. "I usually drive my mother on here. This is much better." I laughed and climbed on the back. I was used to riding on the back of motorcycles.

We set off to the west. "We'll go to the sea," he shouted over his shoulder as we sped down the winding dirt road beside the rice paddy.

"To the moonrise," I shouted back.

We passed through village after village, all alight with color and ornate temples, golden gates, and art in every crevice. We saw carvings along the roadside, carvings of beasts, gods, and demonic masks. I could smell roasting bananas and sweet blossoms, incense and musty bamboo mats. We passed seas of terraced rice fields that looked like green ocean waves. Bali is volcanically active and the fecundity is extravagant. The scent of frangipani blossoms saturated the air so thickly, I felt drunk. Prehistoric tree ferns and passionate wild flowers hung down from the cliffs beside the road. Color burst out of the moist ground. And in every village, in front of the thatched huts, children laughed and waved at us. Outside one village, women with sarongs around their waists were washing themselves beside the road in a bathing place under a grove of trees. They had come in from the end of a day's work in the rice paddies. As we drove by the bathing women, they laughed and covered their breasts, waved at us, and splashed water at each other. We passed high above a lush river gorge and I saw red temples hidden down in the trees, temples to house spirits of the dead. Through a jungled woods we drove too fast around curves. At the edges of my eyes were flashes and movements among the branches, mystical birds, I imagined, and wild, running animals. If I looked directly into the forest, I couldn't see anything but trees. Finally we reached the sea.

"The Balinese don't look to the sea. We look to the mountains. People are afraid of the sea," said Nyoman Bagus when we stopped and parked on the beach. "But I like it here. I like the life of the sea, the things that crawl out of the water and under the sand, the sea beasts."

We walked along the shore examining the sea beasts. Everything we picked up we would inspect with the utmost

attention and fascination. We found vibrant purple coral formations that we stuffed in our pockets, perfect sand dollars,
hermit crabs, and jellied things attached to stones. On our
stomachs we lay down to watch tropical fish trapped in shallow tide pools. We skipped down the shore using giant rubber seaweed tubes as skipping ropes. The white surf crashed
over our feet and the salty wind blew warm sultry air on our
faces as we gazed into the sand. Then we looked up.

"Look, the moon." Nyoman Bagus saw it first, the sea
giving birth to the moon. As orange as the setting sun it
reflected, the moon stirred the sky in a hush too soft for
human ears. The sea beasts must have heard the rising of the
moon because the beach began to transform. Everything
was quieter, more muted. Sharp edges of rocks and even the
cutting surf adopted subtler tendencies, mistier, as details
became lost in shadowy curves and shapes impossible to
define. A sea bird cried out for love down the shore. A fish
flung itself straight up out of the ocean into the world of
air, then down again into the water. I wanted to dive into
the ocean, enter the sea beasts' domain. "Oh no, we can't go
in there. Poisonous snakes, the sea is full of them," said
Nyoman Bagus.

We sat on the sand instead and watched the moon.
Nyoman Bagus put his arm around my shoulder and asked
what my favorite American movies were. It had been
months since anyone had put his arms around me. I felt like
dissolving my entire body into the tender sand.

"My favorite movies aren't American, but I like a lot of American movies."

"The best movies are American," he said. "*Thelma and Louise* is the very best. I have seen this movie four times. I like the part where Geena Davis shows her underwear to the bad boy with the cowboy smile. My brother wanted cowboy boots after seeing that. I laughed at him. I told him Geena Davis wouldn't show her underwear to everybody in cowboy boots."

"I'm sure she wouldn't. Is your brother an artist too?"

"He's a farmer in the day and a dancer at night. He dances the temple dance in our village. He paints his whole body, feathers, masks, beautiful costumes; you should see him. The village women love him. He'll marry soon."

"And you? Will you marry soon?"

"My parents will find a girl for me, but I have things to do first."

"What kind of things?"

"Understand the world, then paint it."

If the world were just slightly lighter in weight, if the moon had remained suspended over the water and deep orange in the sky a moment longer, I could have fallen in love with Nyoman Bagus for saying that.

I stared into the complex organization of his face and wondered what he thought about at night, what he saw in the dark woods to be able to paint the way he did, and why the rising of the moon was important to him, as it was to me.

The stars were beginning to brighten as the moon rose above the sea. "Where's the Southern Cross?" I asked. Nyoman Bagus lay back on the sand to survey the night sky.

"It's there." He pointed. "No, I think that one over there. Or maybe that little one out there." His arm flung back and forth across the stretch of heavens as he tried to find the constellation for me. Finally, he admitted he wasn't sure.

I lay back on the sand with him to fall into the sky's naked eternal mystery and its bursting ecstasies. Soon we were kissing each other. I tasted salt water on his lips and knew that one day he would leave the island of Bali. We must have been kissing for hours, lost in the warm scent and skin of each other, because when we looked for the moon, it was high and alone in the sky, conjuring shadows on the beach.

We drove back through an indigo haze of eerie shapes silhouetted against the sky. The villages we passed were now silent in a lantern-lit red glow, and still; the children had gone. Banyan trees, the enormous Indian fig trees considered holy, with creeping branches that grow back down into the ground to take root, seemed to lurch through the darkness. Nyoman Bagus drove much more slowly than he had before, slowly enough for us to melt into the pure air of the night, slowly enough to be part of a painting. Almost slowly enough to understand the world.

On our way home, as night blanketed the gentle land, I realized that a million years would not be enough to repeat that fraction of eternity when we passed the place where the women had bathed, and I put my arms around his waist, and he leaned back into me, his hair and the moonlight resting on my face.

When he stopped in front of my guest house, I got off the motorbike and kissed him good-bye. "I had a wonderful time. I loved it," I said. "Thank you, Nyoman, Nyoman BAAAAGUS." I tried to emphasize the word *Bagus*, since it meant something good. I said it louder than the Nyoman part, with as much emphasis as is possible to enunciate. But when I said his name that way, something curious happened. Nyoman Bagus narrowed his eyes and looked at me as if I didn't belong in his dimension of reality, as if I were an alien life-form he had allowed on the back of his motorbike. He blinked a couple of times. He made little inhaling noises. He opened his eyes very wide, until they took over his face, as if something was occurring to him that never had occurred to him before. His mouth dropped open. He began to laugh. He laughed without restraint, and continued to laugh while I stood there watching him. He laughed so hard he had trouble sucking in air. The laughing looked painful. He was still laughing when I turned to leave and go back to my guest house.

That was the last time I saw Nyoman Bagus and I like to remember him that way, convulsing on his motorbike with his head falling to his knees. It's a good way to remember someone. I still haven't figured out what cultural gaffe I made and I don't know if I ever want to.

CHAPTER FOUR

I don't travel to see the museums, galleries, and palaces of the glittering cities. I travel to see the faces of villagers in their markets, or the particular sweeping motion of a tree shading someone sleeping beneath it, or to hear what the women say at the bus stops. I watch to see how the moon rises up over unfamiliar land, to check for a deeper yellow, a larger face, a quicker pace. I watch to see if my reflection has changed.

AFTER WE DISCUSS BALI FOR HOURS, I look into the dying fire of the night and consider Taveuni. It's different from Bali, which is pristine and delicate and known by the whole world. Taveuni is heartier, more rugged, closer to the earth. It's also a secret. I'm in love with this place; we're on our honeymoon. The rest of my life could be lived on this little island. What a dream. I listen to Laudi and his cousins sing and hear their voices dissolve into the night wind and ocean waves. Surely they wouldn't sing like they do if this were not paradise. When I lie here at night, I fall back into the world's damp beginnings when animals and insects sang into the trees and filled the earth and sky with song. As I listen to Laudi and his cousins, the singing voices and the sounds of the earth become indistinguishable. Their music must have been on this island long before the first people arrived and simply waited for human voices to stir it. This isn't logical, can't be understood through reason, but like a love that makes our knees shake, it comes from a deeper place than logic. We can't ignore what makes us shake.

This is where my mind flows as I listen to the music pulling in the tide. Until the sounds change. Until the music stops.

At first I think the sounds we hear coming from up on the hill must be emanating from a mentally unbalanced animal, or chickens crying in pain. But chickens don't cry and I hear a rhythm in these blood-curdling wails. The banshee-like crying has to be the wailing of human beings, women specifically.

No one says anything at first. We just sit staring at each other thoroughly alarmed, listening. Then the men put their guitars down on the sand and whisper in Fijian. We hear footsteps of someone running towards us. Pita, Laudi's young cousin, appears out of the bush, breathless. Tears are in his eyes when he announces it.

"Papa's dead."

Laudi asks me to come with him up the hill to his nana's

house where nearby members of the family are gathered. I can see the death of his grandfather has shaken him tremendously even if it isn't a big surprise.

In what they're calling the House of Mourning, which is Laudi's grandparents' house, women sit wailing on the floor, hugging their arms and rocking over the mats they spend their lives weaving, their tears soaking the golden reeds. The men slump in corners, in silence, looking stern and lost, as if something has been ripped from their chests. I've never seen these people this way before. Nor any people anywhere, for that matter. The women continue to wail long into the night, painful moans of deep sadness that echo out to sea. Their cries penetrate throughout the island, enter all our dreams. Even the small children and animals are sad.

A vast collection of relatives is assembling here from all parts of Fiji. They announced the death on Radio Fiji this morning. Relatives phone relatives from island to island and they flock here like geese migrating home. I don't know where all these people will stay. It fascinates me that blood ties are kept sacred for generations, that the human heart holds this much sorrow and memory.

Nobody cancels her ancestors here. Out on the road I see women running at each other: sisters, aunts, cousins, who left Taveuni to marry and live with their husbands' families. They hurl themselves into each other's arms, laugh, cry, scream. The men shake hands. They smile too, smile beautifully, but they never cry. The women are lucky. Their deep sobbing is allowed, even expected of them. Possibly the women's wails help draw the grief out of everyone.

Oi lei! Oi lei! Ai valu! Oi lei! I hear it even now as I write in my tent.

All family members bring with them large sacks of food and kava to be shared during the days of the funeral. They also bring woven *tapa* cloth, whales' teeth, and elaborately decorated mats. Some of these things will be buried with the body and the rest will be divided among everyone at the end. Kalisi tells me the funeral will last ten days. Ten days. The men are drinking kava, planning the arrangements. Up the hill, the women gather under large tents that seem to have appeared out of nowhere. They're chopping vegetables, pounding coconut into cream, cutting meat, preparing tonight's feast. I have a feeling the pig I've befriended in the crate box won't see this thing to the end.

I'm so embarrassed. I want to die! Everyone must kiss the corpse, or, rather, sniff the corpse, which is the Fijian method of kissing. I've never kissed a dead person before and it takes me a while to work up to it. Since everyone seems intensely interested in watching me do this, I want to get it right. When I bend down to sniff the corpse, some dreadful form of nervous hysteria takes over me and I burst out laughing. This is a little problem I have sometimes. I try to cover it up, pretend I'm just upset. I feel like a complete idiot and have come back down here to the beach to disappear into the sea.

Wait. I'm on a tiny faraway island in a far-off country and thousands of miles separate me from my old life. No one outside the waters of this remote island knows I laughed on a dead man's face.

This realization should be more consoling than it feels right now.

I'm spending a lot of time with the women, chopping vegetables and pounding garlic and coconut for tonight's first major feast. I notice the men seem to be having a roaring good time drinking kava.

"Doesn't it seem strange that the women do a lot of work around here while the men just laugh and drink kava all day?" I say this to nobody in particular in a big gathering of women sitting in front of vegetables.

"We laugh too. At them," says Auntie Sala. She cracks me up. I love her. She has a point. The women do seem happy and laugh a lot. But men get away with so much. It drives me crazy. I've attempted these conversations before and never get anywhere.

I'm noticing that women lead hard lives here even if they do laugh a lot. Everything requires so much labor. The women get up at the crack of dawn and go outside to build a fire to boil water for tea. For breakfast they cook the heavy pancakes that drop dead in your stomach, or sometimes biscuits with avocado or fried breadfruit and fried cassava or sometimes all these things. They set the table (a tablecloth on the floor), then they wake the children and get them dressed. After everyone has eaten breakfast the women wash the dishes, put them away, and start preparing for lunch. They grate coconuts, peel cassava, collect food out of the ground, and hunt for firewood. They sweep the whole house every morning with a hand-sized coconut-leaf broom that must break their backs. They fill buckets full of water and scrub the life out of clothes and sheets that aren't even dirty. (Everything here is whitewashed.) They set the table for the lunch they've made, eat lunch, wash the dishes, put them away, and then tell everyone to go and sleep. I like how they do that. "Go, go," they say with their thunderous strong sweeping arms. "Go sleep, all of you." They lay out mats all around the house for everyone to sleep on for the next hour or two. The women sleep also, snore heavily, and so they should. When they wake, there is food to find, wash, peel, boil, and fry; there are mats to weave, children to attend to, plants to gather for tea, and fish to net. All this through a haze of heat and flies. In the evening after they wash the dishes, they roll their smooth dimpled coconut thighs out on the mats they've made and tell stories of their day. They always laugh about it.

Back at the campground, the six campers there tell me that Vix, the drunken unsavory uncle, has given them all invitations for the feast tonight, provided they each pay him ten dollars. He told them he needs the money to buy groceries which he'll give to the women later. I know this is an outrage, a lie, and I know the aunts and everyone else would be appalled to hear he has done this. Funerals don't charge admission. When I ask Laudi about this he looks thunderstruck, swears under his breath and tells me his Uncle Vix will use the money for beer and kava for himself. I ask Laudi what should be done. He shrugs his shoulders and walks away with his head down.

Fijians deplore confrontation. They would walk ten miles to avoid it. They would invent the most ridiculous stories to get around it. Perhaps this has developed from centuries of living so closely together on small islands. It's what works for them. But I wonder, how well does it really work?

Hundreds of people are seated all around me, cross-legged, along both sides of long rows of woven mats. We're stuffing our faces. Next to me sits a mountainous woman, one of Laudi's numerous aunts from another island. She has flying-saucer eyes which grow immense when she eats. She speaks no English. The main phrases I can say in Fijian with any confidence are "Delicious food," "Thank you for the food," "I love the food," and "No thank you for the food, I'm full." The latter never seems to have any effect. The woman beside me lifts a giant prawn from her plate and places it onto mine when she sees my plate getting low. "Eat," she says to me. Her eyes take over her face. An iron-weight laugh rises up from her belly, putting me in mind of Mount Vesuvius. I think back to a century ago when Fijians ate each other and wonder if this woman's great-grandmother's eyes did the same thing before she dug into an enemy's roasted spleen. In every direction, for what seems like miles around me, I see food—fried cassava, spinach in coconut cream, giant clams covered with chilies, pig meat, other kinds of roasted animals—all on its way into mouths. This is just the first feast of the ten-day funeral, two feasts a day. I hate to think of how this scene will look in ten days. I've eaten everything here but the pig. He was my friend; I just couldn't. He was roasted in a pit over heated stones covered with palm fronds and banana leaves. Baked at the same time were chunks of plantain, sweet potato, peeled breadfruit, and taro root wrapped in banana leaves. Roast suckling pig. I called him Bernard. We also eat fish wrapped in leaves and the most delicious curry. Fiji's large Indian population has taught native Fijians to love curry. They stir curry and tiny fresh red chilies into rich and creamy coconut cream, making it taste like mysteries from an ancient earthly time when the world was real. Earthy, spicy, gritty, and no plastic for five hundred miles.

The main topics of conversation among Fijians seem to be food, fishing, the heat, and the relatives. The people in Laudi's family also discuss the various campers at their campground. We're a constant source of amusement and bewilderment for them. They especially love the musical campers, the ones with guitars. Unfortunately, for the first few days of the funeral, no music is allowed. Singing, dancing, even loud laughing are frowned upon by the elders for fear these will insult the ghost. Supposedly, the dead grandfather's spirit is still around us, watching, listening, and even partaking in the occasional feast. When I wake up at night on the beach into an uncontrollable darkness, heaves of laughter from island spirits roll in from the sea. The ghosts find it hard to leave this place. I can't blame them.

THE BURIAL

They're burying the body. The grave is beside the trail that leads from Papa and Nana's house up into the plantation. Papa must have walked on this trail every day of his life, pacing the length of his thoughts with a machete in his hand. Now he'll lie here under a weeping fig tree surrounded by tall ferns and sweet-smelling magic lilies and let the world go by. They made the coffin just this morning. The coffin is on a large platform, covered in *tapa* cloth and woven mats lined with colored wool. All the people he's given life to are here, in silence. The silence goes on for a long time. A priest speaks of the man's life with words that melt into the day's heat, words that mean little to me. My eyes fill with tears I can't understand. I didn't know him well. We'd only smile at each other as if we were sharing a secret. I imagine what his life must have looked like, how he scaled coconut trees from age five to seventy-five, how fast he could run down the road as a boy, how he fell in love with a girl's untamed hair, how he played the radio to find music lost in static, and how he sang his wife to sleep every night for fifty-five years, then counted stars out the window. These things he won't do again because he's been cut loose from the world of people and fish, coconuts and radios. I wonder who will count the stars with him gone. They need to be counted. They twinkle because we believe in them. Perhaps he'll go on counting the stars, name them, pass among them into other tender eternities through a distance he could never fathom outside his window in Taveuni.

As we leave Papa alone and head back to prepare another feast, it strikes me that Fijians, being communal, are rarely alone. They haven't even a word for it in their language. I turn around and through the crowd I see Nana, his wife, kneeling by the grave, hugging the raised coffin with her tiny frame as if she'll never let it go. These two people's hearts have pumped together through years of laughter, tides, sorrow, hurricanes, and children. Nana hasn't a word for *alone* in her language, but its meaning she'll come to know as if it walked up and belted her in the stomach.

Laudi doesn't talk to me during these days of the funeral. Except down at the beach. When we're down at the beach together he acts like a different person. We laugh, sing, tell stories of our lives, and go spear-fishing at night. He acts as if he hasn't ignored me completely for the last six hours up at the funeral. But I can't let him get away with this. It's not in my nature. He finds it difficult to explain what I know: men and women don't communicate with each other in this country. Men talk to men and women talk to women. They're different species who don't understand each other's habits. I'm not used to this. I hate it. Rarely do I come across a man and woman walking down the road together side by side. Only once have I seen a couple on the road who were laughing together, acting like friends, acting as if they truly loved each other. It made me so happy to see them and it struck me then for the first time what an unusual sight that is here. Before I began traveling I always thought of the idea of men and women being friends, whether they're in love or not, as a natural given in the way of the world. But it isn't. When men and women are this polarized they believe the most incredible things about each other. They hold silly romantic ideas like teenagers. Polarization fosters intrigue and it fosters ignorance.

FIFTH DAY OF THE FUNERAL

The atmosphere is getting lighter, the wailing is lessening. People are laughing more and we're allowed to play music again. We're all getting bigger too. Some people are waddling.

I'm a tourist on a male planet. I walk up the hill to find a group of at least twenty men circled around a kava bowl. All these men are acquaintances of mine, if not my friends. I've chatted, joked and laughed with all of them. But now, when they're all together in their circle, a blanket of testosterone hovers above them like poisonous gas. None of them says "*Bula*" or even smiles at me. Even Laudi! I know that if I were to see any of these men alone on the road they would smile their faces off at me, ask me where I'm going and treat me like a long-lost sister. I give them my best What the hell are you doing? baffled look and walk on to Nana's house to seek out friendlier faces. But what I find there is almost as alarming. I find a Fijian priest dressed in a white robe giving a Catholic sermon to a houseful of women. Auntie Uma indicates for me to sit down next to her. Immediately I'm sorry I came up here to this packed house of hot bodies where sweat pours down our backs as we watch a man read in Fijian about the lives of ancient Hebrews. I feel dizzy and my head starts drifting down towards the sea. I imagine hitting the cool green water as I smile down at the fish, envy them their simple lives. On the wall I see a calendar in this house of religious women and realize I've lost all track of days. What's happening on other islands of the world as these days pass? The priest's voice drones on and I wonder if I really can live here forever.

I rave about the chauvinism I see every day to my friends here at the beach. I'm not sure if I could be here without such an outlet. Fijian women aren't seen as human beings with intellectual and emotional capacities. They're baby-makers, cooks, and servants. Everything is the woman's fault. If a man makes a mistake, his mother is blamed for raising him wrong, or his wife is blamed. Men are never criticized. The men aren't expected to be responsible for themselves. They're like big kids. The women go along with this. That's what really gets me.

Early Fijian village life was characterized by tremendous fear and violence. Women were considered property. A wife would be killed upon the death of her husband so she could accompany him to the nether regions. A mother would be slain so her son wouldn't lie in his grave alone. Young girls would often be given to old men in marriage. The girl wouldn't be allowed to see her husband-to-be before the marriage ceremony, and if she ever spoke his name, bad luck would befall the girl and her village for years to come.

I help one of the campers, Patrick from Colorado, squeeze water out of jeans he's washed. Laudi and three of his male cousins come by and acknowledge only Patrick. As if I'm not here. As if I'm invisible. I can't believe Laudi is doing this. One of the cousins tries to make a joke with Patrick about doing women's work. Patrick says he always does the laundry. He tells them he changes his daughter's diapers. They laugh, find it incredible. A few minutes later I see Laudi again on the other side of the trees when we're alone. "Good morning, Laurie," he says as if it's our first encounter of the day. His voice and smile can usually melt me into a puddle with no memory. The heart is easily fooled, but not today. "What's with you?" I say, because I really want to understand this. He appears not to know what I'm talking about and very likely he doesn't know. "How can you ignore me like that? Why don't your cousins ever bring their wives down to the beach at night?"

He looks stunned. "They do. No, only sometimes. I don't know. It's as if they're ashamed of them." I can't be sure if Laudi says this to appease me or because it's actually occurring to him for the first time. He's intelligent in so many matters. It boggles my mind that such a basic issue can elude him so. I assail him with more questions.

"What was that comment your cousin made last night about your Uncle Voulu having a woman's mouth because he gossips? Do people really think women gossip more than men do around here? Your Auntie Uma never gossips."

Laudi stares at me, doesn't speak for an entire minute. Finally I hear these words empty from his mouth: "You're right. It's an insult to women."

I turn around to leave him standing there with the words suspended in the air, so they don't die. I must turn quickly, to hide my smile.

I decide to take a walk to the shop. The humid sea breeze cools me as it drifts through the trees. A flood of morning light streams through the branches as crickets and birds screech from all directions. Poor Laudi, I think, I must confuse him to no end. What a bizarre relationship we have. We're like some sort of exotic pets to each other. Sometimes we can barely communicate. Could I really stay here? Could I live like these women? All that work every day of the year? All that coconut fat? Could I be happy segregating myself from the male species? In coming here, I'm not just traveling; I've arrived in another galaxy. Strange colors and bewildering concepts, unidentifiable sounds and cryptic visions flash through my days from start to finish. I enter this galaxy like a stray balloon adrift from another world.

At the shop, grown men huddled together eating popsicles act like schoolboys when they see me. "Want to drink kava with us?" They're actually giggling.

I walk back under a canopy of trees in the shade of tomorrow, wondering how long I'll stay here. The road rises before me and I look up at the steep wall of dense bushes to my side. I have a passion for the curvature of land, for green rolls and teasing humps on the earth. The eye can't see beyond the hills, can't quite make out the middle distance. To know what's out there, one must imagine, one must dream. But standing on top of a hill, one can sometimes have a private observation of the sea, a view of infinity.

We all need a delicate balance of landforms.

Tonight after the funeral feast, we'll tell stories on the beach. I want lightness back, in my body and in my mind.

The Fijian men looked kavaed out already tonight from

drinking the stuff all day, and it's not even fully dark yet. I wonder how long they can keep up these festivities. I've just come in from a swim and am feeling much better about this place. The evening always does it to me. There's little twilight in the tropics but there is this blue, the bright sizzling blue the sky becomes just before the stars show up, when there's still a bath of light behind the sky. The electric blue only lasts a few minutes, then slips away to give itself over to the slick black you can never quite touch with your mind. Stars that have been waiting all day to present themselves soft-shoe out like Fred Astaire from all corners of the universe. Out there, nothing remains still but the silence.

Kalisi and a few of her cousins, Deseree, Ana, Lee, Laudi, and I make circles in the sand with our feet, spiral patterns like that giant monkey's tail in Peru. We do cartwheels and handstands, sing songs, and splash each other with the waves. We join the men around the fire and drink kava with them. When we want a full coconut serving of kava, we say to the kava server, usually Uncle Adi, "High tide," meaning "Fill it to the top." For a small serving, we say "Low tide." They always laugh at us when we say "low tide." They know how strong kava is. Laudi, Uncle Adi, and the Quiet Cousins (their voices are so soft) sing as they drink too many high tides and gradually fade away into the night, the cousins staggering home. The travelers and I stay up late and tell stories. We talk about searching for the perfect place, our favorite topic lately. I tell them about New Zealand, about how a place really can be perfect, how every so often nature indulges in a creation of trees and cliffs, brooks and valleys, space, light and breezes so precisely unified that it feels like the conception of an enchanted dream.

Life can be this light, I realize as we tell our stories on the beach. No rules are written up in the sky.

SOMETHING OUTRAGEOUS
UNDER A HOLE IN THE SKY

I HATED NEW ZEALAND when I first got there. I continued to hate it for exactly three days. Then I woke up.

New Zealand is very nearly perfect. I find it difficult to identify any flaws in the place at all. The only reason I didn't fall madly in love with it immediately on arrival was I had just left Fiji behind me. Countries are like lovers. Our hearts can't jump from one love to the next so callously. It's betrayal.

Heartsick for Fiji, I resented New Zealand her green and wholesome sheep-smattered countryside with all those narrow winding roads. I might as well be in England. At least England has castles, I complained to myself as I hitched north of Auckland. Everything was too clean and orderly here, too polite.

I like places with too much dirt and passion, places full of, for lack of a better word, love. The kind of love you come across unexpectedly, in sunless back alleys where children hang the whole family's laundry on filthy railings and smile at you anyway. The kind of love that's unprotected by beauty, that's a tender discovery of something brand-new.

But as I said, it didn't take long to love New Zealand. The first thing that struck me was that I must have flown in a time machine and landed somewhere back in the late 1950s, to Canada perhaps. People from New Zealand still stand up for the national anthem before a movie begins. To get a newspaper out of a box on any city street, you open the box, take out the newspaper, then put your money in a little tin. Honesty boxes, they used to call them. Many of the cars on the country lanes seem to be from the '50s or even earlier. The people who gave me rides in those cars drove slowly, as if out for a Sunday afternoon breath of fresh air. "Where are you going?" I would ask them when I climbed in. "Wherever you're going," they would tell me. And so we'd pass pleasantly through rolling pastures and friendly little towns, often stopping on the way for tea with whomever they knew living nearby. Almost everyone in New Zealand seems to know everyone else, or is one person removed from another. "This country's like a big family," they would tell me. "No need to lock our doors here. No need at all."

New Zealand has to be the best place for hitchhiking in the world. Often, elderly women driving alone pull over for backpackers, even male backpackers, even two males with big backpacks. I saw it myself several times. Travelers tell each other stories about how unbelievably good the hitching is. Kiwis, as they're affectionately known, love to show travelers their country. It's part of their national pride. Many times a driver would take me miles out of the way to show me a waterfall or, twice, the country's oldest living tree. (Or possibly it was the country's tallest tree. I saw it twice and still can't remember, but in any case, both my tour guides were extremely proud of that tree.) Several times I was asked to come back and spend the night with the driver's family and continue my journey the next day. One day, a friend and I got a ride from a young redheaded accountant named Percy who was touring the Coromandel Peninsula. He told us he would be driving to Wellington on business in a week and we should give him a call if we wanted a ride there. A week later, I called Percy to see if he'd left yet and I reached him on his car phone. He was already halfway to Wellington. "I'm so sorry! I had to leave at six this morning, quite unexpectedly," he told me. "But I'll turn around and drive back up to Auckland to pick you two up." It actually took a good five minutes to talk Percy out of the idea.

Once we got a ride from a Maori man and his son. They'd been out collecting mussels all morning on the beach, and when we left them, they insisted we take a generous share of mussels for our lunch. They let us off at Hot Water Beach. If Hot Water Beach were in North America, someone would charge admission and it would be overrun with tourists and camcorders and neon and tacky souvenirs. But in New Zealand, it is simply a lovely beach where bubbling surges of hot springs erupt out of the sand just at the place where the ocean meets the shore. At low tide, children dig holes in the sand with shovels and let the thermal waters boil up from below to fill them. Then they sit down in the holes and shriek from the steaming heat until waves pile over to cool them off. They call the holes bathtubs. When my friend and I were there, Hot Water Beach had four somewhat ramshackle cabins you could rent for eight dollars a night and a sunrise rich enough to die in. That was all.

New Zealand doesn't seem to suffer from extremes. It's never too hot nor too cold. I saw no evidence of what one associates with the fabulously wealthy, no signs of conspicuous affluence. Nor did I see squalor, only the very occasional panhandler in Auckland. I often thought the country was a happy assemblage of eccentrics who until recently have had few outside visitors. Perhaps that's why they're so friendly, extraordinarily so.

One evening, a friend and I were hitchhiking on the South Island. On a practically deserted road, we'd been standing for over three hours in the rain and were starting to shiver. We sang every show tune we knew. From across the road in the mist of a field, we saw a man coming towards us, waving. He looked to be in his mid-fifties and he sported a bright yellow raincoat. Underneath the childlike garb, he must have been wearing very short shorts, but all we saw were the Paddington Bear coat, oversized green gumboots and a pair of sturdy pink legs striding our way.

"Won't be any traffic this way tonight. None atal'. Come back with me," he called to us. When we ran over to him, drenching wet, I saw that he looked like so many men in New Zealand his age: robust, with a healthy tousle of wind-blown cream-white hair, ruddy cheeks, and bright blue eyes. As if he'd just bounded out of the Scottish Highlands.

Danny was his name and he took us back to his little shack of a home where he lived alone and immediately whipped us up a meal fit for royalty. We were amazed at how he managed to put so much food on our plates (pheasant he'd shot that day, fresh eggs, spaghetti), cooking it over a sin-gle hot plate. He spent hours telling us about the hell he'd gone through fighting in Vietnam (which surprised the heck out of me, New Zealand fighting in Vietnam) and then he found some musty blankets in his attic and made us a bed like a nest on his floor.

A few weeks later my friend Charlie from Canada and I hooked up, and we decided to walk the Abel Tasman Trek. For a week we hiked along the north coast of the South Island along white sandy shores and through rain forest, spending our nights in cabins along the way. The Germans we met always liked to leave the cabins at the crack of dawn so they could be the first to arrive at the next cabin at the day's end, to ensure sleeping on a bunk bed rather than the floor. I always ended up sleeping on the floor, not being a morning person, nor a German. But I was usually too exhausted to care. Occasionally we would pass whole classes of schoolchildren hiking on the trail and they were always so full of friendly politeness we thought they must have attended a school for good manners. "There must be *something* wrong with this country," we kept saying as we hiked. But we couldn't find it.

Somehow, probably since we were in no particular hurry, we fell behind the group of fellow trekkers, and eventually we found ourselves hiking alone without encountering anyone for whole afternoons at a time. That's when I began noticing my head, or, more specifically, my hair. Something unusual was going on up there, but I couldn't fathom what it was. At first it only bothered me at night. I would dream aliens were invading my head and I'd wake up attacking my skull viciously. Then one day on the trek after a swim in the ocean, I flung my wet hair down on a towel to dry it. When I looked at the towel I saw them for the first time, armies of them: hideous crawling things. They'd come jetting out of my hair, evacuated from their stronghold that was my head. No denying what they were, although I couldn't bring myself to say the word.

"Looks like you've got lice there, Laur," said Charlie too happily. "Hope you don't give them to me."

"You probably don't have enough hair for them to be happy anyway," I told him, distraught. I started to panic. "Aren't there special shampoos to get rid of lice?" Then the thought struck me: What if I have lice everywhere? What if these nasty vermin are all over my body? Where do they come from anyway? I started to feel itchy absolutely everywhere.

"Charlie, you have to help me. You have to check me out. Check to see if I have any more lice, you know, down here." I pointed down.

"You're kidding. I don't think the two are related. They're cousins or something, but I think it's a different thing entirely," he said.

"Charlie, I'm itchy everywhere. Nobody's around. We haven't passed anyone on the trail all morning." I ripped down my shorts and told him to find whatever he could down there. Charlie, a true friend, complied. He knelt down in front of me for up-close inspection as I stood beside the trail in the trees. Like an explorer in the Amazon searching for an extinct species, he searched thoroughly.

"Nope, don't see anything yet," he said with squinted eyes, and he continued his examination.

"Thank God. You're sure?"

Charlie didn't have time to answer. Standing directly in front of me on the trail was a troop of at least fifteen middle-aged German hikers staring at us. Serious German hikers, with hiking sticks, expensive leather boots, and probably lederhosen. Not that I took the time to see any lederhosen. I threw my shorts back on and ran off the trail into the trees faster than I've ever done anything in my life. I stayed crouched down inside a bush watching, trying to remember how to inhale oxygen. Charlie remained on his knees. "It's medical," I heard him say. "Really, it's just medical."

"Yaw, yaw, medical, we believe you, medical," they said and shook their heads. As each new German hiker rounded the corner and came on the scene, the ones in front explained in German what they had witnessed.

"Yaw? It is true? Yaw?" Their eyes would take over their faces and I would see them look for me through the tangle of trees.

"Really, it's just medical," said Charlie.

"Yaw, yaw, medical." I doubt any of them believed us. It must have looked rather perverted, especially since Charlie was inspecting with such intensity, as if he'd never seen a naked woman before and wanted to make sure he was seeing right.

Charlie left for Australia not long after our trek and I stayed in New Zealand. I was having too much fun to leave. I joined an organization where people can work on organic farms in exchange for room and board, and I spent weeks rambling around the country, hiking, rafting, meeting the country's eccentrics and pulling weeds from vegetable gardens.

Then one day I found Happy Acre. On the northwest coast of the South Island lies a magic kingdom called Golden Bay. It's so inaccessible that few visitors ever find it. You have to drive over a mountain on a stomach-churning switchback road for hours before arriving there. With every

turn I became more nauseated and was beginning to wonder if I hadn't made a mistake in coming to such outer
reaches of land. When the driver of my last ride rounded the
last switchback corner of the mountain road, however, I saw
what was on the other side of the mountain, and I understood. I knew I'd arrived in a place unlike any I'd ever been.

It was more than looking down from a mountain and
finding an excruciatingly green sweep of land colored with
mirage-baked dwellings from another time, more than seeing that lush sway of land arch gently to greet the bristling
blue of the sea. It was something deeper than how the place
looked. Something here had collided with the inspiration of
the sun, moon, and stars, with the grace of an unknown
angel. It was an overwhelming feeling that I couldn't shake.
What was this place? I had thought only in fairy tales and
dreams does the world ripen to such subtleties of spirit.

I walked rather dazedly through Golden Bay's little town
called Takaka. People smiled and stopped to talk to me, ask
where I came from, and I had the strangest impression that
I had met them all somewhere before. But that was impossible. They didn't resemble anyone I had ever known. At a
superficial glance this town might have appeared like one of
those utopian green settlements of northern California or
British Columbia, but it felt richer and truer than those
places. It wasn't a large town, nor certainly a wealthy one.
Almost all the cars were over twenty years old and many
buildings were in need of repair. But never had I seen such

serene faces. All the people seemed not only to know each other, but to be utterly and madly in love with each other also. Babies beamed, women flushed, little boys chased their laughing fathers down the main street. Young girls sold fruit and flowers from stands while they played with each other's hair. And from somewhere in the distance, I could hear bagpipes. Who were these people?

Following the directions to Happy Acre in the organic farm-workers' guidebook, I hitched a ride along a country road that wound through violet meadows and over hills, always with the ocean not far from view. When the driver stopped her car in front of an overgrown cottage barely visible behind a tangle of vines and mass of hanging flowers and apricots, she said, "Happy Acre; you're in for something completely different." Then she sped away.

I bushwhacked my way through the front yard and knocked on the door. I hadn't phoned ahead to say I was coming because the guidebook said there was no phone at Happy Acre. It said simply, "Just come." So I came.

The door swung open so fast I thought I couldn't be seeing the man who stood in front of me as he really was. Surely I had lapsed into some sort of mysterious hallucinogenic state peculiar to the area. The man's image as he stood at the door that day is imprinted within the folds of my brain forever. He was in his early thirties, sunburnt and pink-cheeked, muscular, of average height, with singing sky-blue eyes. He wore a Scottish kilt, a red and green jester's hat with a bell on top, a mud-spattered t-shirt that said "Born in the Shallow End of the Gene Pool," a screaming indigo formal necktie, colored pieces of cloth, shells and pebbles entwined in his flaming red hair, and a ring in his nose.

"Oh perfect. You're just in time for dinner! I've been expecting you." I couldn't believe it. Was he psychic? When he grabbed my hand to lead me into his hobbit house I felt as if I were Alice disappearing down the hole. A happy Alice—he fascinated me. As he led me, he skipped. And when he skipped, he jingled. His ankles hosted a stunning array of silver jewelry made of little bells. He skipped me all the way into his main room where a red and white gingham tablecloth was neatly laid out on the floor and covered with bowls of food. All the food looked as if it had just walked in from his garden. There was a bowl of mashed avocados mixed with cherry tomatoes, a bowl of plums, a bowl of nuts, and, largest of all, a bowl containing herbs, lettuces, sprouts and orange flowers. No wonder he looked so ridiculously healthy.

"What took you so long to get here?" he asked as we sat down cross-legged facing each other to eat.

"Oh, I had some places to see first. You know, other countries, mountains, cities, a few rivers, that kind of thing." What was I saying? I didn't even know his name. "My name's Laurie, by the way."

"You look like one. I'm Hank."

"Hank?"

"Hank."

Among other things, Hank was an inventor. He was also a maker and collector of musical instruments. His house was overrun with the most remarkable instruments I'd ever seen: carved dideridoos from Australia, singing bowls from Nepal, harps from Ireland, congas from West Africa, penny whistles, antique fiddles and mandolins. In the corner sat a prized sitar.

"The one I'm constructing right now doesn't even need anyone to play it. The wind plays it. Come and see." He hopped up like a kid and ran out his back door to show me. Standing in the center of his backyard on a little hill in the tall grass was a giant wooden structure which supported long translucent cords of varying lengths and thicknesses. "Listen, hear that?" And I did hear it. The wind was playing music.

While we ate what I felt sure was the best food I'd ever tasted, Hank continued to talk about his life as if we were old friends who needed to catch up on things. His current favorite instrument was the jew's harp which he twanged between his teeth daily on the main street of Takaka for passers-by. He had lived in Golden Bay for only three years but loved it with a passion. When his wife left him for the woman he was having an affair with—I had to get him to say that twice to get it right—he moved north from

Christchurch and bought Happy Acre. On his little one-acre farm he grew enough food to feed everybody who came to work with him, and many came. They came from all over the world. Hank was also a politician, of sorts. He had been nominated to represent Golden Bay as a candidate in the federal elections for the McGilicuty Party, an absurdist party wanting to run New Zealand like medieval serfdoms. Hank campaigned for Golden Bay to break away and become its own kingdom to stand against the world. Already, Golden Bay had a green economy which used barter for services rather than dollars. Hank and I talked for hours that night. He told me about Golden Bay, about the seasonal festivals, mock medieval feasts and battles on the beach, all-night out-door dancing parties and fancy balls where people dressed in the most outrageous clothes they could find. Even after the little I had seen of Golden Bay, I was inclined to believe everything he said.

As unusual as Hank was, I felt as if I had found a lost brother. I think we understood something fundamental about each other from that very first night. Seeking out the rapture of being alive was what mattered to us. And if the world laughed at us for this, so what. When I finally lay down to sleep at four in the morning, Hank called out several times from his bedroom into mine, "Are you dreaming yet? Call out when you start to dream."

I like to believe we're all unique human experiments on the part of nature, but some more so than the rest.

On my first morning at Happy Acre, Hank made us banana almond smoothies with green spirulina and carob powder thrown in. We repaired some decrepit bicycles of Hank's and rode them into town. Just outside of Takaka are community organic gardens where townspeople share gardening and vegetables. Hank went there that morning for a music practice with his Celtic band. They were preparing for an upcoming solstice party. While I explored the gardens, Morris dancers sprang around among the trees to the music of fiddles, penny whistles, durans and a jew's harp. Later, when we rode into Takaka, Hank introduced me to all the people he knew, which was almost everyone in town. I thought some sort of annual town fair or celebration was going on, with all the lively commotion and open markets, the singing, a children's game down the center of the street, and all the people eating homemade ice cream all over the place. In the days to follow, I realized the town is always that way.

Hank and I walked over ten miles that afternoon along the beach behind his house. We were in search of the dolphin. For some reason, a dolphin had separated from its pod and become friendly with the people of Golden Bay. It swims right up to people, plays games with them and even allows children to ride its fin. The water was cold but I couldn't pass up the chance to swim with a dolphin. I was elated when it swam to me, circled me several times, then allowed me to touch its smooth hard back. Touching its skin was magical. It was as if I were entering the shadowy and silent, private world of all sea creatures. I played with the dolphin for two hours, until I turned blue from the cold. I couldn't tear myself away.

I spent a month at Happy Acre with Hank, although I often think now it was probably longer than that. Hank didn't keep track of the days or months and I tended to go along with him on this. In fact, just about everything Hank did eventually made sense to me. That's when I knew it was time to leave.

It was in New Zealand that I first met the crazy Irishman. I saw him while I was sitting in a movie theatre one evening watching D.H. Lawrence's *The Rainbow* and waiting for its second half to start. That's another thing about New Zealand that endears it to my heart; they still have intermissions at movies, reminding me of my childhood in Canada. In the dim lights of the intermission, I felt the stare of untamed eyes aimed at me from across the aisle. I turned to look into the wild eyes, face them squarely. I like to look into the face of insanity when I get the chance. The eyes belonged to a stocky, solidly built man with straggly blond hair and a scar down one cheek, a man in his late twenties, I guessed, or, possibly, his forties. It was difficult to say.

"Hey you, you there," he said. I turned around to see if he was talking to someone else. He wasn't.

"Me?"

"Yes, you. Of course you. Who else? You should do something outrageous."

"Outrageous?"

"Yes. Outrageous. I've raced camels across the outback of Australia. Next month I'm going to Saudi Arabia to race camels there. After that, dog-sledding in the Arctic. What are you going to do?"

His thick Irish accent sunk into my brain like rain into moss. I felt as if I were hearing the most important advice of my life, although that was absurd. I didn't answer him, but when the movie came back on, I couldn't pay attention to it anymore.

I saw the crazy Irishman everywhere after that. He would always yell things out to me—usually from across a street—profound and corny platitudes that I imagined he must have scrawled on bathroom walls or in metro stations.

"Hey you, have you dredged your soul with a rake?" he once shouted at me. "Well, have you?" Another day in Takaka, from behind me on the sidewalk, I heard him call out, "Hey you, do you see beauty when beauty isn't pretty?"

He never wanted to have a conversation. I'm not sure he knew how. In the beginning, when I tried to talk to him after one of his outbursts, his eyes would erupt with supernova passion, but also with alarm, as if he were frightened of the words he found in himself. He would walk away quickly as if he hadn't spoken at all. Later on, when I saw him weeks, even months after, in Asia, I knew not to engage him in conversation. He wasn't made for that sort of talking.

One day I hitched out to the northwest coast of the

South Island, to a place that's so deserted, so desolate and so barren, people from Golden Bay call it The Extreme.

When I arrived I understood why.

On a beach ransacked by eternal wind, swept-back trees in serpentine shapes flung themselves down in suicidal angles. Gnarled arthritic trees cowered behind boulders to hide, not from the wind itself, but from its howling. For protection, little round dwarf trees found homes in hollows and caves. Unearthly forces sculpted trees into human and animal shapes, sensuous curves rising out of the sand. A fine white dust blown up from the spirit world swept over the rocks. Covered with this magic powder, the rocks must have heard the crashing of the sea and felt the sun's heat.

A wind tunnel bore through a tree trunk. I walked through it to pick something up in the sand. When I examined the thing, turned it over and over in my hand, I didn't know if it was a rock or an ancient piece of wood. The thing looked like a rock, round and smooth, but was light enough to toss in the wind, faded of color, almost white, polished by centuries of sea-salted waves. Trees leaned over in alarming reaches to feel the softness of the sand; their branches and trunks curled and melted into one another in agonized relief. It must have fought the loneliness, grasping and touching each other's skin like that. You might have thought those trees were dead, but I say they were alive, only feigning death. They were centuries old, however, lying low like grey hollow corpses so the world would leave them be.

The wind has always blown too hard there. It never lets up and one could go mad. It isn't a place for everyone. It invites the unusual. This is a place to dredge my soul with a rake, I thought. This is beauty when beauty isn't pretty. The crazy Irishman should have lived out there.

I did find a woman who lived on The Extreme. She lived alone. High above the beach she lived in a house on a cliff on the edge of her past. She had left her life behind and, out there, had become young again, like a golden girl of twelve who was in direct contact with her happiness. She read my signs. She told me I'm rootless like the wind and always will be. She said moving on and seeking out are all my heart will ever do and I must follow or die inside. Blowing through that woman, the wind must have imparted its secrets.

How else could she have known me so well after five minutes?

New Zealand is a country lush with everything one dreams of: rolling green hills and alpine meadows, jagged snowy peaks and glaciers, lakes, rivers, quiet valleys and, everywhere, on all sides, the sea. The climate is like an ideal neighbor: it places no unreasonable demands on you while remaining ever pleasant and generous. The people of New Zealand seem to have come from a forgotten time, when caring for each other took precedence over high salaries. New Zealand is a country with little crime, big forests, ruddy-cheeked highlanders, old cars and intermission at the movies.

So I kept calling it the perfect place, but there was one thing not quite right. Just one.

Consider the burning power of the stars. Consider a star so sizzling hot it singes the thin outer layer of a planet's inhabitants ninety million miles away. Like singeing rice-paper red.

The one thing that keeps New Zealand from being perfect is simply this: the absence of an ozone layer. A giant gaping hole in the stratosphere looms directly above that part of the world. The sun, although not excessively hot, cuts through your skin like a knife and sets your veins on fire. It's not even New Zealand's fault; it's not as if they're a greedy industrialized nation deserving that sort of thing. Unfortunately, I don't have tough skin that can withstand sun of that intensity, nor do many descendants of the Scottish immigrants who came to New Zealand a century ago.

Something always stands in the way of paradise. But perhaps this is how it always is. Perhaps this is the only story ever written.

CHAPTER FIVE

"WE MET HIM TOO! Your crazy Irishman! In Australia," say Ana and Lee. "He was on his way to the outback. We met him in a pub in Perth. He said he wanted to walk across the Australian desert to Ayers Rock with camels, like that woman did in the '70s. He drank cranberry juice and sat alone. He was bizarre. He came over to our table and asked us what we ached for. He said, 'Hey you, what do you ache for?' He asked everybody sitting with us. He wanted worthy answers. Long wild hair, crazed eyes. Just like you said. It has to be the same guy."

We talk about New Zealand and Australia until the Big Dipper falls into the ocean. Not everyone loves Australia. The country is harsh, even crude sometimes, especially the men. The ozone problem is even worse there, where it's hotter, than in New Zealand. But Australians don't seem to let it bother them. Many lie under a scorching sun along beaches the way Californians did twenty years ago, thousands of them competing for space in the sand, like guinea pigs for skin cancer research. The men brag to each other about who has the most melanoma scars.

DREAM

My kava-induced dreams transport me to a blinding sunny meadow where I find a trail leading into a woods. I leave the meadow and take the trail. Inside the moist, deeply shaded woods, snow falls on my cheeks. Then I realize this can't be snow because I'm in the tropics. I taste it and realize it's tropical snow, which I had forgotten about. I look up into the trees but can't see the tops of their branches. The trail becomes mistier the further I walk. I come across blossoms the size of human heads. As I walk by the blossoms, they turn and watch me. I walk deeper into the woods. I'm looking for something but I forget what it is. I have a vague feeling I'm seeking an ancient secret library that should be in the woods. I want to work in this library and read all its books. The books will tell me crucial things I need to know. I see an old man walk towards me on the path. At first I think it's my long-ago deceased Scottish grandfather who was a Canadian prairie farmer in the Depression. Then he turns into Papa, Laudi's grandfather. "I thought you were dead," I say to him. "I am dead," he says, "and I've never felt so alive." He does a kind of jig. I notice his old-fashioned leather boots are caked in mud, as if he has just come out of the field, or the grave. "I'm sorry I laughed on your dead face," I say to him. "Oh, I'm glad you laughed on it, lass, I enjoyed that." He carries on down the path with some sort of farming implement in his hand. He's on his way to hoe the sunny meadow. I continue down the trail. On the ground I find a goblet sitting in the middle of the path. I look inside it and I realize the goblet is full of liquid golden-rod. A man with a dark beard and green eyes is hiding in a tree above me. Although I can't see him clearly, I find him overwhelmingly attractive. He tells me to drink the golden-rod. He says drinking it will reveal to me the secrets of the universe. I drink it and it's sweet and creamy, delicious, the best drink I've ever tasted. I feel an immediate rush of warmth spread through my veins. But then I look at the man and notice his teeth are made from pieces of broken glass. He also is now drinking, except he's drinking not from a goblet, but a beer mug. He pounds the beer mug down to the ground for another round. My liquid golden-rod turns into stale beer. The sweet and clear essence of my drink is lost. Now it's murky, brown and salty, like dregs from the sea. Revolting.

I wake in a sweat in the center core of night. Where am I? How did I get here? I wait for the memories to fall back into place, to re-enter this world, reinhabit my body. I don't rush to come back. I enjoy this void that lies between the worlds. I'm no longer dreaming, but I can't place myself in this other world either. Anything is possible in the void. I feel light enough to fly. I hear the sea surrounding me. Yes,

I'm beside the ocean. Images are starting to crowd in, too many at once. I see Laudi float by, and Vix, a fire, stories we told last night, a woman living beside a cliff, a dead man's cold face, too much kava. I feel leaden with coconut oil. I'm in Taveuni, and I had a weird dream.

FUNERAL: DAY NINE

Everyone's going wild. Chaos and craziness have been unleashed from people's hearts. Even adults are throwing water at each other from buckets, screaming with hysterics. Cousins, sisters, brothers, mothers, uncles, and children are chasing each other everywhere. They've plastered their arms, legs, and faces in flour. I'm not sure why, but it sure looks funny. Music and dancing vibrate and pulse deep into the night. Auntie Sala jiggles her body to the guitar music, her entire skin white with flour like an enormous dancing powder puff. I've never seen anyone's hips move like hers do. "I'm shivering. I'm shimmering," she says over and over. People roar and cheer her on. The mourning has lifted. The ghost is gone. After the volumes of food consumed, nobody's clothes fit anymore. I hope to God no one dies again soon. The island would sink from the weight.

Yurgen the Eccentric Romanian, whom we can now safely call pompous, has been experimenting with kava. By this I mean he has been drinking the stuff steadily, morning, noon, and night, since his arrival three weeks ago. He told us he has studied the effects of various natural drugs and narcotics around the world, such as the yage vine in the Amazon, opium from Thailand, New Zealand cactus, Mexican mushrooms, the betal nut from India, toad skins, and snake venom. I was dubious of this at first, but now that I've listened to him further, I see no reason to believe he hasn't experimented with every mind-bending drug known to the universe. He told me that after drinking kava, he paints in watercolors on the beach and everything in his subconscious pours out onto the canvas. He only discovers what he has painted when it's finished. "You mean you Freudian slip all over the paper?" I said. "No, that's what I do when I eat peyote from Guatemala. Kava makes me tell the truth in my paintings." Then he asked me to come back to his tent to check out his retrospective kava-induced early works. Jesus. I told him I had important things to do, like sweep sand out of my tent.

WATER SLIDE

Laudi, Ana, Lee, Deseree, and I have walked through fields of coffee beans and coconut trees to find the water slide today. We're deep in the bush where the ocean is never heard and rarely considered. The sun aches to break into this steamy rain forest but the trees, tangle of plants, even the jungle flowers, won't let it. This place is too full of itself, grows denser by the minute, and smells too wild. We watch fearless children jump from frightening heights into a bottomless green pool. I recognize many of the children from school and they wave at me before they jump. So this is where their happiness comes from, I think. They scale the rocks of the steep hill all the way to the top of the water slide, where water rushes down a long sweep of smooth curved rock made slippery by a thin layer of moss. In Fijian, they try to tell us how to descend, but I can't catch their runaway dialect fast enough. Their excitement about it is sufficient.

Ana goes first and I hear her screams all the way down, then abrupt silence. The children cheer. A young girl, dripping wet and breathing hard, clambers up the rocks and looks at me as if to say "What are you waiting for?" So I go.

You have to put your trust in the water, believe the water won't smash you against a wall of rock. As you drop down with the surging falls you swear you won't do this again, ever. You pray to the god of foolish impulses to let you off easy this time. To stop yourself halfway down the slide is impossible. You'd die. The water never stops itself. At the end of the ride, the water dumps you into a deep cool green pool. It dumps you suddenly and you realize you're still alive inside it. Your heart resumes its beat and you begin to laugh. You do it one more time.

There's a sea turtle held hostage on our beach. We find it there when we return from the water slide. The turtle is massive, with eyes like a sleepy grandfather. An ugly cord ties him to a big rock that says no, no matter how hard he tries to walk back into his old life in the sea. Nobody admits responsibility for this. Laudi suspects his Uncle Vix. Vix suspects everyone else. Neither of them says this to the other.

Fijians eat turtle meat. They love it, they say, even if it's heavy and oily and takes forever to cook; they like it in stew. The size of the turtle means he's probably eighty to one hundred years old, says Jim, a biologist from Auckland. Ana, Patrick, Deseree, and I cringe. Somehow his age makes his fate even worse. He's swum through the twentieth century, through decades of tides, hurricanes, forever-changing hemlines, wars, assassinations, and all manner of fishing boats. He may have swum these waters when Fijians were cannibals. Tonight he'll be stew. One clip of the vile cord could erase all this. Nobody says this aloud, but I know our minds share the thought.

UMA AND KALISI

There are few things to be serious about in Fiji, but superstition is one of them. The word *taboo* (and *tattoo*) comes from here. To go along with their superstition and taboos, one has to suspend temporarily all rational thought.

I'm visiting Kalisi and her mother, Uma, at their lovely ramshackle house at the edge of the woods. From bushes we've just picked fiery red chilies which Uma will cook with tonight. Uma says we can only pick chilies from the left side of the bush. Evil spirits live in the right sides of bushes.

Be especially careful when you pick lemon leaf for tea, she tells me.

We've been discussing men. I tell them I can't understand Laudi. He's such a loving presence while we're alone, filled with stories and quirky passions, questions, and musing. But as soon as one of his male cousins or male friends appears, I vaporize. They don't seem to realize I'm standing right there with them, that I'm an actual thinking, breathing, feeling person. Sometimes they go on talking and ignoring me for so long I have to walk away, pissed off and thoroughly disenchanted. Uma and Kalisi smile at me but don't comment. What would they say? This is the way all men behave in their world. I could tell them I think most men here are stuck in their adolescence. I could tell them that sometimes I can't believe I have anything to do with Laudi at all, that although I find him sweet and sexy and fun, that can't possibly be enough to sustain me when our ways in the world are so different. I could tell them that on the nights Laudi sings to me under the stars, I can almost forget everything else—the chauvinism, the adolescent inclinations—and let his voice drench through me so that the other things don't matter. I don't want them to matter. But I don't tell Kalisi and Uma these thoughts. People don't tell each other their secret thoughts here. Things must be kept light. It's an island rule.

So instead, we laugh and tell jokes about how much kava the men drink and how they howl at the moon. Kalisi waves her hand at the mention of certain men and says "No time," meaning, I suppose, that she can't be bothered with them. They ask me about men in my country and I realize there are many things that wouldn't make sense to them. I say that in Canada, men and women can be friends and they usually see each other as equals. I also tell them that many people in Canada, unlike those in Fiji, are so individualistic that finding someone compatible can be difficult.

"And it's not even necessary anymore," I say. "You don't marry for economic reasons like people used to, or like you do here."

"Then why does anyone bother?" asks Kalisi.

"I don't know. For different reasons. For love. Everyone gravitates to love."

Slowly, Uma nods her head and widens her enormous eyes, as if she has intimate knowledge that what I say is true. Kalisi waves her hand. "No time," she says.

I feel another stomachache coming on as we talk. I get these here occasionally and I think it has something to do with all the flies swarming the food, although I don't say this. Uma brews some special leaves for me from a plant growing outside the house. The brew tastes bitter, but remarkably, it cures my stomachache almost immediately. Another un-published virtue of the earth. She tells me to lie down on my back on the mat and she rubs coconut oil on my stomach with her strong experienced hands. I think she's rearranging my organs. I squeeze Kalisi's hand in agony while Uma's eyes grow completely round as she hovers over me, massaging. Uma laughs and tells me I will sleep well tonight, dream of water. Uma's entirely lovable. She's passion and subtle brilliance, born for a grace of living close to the earth, close to her gods. When it's time to go, I leave them, mother and daughter, collecting more chilies from the left side of the bush. Each of us laughs when we wave good-bye, laughs at the curious world we walk through every day, and at the one we find in each other.

The turtle is free. Someone has cut the cord. Someone amongst us, someone here on this beach, has had the nerve, the whimsy, the sentiment, to perform this outrageous act of defiance. A small crowd of Fijians and a few campers are gathered by the water where the prize turtle was jailed to the rock. Vix is furious.

"Who's done this?" he shouts. His face is gravely angry. Nobody says anything. "I was going to present that turtle to the chief in a ceremony tonight." Earlier, Vix had denied any knowledge of the turtle capture. He storms off, kicking sand as he goes. Over his shoulder he yells back at the group of us: "I'll find out who did this to me."

"Oh my God," Laudi says to me alone. "The chief's not even on the island right now and they hate each other anyway. Vix just wanted to eat the thing."

Why Laudi can't say this directly to Vix I don't

understand, but I don't say this to Laudi. I, too, am falling into this strange world of hiding away one's thoughts.

Vix joins the family at dinner and he's in an unusually good mood. Rarely does Vix eat at Nana's house, his mother's house, but tonight there's excitement in the air and I don't know why. I thought Vix would be especially miserable after what happened today. I try to be invisible, more so than usual at these dinners, and I stare down at my fried cassava. In the center of the table sits a large bowl covered with a cloth. People seem to be talking about it. Some people are looking at me, speaking Fijian to someone else, but looking right at me. I hate this feeling and wonder what's happening. Then Vix tears the cloth off the bowl.

"*Vonu!*" squeals little Kura. *Vonu* means turtle.

I'm amazed. I don't get it. I thought the turtle was free. I feel lost in this world of secrets and confusion. My head swims and can't stay afloat. I look at Vix, at his overbearing untidy body, at his eyes set back in a skull-like hardened face. I wonder if he's ever spoken a true word in his life, if he's ever said a true thing.

It's time to leave this place for a while. I smell smoke burning from the campfire on the beach. I hear the rhythmic beat of kava being pounded into powder. The sun has fallen out of the sky. It's time for night to cool us, replenish us, give us back what the day took away.

Yurgen the Eccentric Romanian begins the night's stories by launching into his drug tales, again. The rest of us settle back and listen. We're getting used to each other.

"I've had hallucinations so intense I've lain down on my back on top of fires like this one. See the scars?" He lifts his shirt to show us his back in the firelight. I don't see any scars, only a tattoo. "This scar came from Papua New Guinea," he continues. "I've lost track of days at a time and regained consciousness in different countries from where I started."

We laugh at this. I see the reflection of the fire in Yurgen's John Lennon glasses and I know he's angry with us already. This doesn't stop him, however. "I believe I'll fly one day too," he goes on. Yurgen's erratic words flow into the night, dreamily entering the world and our minds. Lying on the sand I feel the warmth of the fire and the breeze off the sea with these friends laughing all around me. Traveling tales unravel here, like kite strings into the sky. We're drawn to travel because, like love, it's stepping into the unknown. Patrick tells us about one night in Peru when he thought bandits would kill him. Ana's stories are of Africa: safaris and elephants and mysterious painted people. Untamed, wild places of the heart. Yurgen tells us how he began traveling at age twenty-three. He smuggled himself out of Romania and made his way to Berlin, where he earned a Bohemian's living in sidewalk art. He found more coins in his cup at the end of a day of painting splashy angry faces than after depicting quiet rural scenes of his homeland. So he became the angry-face man. He has wiped the Transylvanian Alps from his palette and his mind.

My initiation to travel wasn't political, or artistic. My initiation to travel planted the Road in my soul. I tell them how I found the Road. I tell them about living in the tree and the five-thousand-mile motorcycle ride with Clarence McQuiggle, the mad Maritimer. I like telling that story.

We talk deep into the night....

TRAVELS WITH CLARENCE

I WAS OUT OF MY TREE the first time I saw Clarence McQuiggle. I mean that literally. I had been in the Redwood Forest in northern California during an unkindly wet spring and my cheap little Canadian Tire tent proved itself useless for those rains. That's when I found my tree. Redwood trees are massive; they dwarf people. Rain was soaking me and my backpack right through to our insides. The enchanted forest was rapidly losing its charm as I looked around an empty campground for a place to set up my tent. Then I spotted her. She was a hollowed-out redwood with an opening like a cave, big enough to crawl inside and stay dry. Once inside I realized this tree was big enough to lie down in. So I found a home for the night, a dry home, and it wasn't going to be another night in that lousy tent. As I settled in with my sleeping bag I wondered if anybody had lived in this tree before. Perhaps a gold miner, an Indian princess, a family of dwarfs. Maybe even a deranged hermit.

I was twenty years old and on my very first solo journey of discovery. That spring was the first time I'd hitchhiked. When I christened my thumb for the first time on the Banff-Jasper Highway in the Alberta Rocky Mountains I believed I was hooked on the freedom of hitchhiking forever. I felt like a female Jack Kerouac on the road, exhilarated with fever for adventure. And so easy. Best of all are the characters who pick up hitchhikers. People of this planet have so much to find out about each other, and what better way than through the noble and neglected art of hitchhiking to discover how different people experience their part of the world. And in case they might experience it in an unpleasant sort of way, I always carried a few cloves of raw garlic in my pocket for chomping on to deter any would-be aggressors. Fortunately it never came to that. I hate raw garlic. So whether in stupidity or what I like to call, in retrospect, wisdom, I hitched out to British Columbia, then south down the queen bee of west coasts, the coast that ballads should be written about. Everything ever claimed about its ruggedness, its cragginess, its wetness, was claimed in soggy mirth. I stopped many times along the way for adventures and various waitressing jobs in Oregon. Then I reached that northern Californian land of the green-leafed giants. A land where trees make people small, practically insignificant.

It was three days before I got out of my tree. It took that long for the rain to stop. But I didn't mind. I was starting to identify with the Buddha: insights, revelations, cramped legs. I don't think I actually slept that much—not that it wasn't comfortable. My tree was the ideal hovel. But sleeping was ordinary. Living in a tree wasn't. Everything around me became electrified and alive: the steady beat of the falling rain as it splashed down through the leaves onto the forest's dark floor, the humming of a nearby brook; the very air I breathed seemed charged with an energizing mist. Towering redwoods took on subtle details. I felt as if I were seeing everything for the first time or as I had seen the world as a child. A vibrant green was taking over the forest, a green that could never be found in a paint store. This green was passionately awake and wildly alive, and for those three days, so was I.

I remember looking out of my tree's entrance, feeling like a spy, awestruck at the stately presence of those ancient kings and queens of plants all around me. They'd seen rain like this for many hundreds of years. The history of the world unfolded while they stood strong and solid, as empires came and went, as wars to end all wars never ended, and as people searched for answers they never found. I felt humbled among those wise observers of the ages because I was learning from them that a constant search for answers was futile. These trees didn't question their existence and their life; they *were* life, perfect in every moment of their existence.

I'm not quite sure now what it was exactly, nor was I even sure a week after leaving the tree, but something happened to me in there that changed me forever. I only know when the rain finally did stop and the sun broke through into the bluest sky I'd ever seen, nothing was the same.

Walking back out to the road, I hitched a ride from an ordinarily friendly kind of guy, or so I'd think today if I were to meet him. But after my monumental awakening in solitude, this particular human puzzled me. He talked on and on about his job as a lumberjack, the economy, the weather. I watched in horror as the words fell out of his mouth, all strung together, yet meaning nothing. The chain of words rattled on until I wanted to scream out the window and at him about how much MORE there was, how he was missing the point entirely. But I couldn't. I barely uttered a word. What could I say? Tell him to go and live in a tree for a while and then we'd talk? I worried that I'd lost the ability to communicate with my fellow humans forever, that I'd gone loony, over the top. But I don't think that happened. Like a powerful summer storm that bolts down on us, leaving behind a freshly stimulated world until the feeling fades, the intensity of the experience gradually diminished. Vibrant green became just ordinary green again. Practicality and crummy tents aren't always a bad thing. It's hard to hold on to that which we try to grasp. Maybe insightful moments of revelation aren't meant to last. But somewhere inside me, three days of living in a tree left an imprint which can never be washed away by anyone or anything, even the wildest of rains.

★

Now to get back to Clarence McQuiggle, which is the story I wanted to tell before getting sidetracked by the tree.

When the alien-like lumberjack dropped me off at a gas station on the coast I was dying of thirst so I bought a drink at the roadside store and sat outside on the porch. I shut my eyes to aim my face into the sun. That's when I heard it: blaring country and western music, the worst of its kind. I opened my eyes to observe the spectacle in front of me.

He wasn't what one would call a big man although he must have weighed a good 250 pounds. Most of this girth seemed to be concentrated into some sort of eerie tabloid image—"Man Gives Birth to a Giant Watermelon"—set above his low-riding polyester brown pants. His sweep of slicked-back silver hair blocking out one eye was intended to give the impression of distilled youth, but fooled nobody. He was probably sixty-five years old. Oddly, his legs were short, skinny even, which struck me as funny since he and his stomach took up so much space perched on top of his equally large luxury-style motorcycle. Yes, it was the legs that made him appear ridiculous.

More impressive than his extraordinary appearance was the collection of sprawling odds and ends strapped onto the back of the motorcycle: a Disneyland pillow, a frying pan, a clear plastic bag of socks, a bag of squished hot-dog buns, a carefully folded Texas flag, a box of assorted chocolates, a sombrero.

Country music exploded from the stereo speakers of the beast-like machine. It had to be an expensive bike, probably brand new too. The man wore a brown leather biker jacket, far too small for him, and '70s-style zippered ankle boots, very cool. He made his way up to the porch to buy a double ice-cream sundae at the counter. Extra chocolate sauce, no nuts, I heard him insist to the young girl at the counter. The country music he left on for everyone's enjoyment.

"Howdy there. Where ya from?" Damn. My backpack was giving it away that I wasn't a local. I felt like saying I wasn't from this planet but decided it would be safest to say I was from Los Angeles instead of Canada. It might deter further conversation. It didn't. He proceeded to tell me how he'd just been "verbally harassed" by Californian delinquent brats, even worse than the kids who had laughed at him going through Texas. I didn't laugh. I held back. Instead, I tried to imagine the reaction he must have been causing across the country on his motorcycle crusade promoting sappy country music with a fully bloated ego and belly. Stereotypical loud American, thought I.

"Clarence McQuiggle's my name. From Yarmouth, Nova Scotia."

"Nova Scotia? You're Canadian?" So much for stereotypes. "Me too," I confessed. "I haven't met another Canadian in ages. I'm from Ontario." We shook hands. He didn't seem to notice I'd changed nationalities.

"Well, they had a big tornado in Ontario," he told me

proudly. "Most of them up there in Ontario are dead. Yep, big tornado." He smiled as if he had something against Ontario, as if they would laugh at him there too.

"What! There must be ten million people living in Ontario. They can't all be dead!" I thought about my family and friends lying devastated or dead while I'd been contemplating the wonders of rain and eternity in a tree.

"Well, maybe not all dead. It hit one town, couple farms too. Yep, pretty bad, pretty bad. So where ya headed?"

Where I was headed was difficult to say. A debate had been going on in my brain between the *live for the moment* version of life versus the *plan ahead, set goals, work towards the future* perspective. I wasn't clear which side was winning. Living in the tree scored points for the *live for the moment* side, but I knew I couldn't have kept that up much longer. It was one of those summers when we try to figure it all out, think we have, find out later we never really knew anything but at least had a good time trying. I had just finished my second year of university and was on my disaffected-youth quest for deeper meaning and more immediate experience with life itself rather than just reading about it. I loved my free-spirited wanderings which faced life head-on, even if the occasional rainstorm or dark night did put me off sometimes. Living for each moment—the accumulation of which actually makes our lives—and living for the journey itself rather than the destination seemed reasonable to me. But it was a lot harder work than I thought it would be.

"I'm headed for adventure."

"Adventure? Nope, don't know that town. All kinds of crazy names for these California places, eh? How'd ya like to go for a ride on the bike with me? Great day for a ride."

"Geez, that'd be great. But are you kidding? Look how packed down it is already with all your stuff. My backpack's pretty heavy."

"Nah, there's always room for more," he told me, picking up my backpack and shackling it down. Amazed at the ease with which he could accommodate my backpack on top of everything else, I thought of protesting further, then thought, Why not go?

"Well, okay," I said. "I'd love to go and it *is* a gorgeous day."

He handed me an extra helmet and off we sped up a winding steep road that ran along a cliff overlooking the ocean. When I looked down I saw monstrous waves smashing against the cliff bottom. They were the kind of cliffs that are hacked off like a piece of rye bread, so you can see what the earth looks like inside. Beyond the cliffs, the violence and expanse of the sea thundered out into forever. It was spectacular. I couldn't believe how undeveloped this part of the coastline was. I'd always imagined California to be packed with people, the last stop for twentieth-century pioneers in search of a Barbie and Ken existence who had left their lives and the cold back east, people on a golden quest for a "lifestyle." Other than an occasional cluster of aging hippies, however, the northern part of the state appeared largely people-free.

"This is fantastic!" I shouted over the roar of the engine. Adrenaline-laden ecstasy tangoed all through me. The wind wrapped itself in a rage around my body and raided my hair. Ocean mist cooled and dampened my skin while the sun enlisted itself straight into the navy of my bloodstream. I was part of it all.

"Yep, fantastic is right," Clarence shouted back. "She's a beauty."

I didn't mean the bike but I guess it was okay too. I meant the whole thing. I meant roaring along the edge of the breeze through earthy elements that had taken on the musical substance of a drifter's cabaret, the world split wide open, open sesame, for motorcycle entry only. The world does the can-can for anyone on two wheels. I felt free and alive. Future and past melted into a clear and golden now, like maple syrup, like patches of snow in the spring. I realized this was it. This must be the way to live.

If I'd only known the path to enlightenment could also be found by bumming a ride with a Hells Angel wannabe bound for the Open Road, I might never have bothered living in the tree. Then again, who can say? We're only twenty years old once, and must make use of every hovel and eccentric we come across. Otherwise, how are we to know what to make of life?

Maybe an hour passed meandering along that coastal road but it could have been much more than that. Ordinary conceptions of time had exhausted themselves out the muffler far behind us on the road. Clarence pulled into a scenic lookout far above the spray of the sea and took off his helmet. He walked John Wayne style to take a look at the cliff below.

"Some view this is. They call this a scenic lookout? They've never been to Nova Scotia." I think he was trying to impress me.

"But this is beautiful. Look at the way those waves are crashing against those jagged rocks down there and there's no development here at all." I tried to be polite. After all, he had just given me one of the most blissful rides of my life.

"Nope, sure ain't like Nova Scotia."

Forget it, I thought to myself.

"I'm headed back there now, can't wait," he said. "I'm going north to B.C. and straight east all across Canada to Nova Scotia. Should be back home in ten days or so. Wanna come with me? It'd be free for you and I've got this extra helmet anyway." I fixated on his face for ten seconds without saying anything. Was he serious?

"Oh no, I couldn't. That's crazy." A thousand thoughts railroaded through my head on the pros and cons of this unusual offer. He was a total stranger. Yet, he did have an endearing kind of helplessness or naïve quality to him; I knew he was perfectly harmless. But travel thousands of miles across the continent with the guy? My head reeled. It would solve my current financial problem of having next to no money except for an uncashable Canadian paycheck. And I always wanted to travel by motorcycle. It could be the perfect way to get back to Canada.

The idea, absurd at first, began to grow on me like seaweed. I thought about rising through crude passes of the heathen Rockies, flying straight and reckless across the endless prairies, migrating back to my forested home province of Ontario, then maybe further east through Quebec, and out to the dampness of Maritime fishing villages. All that light and heat. All that wind. I would contemplate the raw power of speed, able to see, always, in all directions, as I reveled in the pure moments of the journey itself.

The idea of going had already taken me. I could steady myself against it. Besides, I've never been one to overlook the whimsy of things. If only I could get him to lose the corny country music station.

"Okay, Clarence. I'd love to go with you." For the second time that day, Clarence McQuiggle and I shook hands.

Clarence McQuiggle was a terrible driver. So bad, in fact, that I considered changing my mind about the entire whacked-out notion even before we reached the Oregon border later that afternoon. But it was too late by then. I was hooked. I'd become a full-fledged motorcycle mama in a Zen-induced two-hour ride of rapture. Except for the drone of the engine, we were experiencing glory and eloquent silence. Or at least I was. Clarence enjoyed the experience of speed.

When we veered away from the coast for a time and blasted along a quiet road obscured from the sunlight by a forest of two-hundred-foot redwoods, I felt a twang of remorse for zooming past these intimate giants, now my friends, at such a pace. These tree gods deserved reverence and quiet contemplation but I could hardly shout that out to Clarence. He was like a madman possessed, intent on taking off through the forest into flight, trying to defy gravity and beer gut all at once.

He did eventually come to a squealing halt, thank God. A sign saying "WELCOME TO OREGON" by the roadside caught his attention, as would every other "WELCOME TO" sign for the next five thousand miles. Clarence began his camera search through every luggage container and duffel bag strapped onto that machine. I stood by, completely in awe at how much junk we were lugging. Clarence McQuiggle was a pack rat, a souvenir storer, a heavy hoarder.

"Here's the damn thing. Now take a couple pictures of me in front of the sign. Make sure I'm not blocking out 'Oregon.' Gotta show my friends back home."

Clarence had friends? I tried to imagine who they were as I stood, camera in hand, while he posed with his weight on one leg, hand on hip, head cocked. His half-zipped leather jacket tried hard to conceal its portly contents.

Snap: The state of Oregon welcomes Mr. McCool-quiggle.

Look out, all you West Coast night-riding biker-gang scary types. Clarence McQuiggle has arrived toting enough tacky souvenirs to offend and bully even the most tasteless angel from hell right out of you, country music to nauseate the sappiest, and a twenty-year-old Buddhist biker chick on the back to utterly confuse the grievous tattoos off all of you.

Night fog from the sea had rolled ashore and the escaping sun's rays had long since cast their good-bye glow on our faces when Clarence finally cooled his various engines for the night. It was a neon, flashing red sign that lured Clarence off the road this time. Apparently, "ALL YOU CAN EAT" proved as powerful a Pepto-Bismol for seizing engines as "WELCOME TO (anywhere, nowhere; population: 14)" and "SOUVENIRS FOR ALL." Those three signs, in their varied and enticing forms, are about all that ever did coax Clarence off his road.

I felt windswept and groggy inside the restaurant but luckily its crass interior awakened my numbed senses. Clarence delighted in the place. He was truly in his element. He didn't even wait for our overly friendly waitress to present herself and offer the all-you-can-stuff-into-your-gut plate before he herded into line at the trough. That surprised me. I'd ascertained that Clarence aspired to be a womanizer, and roadside waitresses always seem doomed to be the compliant targets for the Clarence McQuiggles of the world. Instead of chatting up the waitress, Clarence found someone's used plate on a vacated table and wiped it clean with his handkerchief.

I wished I hadn't seen him do that.

It was to be the first of several unforgettable moments on the momentous journey. Hey, who is this guy? I would ask myself. What the hell am I doing this for?

Between grazings, Clarence told me that he'd started out on his continental trip from Nova Scotia with his then ladyfriend (ladyfriend?) but she had tired of travel (travel, not Clarence) somewhere outside of Portland, Maine one evening in a torrential downpour when Clarence insisted on making Boston that night.

"Yep. Gladys just threw her helmet into a big puddle, unstrapped her suitcase, and by dang, she was a goner. Can't take a little wet."

Gladys was a wise woman.

That night, I learned something else about Clarence which, if I'd given it any serious thought, I would have anticipated. He snored. I don't mean the acceptable-decibel-level snore. I mean something light years and two football fields beyond that. I couldn't escape it inside the hotel room even though I slept on the floor with a pillow and all my clothes over my ears, the maximum distance away from the artillery fire. I had to trudge outside with my sleeping bag and sleep on a lawn chair in the hotel's backyard. Even then I could still hear the Maritime Marine Battleship thundering off shells in the distance.

Clarence's weakness for souvenirs was getting out of hand.

After all, we were traveling on a motorcycle, not a tractor trailer, and although this vehicle, like Clarence, was of ample size, it did have its limits as to what it could carry. At the "WELCOME TO WASHINGTON STATE" sign picture-taking session, Clarence learned from a retired couple about a souvenir shop that sold redwood carvings just ahead, five miles off the highway. Clarence rarely ventured off the main highway—a point of contention between the two of us—but he made an exception for the ultimate in souvenir shops. Thirty minutes later, we rocketed down the highway towards Seattle, country music blasting, forty pounds heavier, and a tad lopsided. Clarence had just purchased a four-and-a-half-foot carved redwood totem pole. Easy Rider here we come.

As if the totem pole had given us wings, we found ourselves gusting through British Columbia's Okanagan Valley in no time at all, passing all manner of traffic in our way. Clarence was still possessed. Whenever I suggested we slow down for a while, or maybe even, God forbid, stop somewhere along the way like a lake, a small town, or a fruit stand, Clarence would bellow back to me, "Can't stop, gotta make time."

Make time? What exactly does that mean? Time isn't something one makes, like bread or a bed. Clarence was retired and had no appointments to keep in Nova Scotia. What was the rush? Why had he even bothered to take a trip around the continent if he didn't want to see it? All he seemed to care about was getting back to Nova Scotia. He was missing everything along the way, thousands of miles' worth of irretrievable moments, all just to GET THERE. I tried to convince him that somewhere is right here, now, along the way, but he never stopped to look, not even once. Most of us live our lives like this, I thought, so focused on a hazy future that we miss the journey of our lives along the way. But for now, seated behind the heavy hand of a motor-fiend, I'd have to take his cue of getting my kicks out of speed and the open road. And really, that wasn't such a bad thing at all.

The Trans-Canada Highway, which I like to call McQuiggle Highway since that road was Clarence's religion, passes right through Banff National Park in Alberta, and that is a place of splendor and magnificence. The morning we sliced through there, hawks and eagles soared above us so high into the deep blue they disappeared into another realm. The groaning upheaval of the Rockies reaching for their maternal clouds stirred my soul and breathed life into me. I was trying to feel each moment, take it in with all my senses, notice every detail I might normally miss. I let the ecstasy of being alive and awake take over my whole motored-out being. We whirled by a turquoise lake cradled inside a near-translucent glacier. Clarence refused to stop.

Honest to God, he refused even to look.

As loudly as possible I shouted this in his left ear: "Every moment stolen from the present is a moment lost forever.

There's only NOW!" The words floated up into the mountain air somewhere and lingered, catching some hawk's ears perhaps, but not Clarence's. Yarmouth, Nova Scotia lay ahead, and by dang, Clarence McQuiggle was going to make time that day.

I shivered all the way through the Rockies because we forged through a blizzard unleashed from hell and Clarence maintained a determined perversion to battle the blizzard and win. I thought shelter from the elements and hot soup might be a better way to beat the nasty onslaught but I'd learned by then that trying to persuade a tomorrow-bound maniac was futile. Besides, I was far too cold and exhausted to shout out my suggestion over the racket of storm and engine. Luckily, the agonized tunes of lovesick wailers weren't part of the racket just then. Although the mountains stood cruel and austere that day, I thanked them for their compassion or good taste in refusing to allow country music radio waves to trespass through their valleys.

Somewhere out on the prairies of Saskatchewan one afternoon, we came to a turning-point of the journey. In a moment of clarity, I think I actually understood Clarence McQuiggle. We'd been driving flat out under a creamy summer sky when a greasy-looking roadside restaurant netted Clarence. The place was called Farmers' Co-op, and upon entering, Clarence nudged me, whispering, "Don't talk too loud in here. They're all gonna be Commies."

"Commies? You must be kidding. Why? Because it's called a co-op?"

"Yep. This province is full of Reds."

That's it, I thought. I'm exasperated. I can't take him another second. But Clarence was just warming up. Inside the restaurant, Clarence explained that the best president the United States ever had was Richard Nixon because he had introduced Coke into China. That's when the turning-point came. I could have screamed and walked away forever, towards freedom, or an asylum. But then it came to me. Okay, I get it. This is Clarence McQuiggle. This is a lesson on the journey of life. Life is what you see in people's eyes. Virginia Woolf said that. Accept, if not appreciate, the differences in people. I chose to laugh, do the smart thing, maybe because I had grown slightly smarter, or maybe because we were at a dumpy truck stop smelling of cows and greasy fries, somewhere between Nowheresville just fifty miles up the road and Hooterville, and the thought of being stuck there was actually even worse than the thought of indulging Clarence in more twisted political paranoia. Besides, I'd come to see this journey as something of a challenge. I couldn't just bail out. That would be too easy. This was the ultimate endurance test.

I've always thought the true beauty of the sunset comes not at the moment when the burning ball falls into the lake, mountain, ocean or prairie, but in the moments after, when it scars the sky in colors too transcendent for description.

But Clarence McQuiggle refused to watch any of the sunsets. Not an hour had passed from the time of our last speeding ticket when Clarence was once again tearing across the Manitoba prairie at law-breaking velocity. The fallout from the sunset had plastered the entire western sky in a flush so deep it burned. I thought I should point this out to Clarence.

"Nope. Can't look," he shouted over his shoulder. "Wouldn't be as good as the sunset over the Bay of Fundy anyway."

We blasted on towards Ontario, breezing past the lucky ones on the other side of the road, the ones driving into the sunset. Those who would never have to question the logic of a faceless fellow journeyer on McQuiggle Highway.

Northern Ontario takes forever to drive across, and since I happen to be from Ontario, Clarence concluded that the province's immensity was my fault. I think the long days of driving were starting to get to him so I thought I'd accept the blame for the size of my province. But his edginess continued all across the north shore of Lake Superior. The strapped-on collection of souvenirs all over the bike was really becoming annoying. Clarence was constantly rearranging things. Somewhere between Sault Ste. Marie and Sudbury, Clarence pulled over to the side of the road and stopped. I instinctively looked around for one of the "ALL U CAN EAT," "WELCOME TO..." or "SOUVENIR" signs but could see none of them. We were in the middle of nowhere and Clarence McQuiggle had stopped for no apparent reason. We were in the middle of nowhere when Clarence McQuiggle finally lost it. The totem pole, I mean. He unloaded his stockpile of souvenirs amassed across two countries and proceeded to throw everything into the ditch.

"I can't take these god-damn things anymore. They're slowin' me down. They're falling off. I don't want 'em."

Clarence was having a fit, a temper tantrum, and I thought it best to keep quiet, try not to laugh, and let him do his thing. He was right to liberate the totem pole. I sometimes wonder what became of that Washington State genuine carved redwood totem pole that got turfed into the ditch up there in northern Ontario, so far from its home. Quite possibly, it's still there.

Days tumbled over each other. On some days I had no understanding of why I had taken flight with a madman across my country. Other days I knew exactly why. It was for those rare moments when we would rub through small passages of life along the road that could never be encountered the same way again, when I knew the only place on earth to be was on the back seat of a motorcycle, when that conflux of place and time and joy and godliness would lift that piece of the world, that piece of life, into something magnificent, something golden. On those days, even Clarence seemed like a swell guy.

The further east and the closer to Nova Scotia we

traveled, the more urgent it became for Clarence to GET THERE. We'd set off each morning at five-thirty or six after Clarence had consumed massive quantities of greasy breakfast food substitutes and the first of his sixteen diet sodas of the day. We wouldn't stop until eleven or twelve at night, having ripped through eastern Canadian places of grace lost to those whose eyes are more enamored of highway asphalt.

Clarence seemed to have an unreasonable dislike for Quebec and insisted on speaking English louder than usual at gas stations in that province's villages where little English is spoken. By that time, I was well on my way to proficiency in embarrassment and I always tried to compensate for Clarence's lack of social graces by smiling, rolling my eyes and shaking my head behind Clarence's back as we roared off so the bewildered gas station attendants, store owners, and anyone else around would say to themselves, "Oh, she's not really with him; she's just getting a ride, poor thing."

On the outskirts of Quebec City one night, I almost fell off the bike. I was nearly asleep with exhaustion. When I jolted myself awake to see my favorite Canadian city approaching, I considered getting off right then and there. Why was I staying day after day on a motorcycle with a country music fanatic whose speed limit exceeded his I.Q.?—and I'm not talking metric. Not only was it frustrating, deafening (engine, twangy radio, and snoring), often embarrassing, and generally absurd, it was now dangerous too. But somehow, somewhere, this journey, the Road, had become an obsession for me. It should have been easy to turn in my biker jacket (not that I had one) but I couldn't do it. Back in northern Ontario I could have said *sayonara* and simply headed south for home. Maybe Clarence's determination to get to Yarmouth had blown its irrational zeal onto me. All day long I'd see his shoulders hunched up, his head aimed into the wind bound for THERE—I guess it gave me a thrill. Not Clarence, of course, but the ride—a twelve-day amusement park ride to which I was shamelessly addicted. If I'd spotted a billboard advertising a motorcycle-crazed passengers-anonymous support group, I'd have joined up immediately. Yes, I'm a Road Junkie. About eight days now. How could I tear myself off the back seat? No time to chat about it. By dang, Yarmouth, Nova Scotia lay ahead and I was just dying to get there.

Clarence made a call home one afternoon from a restaurant in New Brunswick and it made me wonder about what he called "his people." I suppose it was all part of the curiosity I'd built up about Clarence, the compulsion to see this thing through to the end, make sense of it all, rather akin to being compelled to snatch a glance at a traffic accident's aftermath. The restaurant served lousy food although Clarence happily devoured three hamburgers before continuing his binge by gorging on the white lines of the highway. But his demon driving habits no longer bothered me. I felt so weary towards the end that Clarence's road gluttony had become a good thing. We were almost THERE and I think I could even smell fish, or fish factories.

Clarence swelled with as much pride and swagger as a prize-winning pig on the sun-blazing afternoon we pulled up to the "WELCOME TO YARMOUTH" sign. He'd finally accomplished his feat of GETTING THERE, and as I peered through the view finder of his little camera to snap that last noble shot of him, I couldn't help but feel a rush of gladness for my friend. Never mind the lunacy of two diametrically opposed humans raging across the continent together. The journey had been kind of fun.

We rolled into Yarmouth and for the first time on the entire journey, Clarence drove without breaking the speed limit. In fact, he moseyed. We held up traffic. Clarence honked on the motorcycle's horn and waved at people on the street as if we were in a parade. He offered the royal glaze of not looking directly at anyone in particular, just a general gaze for the masses welcoming home their king. This home-coming affair embarrassed the heck out of me, but what else could I do but pray to the god of random chance that I wouldn't know anyone in town?

I looked at the faces of the Yarmouthians strolling down the main street, smiling and waving at Clarence. Most of them seemed to know him or, at least, know of him. All of them gave me a thorough look-over and smiled as if they knew something I didn't. A young man shouted out, "Hey Clarence, how long did it take ya?"

"Eighteen days and a half," Clarence shouted back.

"Have a nice time, Clarence?" called out a woman with a squeaky voice, wearing a cotton print dress and rolled-up hair. I wondered if she might be Gladys.

"Yep. Eighteen days and a half," was Clarence's proud reply.

A few more townspeople asked about Clarence's trip as we continued our crawl down Main Street. The men all asked how long it had taken; the women all asked if he'd had a nice time.

As I sat contemplating this difference between men and women I noticed the signs above the stores: McQuiggle Furniture was next to McQuiggle Draperies, which was two doors down from McQuiggle Hardware and Appliances. My God. Clarence owned the whole town. Clarence was the Big Cheese of Yarmouth.

"Clarence, are these all your businesses?" I asked, expecting him to reply "Yep, eighteen days and a half," since he seemed rather stuck on that particular phrase.

"Yep, sure are. Most of my ladyfriends run them for me now."

We pulled up to a corner store and Clarence bought a tootsie roll and the local newspaper. He opened up the paper to the local affairs section. "Good, they got the day right." He handed it to me to read.

YARMOUTH YACKINGS

Clarence McQuiggle is expected back today from his well-known, much-talked-about motorcycle caper which took him from Yarmouth last month to Maine down to Florida, all across the southern United States to California, up to British Columbia and back across Canada to his and our fair town. Word has it that Clarence has a traveling companion with him. Who will she be and how will she have survived travel with our Clarence? Welcome home Clarence and a warm welcome to Clarence's companion from all of us here in Yarmouth.

I ended up staying a few days in that friendly little town of Yarmouth before heading back home via the ferry to Maine. Clarence's oceanside house outside of town was far too large even for him and for all the souvenirs that didn't make it. Too bad. They would have been perfect. Clarence gave me a room with shag carpet on the walls, a round bed, and a life-size, last-concert Elvis poster tacked to the door. Now I'll never have to worry that the decade of my forma-tive childhood years is dead; the '70s are alive and sweating at Clarence's place.

Clarence and I watched the sunset every night over the Bay of Fundy and I realized he was right about it being more beautiful than the sunset over the prairies. Not because it was more red, or any more spectacular, but because it was home, Clarence's home. Since my home was the Road at that time, all sunsets were beautiful to me, but in this also lay a loneliness and a longing for one place in this world where a sunset moved me more deeply than anywhere else.

Although Clarence missed so much of the journey along the way, there was one thing he talked and cared about more than anything else: his town, his home. In Yarmouth he was a somebody, a comical somebody, but a somebody nonetheless. And that made him happy.

Maybe some things, some people and certain places have to mean more to us than others. Maybe we all need to find our Yarmouth, a place we know we finally belong.

So I learned something from Clarence McQuiggle, something I'd never appreciated enough before: home and friends. But to this day, I draw the line at appreciating country music. I just ain't never had no hankerin' for it.

CHAPTER SIX

LAST NIGHT'S STORIES around the kava bowl made me realize that travelers battle a constant and raging struggle between two forces: to stay or to leave. To leave, to travel, is to live for the moment, freely, wildly, to be vital and alive, having ties everywhere but no one place to call home, and, at times, feeling too close to an uncertain edge. To settle is to know security, possess something stable and cared for, built up over years by the warmth of your own fireplace. Unlike travel, a steady home is rarely wild and freeing; yet to me, it's a dream I often long for when I travel, but fear I may never know.

I'd love to have faith in one single place, in all its familiar beauties and strengths and human connections. Constant exploration doesn't have to be my religion.

DAYS LATER

I can't leave this place until I understand why it's impossible for me to stay. For its beauty alone I should stay forever. For the way the green and vast sea keeps so far away any thoughts of factories, miniseries, highways, fluorescent discount stores. For the way the moon creeps up like a whisper so fat and orange over the mountains of coconut grove. For the way the people smile at me when I walk by on the road. For the way they are as wise as the redwood trees, not questioning life but part of its rhythm. But something else lies deeper than these things, something that makes me uneasy. I can almost touch it, realize it, then it's gone and I'm enveloped again in the sultry ease of the place. Days pass by in this trance-like state. I try to speak the language, cook the food, enjoy the politeness of the kids at the school, laugh and gossip with the women. I'm never alone. I forget myself.

They always tell me what to do, as if I have no mind of my own. This could all be so easy if I weren't resisting. But I hate easy. They think everything must follow straight and predictable lines. Everyone must think the same way, say the same things, not say the same things, obey, conform. They think everything, including the stirrings and journeys of the heart, travels along prearranged paths. But I've learned from the world this isn't true.

MANDARIN GROVE

On this early morning, pink and soft, the birds wake up the woods. I walk up the path to the plantation, as I've done at least thirty times before, and say hello to Papa in his grave. He's been buried for over two weeks now and his raised coffin is still covered with colorful mats and flowers like a shrine. I go on in search of plantain for one of the Giant Aunts. Through dense vegetation of ferns and fig trees, I see Laudi coming toward me down the path, bushwhacking, machete in hand. "Oh Laurie, come, I'll take you up." He takes my hand to lead me back up the trail behind him. How does he think I made it this far on the trail by myself? How does he think I made it to the other side of the world by myself? This isn't Victorian England. I'm not so delicate.

We discover a grove of wild mandarin trees pregnant with juicy fat oranges dripping low to the ground. Laudi climbs the trees and throws the fruit down to me. We can't stop eating them. They're too full of sweetness. We eat, laugh, chase each other and squish open oranges into each other's faces. A tree close by bears X-rated fruit that shocks me. It's red, fleshy, moist, and has no skin. I pull one off and taste it like I've never tasted anything else. Inside my mouth is an explosion of all that's forbidden, all that's sweet and sour at the same time, and as I swallow it, I realize that nature folds secrets into out-of-the-way places. We could live on this island forever, Laudi and I. But I forget we're in a grove of wild mandarins way up high, where life is lighter, where the world below is a faded dream.

I try to avoid writing about him, just as I avoid him. I'd love to keep the pages of this journal lovely and untarnished. But that's silly. We can't ignore what we don't like. We can't pretend that which we despise doesn't exist. Everything seeps into our consciousness, whether we're aware of it or not. It seeps in without defense. Just as passing images, shapes and patterns we don't notice consciously are etched into our psyches and show up in our dreams, so too are the things we try desperately not to see. These things become nightmares in and out of sleep.

Vix. He's the keeper of a secret evil stored in a sour heart. He comes to me wanting money, just to borrow. He comes back drunk and I never see the money again. He frightens the campers. He invades our quiet nights like a torrential storm, intoxicated, yelling at us, spewing unintelligible insults into the campfire. We see his face burn red with hate and we try not to shake. Some days he laughs and plays with children and we almost forget the nights. The sun is so blinding and hot and high in the sky here that night feels impossible and forgetting is easy. But night always comes and too often brings him with it. Surely not from these gentle people he came into this world. He must have originated from a thorny and wounded place, a place cut off entirely from the sun, from any warm softness at all.

I hear him now as I write in the tent, his voice shattering the waves. This time, he's yelling at his wife. A millimeter of canvas hides me from his rage. I have a feeling I'm not alone in cowering from him, but none of the Fijians talk about it. The campers do, however. Most of them form a vague but persistent idea that Vix must be dangerous in some undetermined way. They see it in his eyes, which look like hardened glass balls that stare and don't see, like marbles you can't get rid of.

GOSSIP

Laudi sits next to me most nights at the family dinners. He takes food from his plate and puts it onto mine, always the best pieces of fish. I feel like a helpless alien who has to be taken care of. I hate this feeling. Most people are used to me now and few pay attention to me anymore. What a relief. Tonight at dinner, some sort of gossip is heating up the room. This isn't unusual; there's always gossip, but tonight seems different. One of the Giant Aunts says my name quickly and a few people look up at me from their food, then look away just as quickly. I have the distinct and uncomfortable feeling they're gossiping about me. I hear other names that are familiar, names of some children at the school. I'm sure they're discussing something horrible they think must have happened at the school today, although I have no clue what it could be. Nothing strange happened there today. Nothing that anyone told me.

"Are you talking about the school?" I blurt out in English because I don't feel like hearing them laugh at my broken Fijian just now. A suspicious silence lasts too long before one of the aunts pipes up: "Oh, the school. It's a good school." Her eyes flash to another aunt after she says this, a flash of conspiracy. They resume their talk and twice more I hear my name said in the way they disguise it. This is dreadful. Laudi smiles at me and turns to tell them in English that I love teaching there just as the kids love me.

When we're washing the dishes I ask Laudi what the conversation was about and he tells me not to worry about what silly old aunts say. This doesn't make me feel better. Gossip cuts deep into island life. I hear it all the time from men and women both. They pass around a secret and pretend nobody knows a thing. Sometimes they're trapped in events from a lifetime ago, as if current gossip isn't enough. They go back generations, judging the faults and failures of people now old, even dead, people who passed through their lives, however briefly, and didn't pass through quite right.

A F T E R   D I N N E R

Laudi and I climb to the top of the plantation to see the moon rise. As Laudi bushwhacks our way, he tells me how, as a boy, he would run away and live in this bush for days at a time by himself. I find this incredible since Fijians deplore being alone. "Did you want to get away from your family?"

"No, I wanted to live in the bush." Of course he did. I feel mean for asking such a question. To Laudi, tight family control and gossip are part of daily life. He himself is constantly victim to gossip and lets it slide off his back like water. Once again, I'm amazed at how quickly the darker side of Fijian life falls away as soon as we climb up to where the jungle creeps inside us. It's this wild part of Fiji that keeps me here. It overpowers the senses, making all else seem paltry. This wildness of Fiji lives in Laudi. I try to imagine him living in the bush as a boy and think of the skill and knowledge needed to survive, to understand which plants are good for various purposes. I try to imagine Laudi's life, year after year of it, running parallel to my own and now the two lives colliding, running together, yet still a world apart. And I wonder, how deeply do I fall into this love, into this place?

"What did you think about on all those lonely nights up here?"

"Evil spirits."

We reach the top just in time. The moon lifts up out of the water and approaches the sky slowly, like a tired hobo who has been places and has news of the world, but only if one were to ask for it. The moon is bulging yellow as full as our stomachs, overbearing on the land, and we can't believe that soon it will be lost and small in the sky, icy white and distant. Not this time. This time it's too much with us.

We have to come up here every full moon. Both Laudi and I say this. Both of us believe in it too. The full moon has a way of swaying you back into your heart, just as some people have a way of slipping unintended beneath your skin.

Someone has riffled through my backpack. This isn't the first time. Fijians have a different concept of sharing than Westerners. In this communal group where individuality is impolite, nothing can really belong to just one person. At first I thought I was being careless, misplacing t-shirts or hats or books. But then I'd see my clothes materialize on a Fijian. It's strange. They always seem so proud when they pass me on the road, wearing my clothes. I never know what to say. "Hey, nice shirt. Can I have it back?"

This works two ways. If I happen to tell an aunt that I like the scarf on her head, or I think it's pretty, she'll take it off and give it to me, and won't take no for an answer. Sometimes all I do is show interest or curiosity in something and they give it to me. I've learned to restrain what I say. Already I have a collection of Pope coasters, seashell necklaces, and photos of total strangers in my tent.

LATER

I have no control over my life anymore. My life slips away with the days until I'm a shell that forgets what used to live inside her.

I've just been washing clothes in a tin bucket outside Nana's house. The cold soapy water felt good sloshing against my hot skin and I enjoyed watching the water turn from white to varying shades of rust-brown like the earth. I tried scrubbing the clothes against the old-fashioned washboard as I imagined my grandmother would have done.

"You do all wrong!" boomed a voice above me, hovering, blocking the sun. In the shade of a Giant Aunt, I felt like a scolded ten-year-old.

Okay, so I'm a failed clothes-washer. A month ago I

would have laughed at this and simply learned how to do it her way. Why can't I laugh now?

I don't really care about losing things from my tent. Losing myself is what worries me.

Every day I swim out further and deeper. I swim until the reef disappears and underneath me is a calamity of startling blue, then black. Deep water doesn't frighten me but this is like looking down into an abyss, bottomless, timeless, like the universe. I do back flips in the water with my eyes open. A tumbling succession of sky, sea, sky, sea, sky, until sea and sky join together in a streaming blue dance linked by a diamond necklace.

After Sunset

I'm in my tent. Nobody is on the beach tonight to share stories with. I need the stories to remember myself. This place swallows me up. I can't allow this to happen.

Oh God. I hear them calling, the Giant Aunts. They're seeking me out.

"Laureeee, Laureeee, where are you?" I'm not answering, hoping they'll go away. Damn. Here they come.

"Laureee, why are you down here like this? Where's Laudi? Where's Kalisi? They should be with you. Come back up the hill."

"Oh no. I'm fine. I'm just tired."

"Come eat."

Eat! Eat! We just ate a glutton's feast less than two hours ago. I could give birth to the *Hindenberg*. "Oh, thank you. I'm fine. I'm not very hungry."

"You need to eat more. You swim too much."

"I love swimming, especially here. You're so lucky to live right next to the sea."

"Come eat. We can't let you stay here like this."

Like what? I wonder. "No, I'm fine. Actually I'm tired. I think I'll go to sleep." They shake their heads at me and mumble in Fijian to each other.

"See you tomorrow morning then, skinny girl."

I'm not skinny and haven't been since I was fifteen years old.

Is it merely by chance I ended up here? I could go crazy thinking the world is so haphazard. There has to be order to the universe. Maybe in another life I'm on another South Pacific island, like Tonga, or Bora Bora. I wonder how the Giant Aunt situation is there. Maybe I'm riding horseback in Mongolia. Or shopping for sunglasses in Brussels.

I leave the tent and walk along the shore to the group of long black smooth rocks that rise up out of the water onto the sand. These rocks I call the Beached Whales. I climb on top of one and lie on my back, feeling its stored warmth while the wind breathes sea salt into my lungs. The moon hasn't risen yet, and up in the sky, impossible stars detail the night. I'm still looking for that elusive constellation, the Southern Cross.

I think back to what I've read and heard about the

Southern Cross. Crux, or the Southern Cross, is the smallest of all the 88 constellations. No wonder I can't find it. The origins of Crux are lost in history, probably because it was considered to be part of another constellation, Centaurus. To the ancient Greeks, the stars of the Southern Cross were the hind feet of the centaur.

Not until Dante, a man of extraordinary imagination and poetical genius who was once called "the spokesman of ten silent centuries," was the Southern Cross appreciated for the celestial treasure it supposedly is. Dante referred to the Southern Cross many times in his *Divine Comedy*:

> To the right hand, I turned and fixed my mind
> Upon the other Pole, and saw four stars
> Ne'er seen before save by the primal people

Dante never saw the Southern Cross himself, and where the poet learned about it, no one knows. It wasn't until two hundred years after Dante's death that any published accounts of the constellation appeared. He may have seen some of the Arabic celestial globes or even talked to travelers. Perhaps he heard about the Southern Cross on the return, in 1295, of Marco Polo, who had ventured as far south as Java and Madagascar.

The earliest reference to the Southern Cross's present name was made in 1515 by the Italian navigator Andrea Corsali, who called it the Marvellous Cross and described it as "the most beautiful among all the southern constellations, compared to no other heavenly sign." Another Italian navigator,

Amerigo Vespucci, called it Mandorla (Almond). English writers and explorers of the sixteenth and seventeenth centuries gave it similar titles, the Southern Triangle, the Southern Celestial Clock. After long and treacherous sailing voyages to the Southern Hemisphere, European navigators celebrated the sighting of the Southern Cross with great joy.

The precession of the earth's axis has moved the Cross farther and farther to the south. It was last seen on the horizon of Jerusalem at the time of Christ's crucifixion.

Southern Cross, where are you? The Greeks thought you made a great set of feet. Christ may have watched you from his cross. Dante dreamed of you. The Italians named you. Spanish sailors danced and cheered when they finally spotted you. When will I find you? I must be patient. We must be soft-spoken among the stretch of constellations. In looking at them we're wandering through the centuries. I look for a peephole, a place where there is no star, but can find no such place. If you look hard and deep enough, you can always find a star. Everywhere. That's what they say about China. No empty spots. A person in every plot. They have to bury people standing up. But Fiji is filled with stars, not people. So many things draw me here, yet so many things repel me. Down the shore I hear Laudi's voice calling me but I don't answer. I think back to the first time I heard his voice, when it came out of the dark. Although we've never discussed that night, it affected me deeply. I think back to almost a year ago when I came to Taveuni the first time, in the beginning, how I found this place.

RAMBO REVELATION

I THINK I WAS IN LOVE WITH FIJI before I ever set foot on it. I'd been in Hawaii for ten miserable days—yes, miserable, a God-awful place—and I escaped on a midnight flight out of there to Fiji. I was willing to let Fiji take me in with the warm open embrace of somebody's grandmother.

I know that's how I must have felt because from the pages of my journal I find this:

H A W A I I

Without a doubt, this is the worst place I've been in the world. I'm stuck here for another twelve hours until my plane carries me to Fiji. Sitting on a rock outside Honolulu's library, closed on a Tuesday afternoon, I watch traffic pour hot and choking exhaust into an intolerably hot and humid atmosphere of filth. There's a terrible apathy here—no music in the streets, no people arguing politics in outdoor cafés, no culture at all except overpriced fast food, pretentious hotels, and plastic smiles. I feel sick from it all, sick from the ice cream I was

bored enough to pay a ridiculous price for, sick from Hawaiians'
frightening conformity, sick from knowing I was born an American.
From now on, I renounce my American citizenship. Canada, my real
home, is teased for being bland, but surely it's not as bland as this.
Extremes of any kind are dangerous and these islands have co-opted
the worst extremes of the mainland. Hawaii is utterly American,
allowing no space for anything but America.

Fiji will be different.

I think the ice cream must have got to me when I wrote
that, put me out of sorts, but I did have a wretched time in
Hawaii. The first three days turned out to be the best,
although I didn't know it at the time. I flew from Honolulu
to the big island of Hawaii to look for an acquaintance from
Canada. In a letter she had told me she lived beside the
ocean off a certain road where a tree pointed to a path leading to her wind-shelter home. I was hitchhiking and the driver thought I was nuts to get off in such a deserted place
with those sketchy directions. I found her though, walking
along on the path and carrying a box of pineapples on her
head. She was naked. When she saw me, she dropped the
pineapples, ran towards me and called "Sabina, Sabina!" She
had my name wrong. We'd only met a couple of times. She
and her husband, a native Hawaiian, lived off fish they caught
in the ocean and fruit they swiped from an orchard over a
fence at night. I think they believed stolen fruit was an oxy-
moron since they picked it right off the trees that Mother

Hawaii provided for them, and perhaps they were right. A volcano on the island watched over them, they said, and often got angry at tourists.

The ocean was violent there and woke me several times a night, sounding like hot-blooded thunder as it smashed against molten lava rocks on the shore. After three days I left the couple bathing in sacred spring pools in their spaced-out bliss and hitched to the other side of the island with a crazy woman and her dog. I went to a place called Kona, which must mean The End of Western Civilization. It's all there: blinding-white skyrise hotels with little balconies to see the "some view, Ethel" and souvenir shops lining the streets like cholesterol build-up; t-shirt and postcard and coffee-mug shops; macadamia nut cookies for three dollars each. And designer poodles. They're everywhere. Don't look for an escape because there isn't one. This is what people come for. It's their golden dream: rip-offs and rich people who talk about taxes and tans. It wasn't my kind of place. And the people whose kind of place it was, I never want to sit next to on an airplane.

I did meet one interesting person in Kona. He was a fif-teen-year-old upper-class black kid from England whose parents had sent him to boarding school in Hawaii. He hated Hawaii as much as I did. We met in an overpriced bookstore that sold trashy bestsellers and Hawaiian scenic-beauty cal-endars. In his posh accent he asked me where the classics section was. "Are you kidding?" I said. We went for a walk to the beach and he told me about his futile search for interesting life in Hawaii. Over the past week, in an attempt to lift his spirits, he'd been on a five-day cruise and a helicopter excursion, and was currently staying at the Hilton for four hundred dollars a night. It wasn't helping. Obviously he wasn't looking for happiness in the right places. At sunset, we burned our feet walking along an ocean-side wall of black rocks that had absorbed the day's mean heat. The wall separated the ocean's crashing waves from the backyards of monstrous movie-star houses. One of these houses, the boy told me, was owned by Sylvester Stallone. In Sylvester Stallone's backyard was a Japanese swimming pool that lapped against the stone wall. Its green waters lay so close, so clear, so cold and inviting; a mere jump off the wall and we'd be immersed. Oh God, it would be heavenly to have cool skin, to escape the debilitating heat and ugly boredom that was Hawaii, even for a few seconds. Nobody was around, certainly not Sylvester.

"Oh, we have to do this," I said. "We have to jump in. Come on."

"Oh, I wouldn't advise it. That's hardly the thing to do now, is it?" said the fifteen-year-old.

Clearly, something was wrong with him: he didn't know how to live. So I showed him. I jumped in. I've never been a Sylvester Stallone fan, but those ten seconds in his pool changed everything for me. The pool must have been a magic source for something powerful because its cold water rushed into my burning skin and swirled a quiet internal storm that made me shiver with life's possibilities. I knew I had to get out of Hawaii after that. I wanted to be part of that magic all the time. What little Hawaii offered, I had just sucked dry.

The next day I changed my ticket to get to Fiji as soon as possible. The sun woke me early that morning on the beach. It burned through the flimsy nylon of my tent and swam directly into my blood. It wasn't yet six in the morning and I was sweating. I went for a swim but started melting again as soon as I walked out of the water. By the time I'd packed my tent and walked a mile along a paved black airport runway to find the strip mall with the travel agency, I had heat exhaustion. Never having suffered from that before, I wasn't sure what to do. I felt as if I were in a desert and the only oasis was a Burger King across an intersection. There would be water there, and air conditioning.

I stayed three hours in the Burger King, drinking water and orange juice and reading a book about Ireland. They don't like you to linger long in fast-food joints. People get paid alarming sums of money to come up with clever ways to make people want to leave after ten minutes. Whoever came up with the elevator music, back-breaking swirly little chairs, strategically dispersed tabloids, and screaming child implants was a depraved lowlife and very smart. I finally realized I couldn't spend the rest of my life hiding from the heat in Burger King. When I walked out into the day's furnace, I tried to imagine Ireland: cool misty rain, green dales, and a deeply buried sun.

At the travel agency, a bronzed woman of undetermined vintage, with dyed hair the color of Wonder Bread and strips of blood-red make-up aligning her face, told me I couldn't fly to Fiji for four days. Her girlish knees bobbed over her cowboy boots and under the frills of her miniskirt as she told me about her grandchildren. Such a surprise was she, with her face that might have been painted by a child with crayons, that I hardly comprehended what she was telling me: I would have to kill four more days on the infernal planet of Hawaii.

I have only scattered memories of those next four days. I remember that upon leaving the travel agency, I felt so attacked by the hostile sun at a congested intersection that I decided to walk in whichever direction the light turned green first. Since I had no plan, it made no difference. Of course in the end it would make all the difference, but I was too miserable to be philosophical or poetic. I wanted a green light. There's a freedom in having no plan, having no idea at all what you will do for four days, especially when you feel like an alien. Being a stranger is sometimes a thrill, like being in disguise and full of possibilities. If there had been a wind, I would have let it blow me someplace wonderful, because I'm sure there are wonderful places in Hawaii. But I don't recall a wind, only a sun that burned me inside out.

When a light finally turned green and I crossed a street, I

presented my thumb to the oncoming traffic. A Jeep swerved to the roadside and stopped for me. The driver's thinning hair was what they call bleached blond and it flew out behind him in mad fury as the Jeep sped into the hills. The man blared a Madonna tape and asked me when I was going to move to Hawaii. "Everybody ends up here eventually," he yelled over to me. This was an alarming thought, although I didn't argue; I was getting a free ride. That's one of the rules of hitchhiking—agree with everything the driver says. My next ride was from an Iranian man who worked at a rental-car agency. He said I could rent an air-conditioned car for free. "What's the catch?" I asked him. He told me there wasn't one and something in his manner made me believe him. I spent the rest of the afternoon driving around in a car that blew cold air in my face. I liked that.

Another day, I was walking down a street in Honolulu, minding my own thoughts, when an aggressive little teenager herded me into a church where people were serving free lunch to passers-by. "What's the catch?" I asked him. He told me there wasn't one and I didn't trust him for a second, but I was bigger than he was and felt rather hungry. Inside the church basement, I was invited to sit at a table with some excessively friendly people who ate sandwiches of processed cheese slices on white bread, and jello from paper cups. I ignored the jello. There was something strange about the people, something unnatural. They were too happy. The woman across from me had two long braids and shiny eyes.

She asked me if I had invited Jesus into my heart. I told her my heart was pretty full as it was but I wouldn't kick him out if he was a good dancer. They saw me as a project. They told me everyone who didn't believe what they did would get a one-way ticket to hell so I argued until it made me angry and I stormed out. Soon after that I found my way to the ice cream and the rock outside the library.

Fiji will be different, I believed with my full heart.

My getaway plane landed on Fiji at six in the morning. Immediately the place made me happy. The airport had a scuffed wooden floor, a Second World War paint job, and a 1940s relaxed feel about it. The people working there acted as if they were at a garden party sipping fruity drinks from tall glasses as they swayed to an inner rhythm, slow and breezy. They all smiled, all the time. The next thing of interest was the men wearing skirts. The skirts had prints of hibiscus flowers splashed on them, except for those worn by the men who worked at the airport, which were solid blue, un-flowered, and official-looking with snazzy fringes along the bottom edges. All the men were big, strong, and muscular, their calves especially.

My backpack didn't arrive with me and no one could say where it was. It wasn't Fiji's fault, they told me; blame Hawaiian Airlines. That figures, I thought. The woman in charge of "Missing Items and Personals" took me into a room to fill out a lost-luggage form. Her name was Mary-la.

As I wrote, she began to talk excitedly. "You go to Lautoka town and buy little things you need, like a toothbrush. Then you come back here. You come home with me, stay at my house while you wait for your backpack. My children will love you. I'll show you Fijian cooking. We go around at night. We'll visit my friends."

Leaving Mary-la, I passed a room containing more airport employees. Two young men and a woman were playing crokinole, laughing hysterically, and drinking brown murky water from a big wooden bowl. "Come, come." They waved me in. "What's your name?"

I told them.

"What? Say it again." I did and they laughed. "We've never heard this name before. Please sit, we don't laugh at you." So I sat and they gave me kava to drink and invited me to stay with them at their airport-staff housing. "You'll love staying with us. Plenty room. Too much fun."

A jolly round man, whose smile displayed the largest lips I had ever seen, introduced himself as yet another airport employee. His name was Sunny, which suited him fine. Sunny drove me in an airport Jeep to Lautoka, twenty miles north of the airport, so I could buy a toothbrush. I could have bought a toothbrush in Nadi, the town close to the airport, but for some reason the airport people felt I should go to Lautoka for my toothbrush. It was all rather complicated, this toothbrush affair, but I was having such a good time, who cared? Sunny drove like the wind on a potholed rumpled road through fields of sugar cane that stretched from rolling Irish-green mountains. The sun poured down on us like golden honey with such quiet grace that I wondered whether I had flown into another universe, a universe with a gentler sun warming a gentler people. I would check the stars when it got dark to see how differently they were arranged in the sky.

"First time in Fiji?"

"Yes," I told him. "I love it here."

"Where will you stay tonight?" He didn't wait for a reply. "You come stay with us. My wife loves Europeans."

"I'm not European. I'm Canadian." He looked over at me, mystified. Then he held his round belly, tossed his head back and laughed as if I'd said something absurd.

"You're white, you're European."

I searched the streets of Lautoka for the much-discussed toothbrush, then ate lunch in an Indian restaurant which served rich curries and mango shakes. Jet lag finally hit me after that and forced me to look for a place to sleep immediately. In the town park, I found a kind old tree with swooping, open-curved branches and lay down in its shade to take a nap. I hadn't been sleeping long when I heard a whistling sound. Someone calling a dog, perhaps. I looked up to the balcony of a little building on the edge of the park, and there I saw my first giant Fijian woman. She wore a white flowing dress which billowed in the breeze and flapped around her legs as she waved at me. Her bushed-out hair was truly wild, like a living species of its own. "Come, come," she called. I picked up my dog-tired body and walked over to the foot of the balcony. Getting closer, I saw that her shape was reminiscent of those ancient figurines molded long before Christ, round fertile-looking sculptures with huge thighs and breasts, depicting a goddess worshiped for centuries as the mother of earth. "Sleep here, inside my office. Come up," she said.

The Mother Goddess's name was Makareta. Her eyes were large and round and perpetually surprised. Makareta made me a bed on her office floor by laying down a mat and borrowing a cushion from someone in another room. What she called her office was a green-painted room with open windows along the walls, a desk in the corner and, on the door, a tattered poster of an aquamarine sea proclaiming "Yasawa Islands Call You." A travel agency, perhaps? I spent the rest of the afternoon dozing on and off in the corner on the floor as every person in the town of Lautoka passed through Makareta's office to chat. In the middle of an especially confused dream, a ponderous woman with a deep-barreled voice woke me trying to feed me fish and fried cassava. I woke up to her enormous inquiring eyes four inches from my face. Another time, I awoke to see a group of women sleeping on the floor just as I was. The next time I awoke, the women were circled on the floor, sharing a platter of fried fish, licking their fingers, laughing loudly, and shushing each other not to wake me. Makareta's job looked like fun. Eventually, Makareta said, "Okay, that's it. Work over for the day. We go home now." Evidently, I was going home with Makareta. All this hospitality was a little overwhelming after the strange coldness of Hawaii. I hadn't been in Fiji twelve hours and I felt as if half the country had befriended me.

I followed Makareta out into the streets, where she hailed a taxi by threatening to walk directly into its path. We picked up her husband, three other people, presumably neighbors, and Makareta's three children. It was a little cramped, careening through the streets with my head out the window and two children on my knees, but I loved it. Makareta's family lived in a village just outside Latouka. The driver slowed to a crawl along the dirt roads as the sun set crimson through the trees and it seemed we had entered a ruby jungle rather than the suburbs. Their house was a wooden structure with a corrugated tin roof. Three rooms were separated by handmade curtains: a kitchen, a living room with two beds and a couch, and a bedroom. I was warmly welcomed inside their humble home with its tidy dignity and heartbreaking neatness. Makareta's five-year-old daughter, Meme, was the most adorable child I'd ever laid eyes on. She already had more hair on her head than most people grow in a lifetime. Meme sat on my lap, sang me songs and showed me clapping games. Makareta showed me how to peel cassava and then shooed us all out the door to tour the neighborhood.

At the end of a dirt road we came to a stream and a small thatched hut set back in the trees. Meme led me to the door and whispered, "Papa Jimbi live here." She creaked open the door and called his name. A crinkled and weather-worn man, smiling and built like an ox, came out of the dark corner of his home to let us in. He wore a tattered *sulu* around his waist. Judging from his eyes he looked old, centuries old. "*Bula,*" he said as he shook my hand. "Papa Jimbi." Papa Jimbi had no teeth. He invited us inside and told us he would make us sweet ginger tea. Through some complicated genetic connection he was related to Makareta's family, as all Fijians are related, and clearly, he and Makareta shared the entertainment gene. He began talking as soon as we sat down. Since I'm plagued and blessed by the urge to explore the wonders of the world, I asked him everything a stranger from one side of the earth could reasonably ask a stranger from the other side. Soon Papa Jimbi was telling us stories of his childhood home on a faraway island. I fell into his stories as if they were a warm bath. He talked of his island of jungle flowers, rare birds, secret lakes, and mountains, surrounded by deep seas feared by Captain Bligh and his sailors. After the mutiny on the *Bounty*, when Captain Bligh was cast adrift with a small crew, he had to pass through the Fijian Islands, known then as the Cannibal Islands, and he feared the island of Taveuni the most. For hundreds of years, eating human flesh was a normal part of life in Taveuni. Eating your enemy was a disgrace to the victim's family.

"The feuding families would never speak again," said Papa Jimbi. "Eating your enemy was the biggest insult you could give somebody and his family."

"I can't imagine anything more insulting."

"There was nothing more humiliating than being eaten. Taveuni was the best at eating people. The fiercest cannibals in Fiji were from Taveuni. We used to feed missionaries roasted fingers and not tell them until the next day. Now, Taveuni is a quiet place. Don't eat people anymore. Those days all over."

He laughed and said this as if he was talking about the good old days and was a little sad to see them gone.

"What's the name of it again?" I asked.

"Taveuni, far away. You should go there." Light passed through his ancient eyes as he poured me more ginger tea.

The children and I returned home to my first real Fijian meal of fried cassava, fried fish, boiled taro root, and fried breadfruit. After Meme and I washed the dishes, I joined the family in what was presumably their nightly ritual of sinking into the couch in the living room where they would talk, tell stories, read aloud, and laugh until it was time for bed. Television in Fiji hadn't yet arrived, although I kept hearing it was on its way. The children told me about school and the two boys played with math puzzles. Makareta's husband asked me about snow and winter and they laughed, howled, and slapped their thighs when I tried to tell them how we live through it.

This is how it should be, I kept thinking, a family all together after dinner in one room, talking and laughing and loving each other. It's what our ancestors must have done for millions of years, cultivating the warm and affectionate side of human nature. Life is pure and simple and extraordinary when shaved down to its bare bones of connection.

That night, sharing a bed with little Meme, I lay awake for hours as trees and flowers and faces of Fiji sailed through my head. This country was pulling me in with hot jungle arms and smiles so wide they took an hour to walk across. I knew I'd go to Papa Jimbi's strange and magical island, but I kept forgetting its name. I looked out the window at the stars to check whether the universe had changed. This was the first night of my life in the Southern Hemisphere. I scanned the skies for the Southern Cross and realized I had no idea where to look for it.

After I picked up my backpack, it took me another four days to leave that side of the main island, Viti Levu. Fijians kept inviting me to stay in their homes. Several times I tried to head east to the capital city of Suva, then forged on, eventually to Taveuni, but I was in no great hurry. Every person and family along the way stirred and warmed a piece of my heart.

In Suva, I inquired about possible teaching positions in the outer islands. At the Ministry of Education I met the Fijian Education Minister within five minutes of walking into the building. With his feet up on the desk in an ordinary wooden office, he was a friendly man who told me that, since the time of the 1987 coup, it was impossible for foreigners to get paid for teaching positions. Then he wrote me a list of schools where I could apply anyway. One of the schools was on Taveuni.

I sailed overnight and part of the next day on an old steamer to Fiji's second-largest island, Vanua Levu, to meet some relatives of people I'd met in Nadi. They lived in a traditional village of grass-roofed huts beside the ocean. I brought with me kava and varieties of food I was told they would appreciate. In the evening, the women took me to the village meeting hall to watch a video. For some reason I expected to see an Australian movie, but instead, we sat on the floor and watched three black-and-white hours of Fijian choirs singing Christian hymns on a tiny screen. The missionaries should have left them to their cannibalism. At least that would have made for an interesting video. When I returned with the women to the hut, twelve groggy men were circled around a kava bowl celebrating my arrival. They didn't look up when we entered, the head motion being too much for them.

The next morning I asked one of the women where I could brush my teeth. She called her youngest son to take me to the village pump. By the time we reached the water pump, a herd of curious followers was on my heels. Unlike the Pied Piper, I carried not a flute but a toothbrush.

Surrounded by an audience of at least twenty people, I brushed my teeth to giggles and wide-eyed amazement. I wondered what they would have thought of multiple body piercings, donut shops, and bank machines.

I left the village that day as the "European woman who scrubbed her mouth like laundry," entering the folklore of that village and every surrounding settlement. After a four-hour ride on a jammed bus through a jungled land full of hidden villages, I boarded a motorboat for another three hours. I sat out on the bow with another woman as the ocean sloshed and soaked us with every hurtling wave. We held on to a rope and let our lives hang in mad peril, some-where between hysterics and terror. In the distance ahead, through the haze of ocean spray, I saw something come alive before us: a long volcanic island that rose from the turquoise waters like a glorious sea monster. The island of Taveuni.

When we reached Taveuni's shore, a man waiting in an old-fashioned van took away my few fellow passengers. The van sputtered off, leaving me sitting alone on a rock gawk-ing at fifty-foot exotic house plants. A friendly Indian man came by and offered to drive me in his taxi up the western side of the island for the price of the local bus. The sun was touching the ocean horizon as I bounced along that wild road for the first time.

"First time in Taveuni?" he asked.

"Yes. This place is a secret, isn't it?"

"It's your secret," he laughed.

As the forest and the evening closed in around us, we followed the road, which followed the ocean. I was surprised to find villages lost in the dampness of such drowsy, thick, sensuous vegetation. We weren't driving further and further; we were driving deeper and deeper. Yet, the route seemed to be leading someplace familiar. As the rich life of the island whirled by, I felt as if I was taking everything with me; that is, the most profound and private part of myself. Then I saw it. And smelled it and breathed it and felt it. I asked the driver to stop. The first thing I saw back in the towering woods of Buvu Beach Campground was a thatched little *bure* beside the now pink and muted sea. I left the taxi and walked through the trees toward the hut and laid my backpack outside its door. Not a soul was around. Lashes of cranberry wine, mandarin oranges, and lilacs streaked the sky. Had I really seen sunsets before? I stood by the hut and looked out at the water as if what lay beyond it embodied who I was before and every place I had been. Here and now I cast myself apart, had found my place. Something was happening inside me, something unaccounted for that uprooted me from all sense of the present moment and carried me through unexplored regions of the mind. I felt overwhelmed by ancient memories of a place I had only just arrived at.

I slept that first night on a cot in the *bure*. It wasn't until the next morning that I saw other people. I did hear someone though, on that first night. It was a man's voice that came out of the dark into the deep sleep I had fallen into.

"Is someone here?" said the voice. I froze and couldn't answer. After all, I had just walked in, uninvited, and it was pitch-black. After a few seconds, the voice said, "Oh, it's okay. Good night." I heard footsteps dissolve back into the night. The grace of angels lay in the chambers of the stranger's voice and I knew this would be a place I would stay a long time. A place that would touch my life.

CHAPTER SEVEN

SOMETHING WAKES ME very early this morning. Much too early. Night is barely over, I think, as I stumble out of the tent. Halfway out of my dreams I walk groggily to look at the sea, the disappearing stars, the mountains of the next island. This view of the sea is just as miraculous as the first time I saw it, that evening almost a year ago. But now, as I look at the water from the trees, I see something new, a sight entirely shocking to my sleepy self. The Giant Aunts, the overbearing and jolly Fijian women, five or six of them that I thought I knew so well, are walking into the sea, dressed in bright floral *sulus* that engulf their bodies from their breasts down to their knees. They laugh and talk and tease noisily, splashing each other as they walk out deeper. Then they plunge.

Their glorious bodies split open the water and their red soaked *sulus* cling to their soft mocha skin. They continue to laugh and splash, but then, as if by cue, as if they must, they fall silent. Each woman floats her gorgeous vessel body adrift, face up, arms and legs stretched out like the sky's fading stars above, the ocean's starfish below. They welcome the opening dawn. The sea's lapping swells make no noise. There's no noise at all.

As I watch, I think it must be the aqua green of the water alit with the vibrant pulsation of the women, human lilies, that can cradle them this way, push them off in different directions. As they float, they're inside some kind of deep Love, and I'm aghast at the alarming beauty of it all. I watch them secretly, fascinated. This is something I didn't know about them, about this place. I had no idea. It touches me, shakes me. Things are simpler, and far deeper, than I'd realized.

They never speak of it. If it weren't for the footprints in the sand, I would believe it was a dream.

O N E   W E E K   L A T E R
Laudi's ex-girlfriend, Vaneesa, has returned. She appeared this afternoon off the boat while I was showing Nana how to make spaghetti (her request) and while Laudi was net fishing with his cousins. She wants Laudi back. This is the news Kalisi whispered to me as Nana and I flung spaghetti against the wall to test its readiness (an activity Nana decided is the best thing she has ever done and has taken up wholeheartedly with tonight's yams). Kalisi dragged me outside, led me up the path to the plantation, and by her grandfather's grave with firecrackers bursting out of her eyes she said: "Vaneesa

left Laudi for another man but he's a bad man. Terrible time they had. Everybody knows about it. Now she has come back for Laudi. We don't like her. Bad woman. What are you going to do?"

"Do? I have to do something?"

"Yes, you have to fight for Laudi. She'll steal him away. Poor Laudi."

"Poor Laudi? Can't Laudi stand up for himself?"

"Some women have evil power. Vaneesa has it."

As we walk back down the path I realize it's exciting to be a player in this drama. But I have to remember these are people's lives. If Laudi wants to go back to this Vaneesa woman, I certainly won't stop him. Sometimes I think it's only the feeling of being in Laudi's arms that matters, that I would miss if it were gone. It has very little to do with him as a person, or with sex, or with anything he and I discuss. I've narrowed it down to those few seconds when I'm engulfed in his arms. It's not his smile, nor the honey dark-ness that shades his eyes, nor even his singing, but this: the empty pocket between his arms and how that feels and how that smells.

What Kalisi said, however, makes my head reel. The men get off so easily in this country. Can't they take responsibility for anything? Evil women? Fiji's superstitions never seem very friendly to women. Fijians believe that if a woman is pregnant and doesn't tell anyone about it, she will cast an evil eye on everyone she looks at until she confesses her pregnancy.

Everywhere she goes she'll leave a trail of misery in her wake. They also believe an injured woman causes bad luck.

When I broke my toe, a Giant Aunt told me not to look directly at anyone on the road because whomever I looked at would also break a toe. As an experiment, I looked at her husband that afternoon as he strolled down the road from the shop. That night when he was singing at the campfire, he drank too much kava, keeled over on his back with his guitar on his belly, and groaned. "See what you did?" said the Giant Aunt to me the next morning. When I replied that he drank too much kava, keeled over on his back, and groaned every night, she said, "No, last night different. Last night he staggered home, like a drunk man, like a man with a broken toe."

I have seen Vaneesa and she is beautiful, the kind of beautiful that makes you take a second quick breath when you see it coming at you down the road on a hot day, like a piece of shade in the distance. She's different from the other Fijian women, even the teenage women, who always hover near the seductive edge of being overweight. Vaneesa has long thoroughbred legs that pour down to the sand she walks across. Golden legs striding golden sand.

She hates me, though.

Laudi tells me they fought for three years. He says she's like a house on fire. They were married too. Laudi didn't tell me this. Kalisi and Uma did. Another Fijian secret, I suppose.

She looks at me with suspicious eyes. She's completely captivating. What am I supposed to say to this woman? It's my natural tendency to befriend people but she's like a gnarled piece of wood around me. I try to ask her about her life, talk to her. She barely responds and turns her back to speak Fijian with the others. Snob. She even dresses differently from people here. Tonight she's wearing a plunged-neck dress and leather sandals. Imagine. Leather sandals when everyone on this island goes barefoot or wears flip-flops. She's tall, she towers above these people. With her slim ankles and narrow limbs she seems out of place among the rounded aunts whose loving brown flesh is suddenly friendly and welcoming, a warm refuge. "Suva's getting boring for me," she announces. "I need some country life." We all eat dinner together at Nana's house and it's painful, so painful I have to slap myself on the knee to remember I don't have to be here. This is a holiday, or something. No, it's not a holiday. I'm exploring the wonders of the world. This situation is especially pleasing to Vix. He loves smashed pleasure, lives for it. Laudi smiles at me. Everyone else is talking so quickly I haven't a clue what they're saying and I hear my disguised name several times. But I don't care.

I don't care because Vaneesa finally turns around to face me, and although her tumbling Veronica Lake hair completely covers one eye, she winks at me with the other.

She disappears immediately after dinner.

"Who she think she is?"

"Why she here?"

"Leaves without helping us with the dishes. Umh!"

The Giant Aunts are enjoying this. I know they are. Vaneesa's arrival is the most exciting thing to happen around here since the funeral.

I love a good caper and I'm in one now. It's pitch-black. My friend the moon (who I've decided is utterly female) is nowhere to be seen tonight. She's taking a break from the sun. In this heat, who can blame her? I'm on the beach and can't see one single thing. I hear voices break over the waves. They're getting closer, the voices, and I stand absolutely still, let the voices walk right up to me. It's Laudi and Vaneesa. They don't know I'm here, inches away from them in the dark. If only my Fijian were better. They're arguing. I hear my name spoken several times. They stop talking for a few seconds and I think they must be able to sense my presence; for God's sake, I could reach out and touch them if I wanted to. I strike weird poses, inhuman shapes, any formation a person wouldn't detect in a silhouette. (I read about this once in a book.) If I change my body shapes enough, I won't even be human anymore. I'm invisible and silent; I've lost that much of myself as it is. I stretch my arms in twisted angles, catlike, make faces, con- tortions. Like Nana throwing spaghetti against her wall, this is the most extraordinary thing I've ever done. If lightning flashed right now, though, I'd feel extremely silly. They continue to argue although it's not hateful arguing; their voices sing. The words are fast and fly through the dark. I feel electricity shooting off our limbs in silver strands, whipping through the air like cosmic fireflies. It strikes me that we know where each other's happiness comes from. Don't they feel it? I don't think I've ever felt so alive. We're all flickers of the same flame, the whole world is. I try to gather this message into my throat, to tell them.

Can't do it. What would I say? "Tag, you're it," and run away?

The stars have swung well past midnight and I hear Laudi singing through the trees. I walk over to the kitchen shack and find him sitting in there alone, the warmth of his face glowing against the oil lamp. His fingers strum the rickety guitar while he sings "Isalei," my favorite song. It's like watching an angel sing. I sit next to him.

As he sings I recall a night in this kitchen almost a year ago, my first time here in Taveuni. I had been on Buvu Beach for two weeks by then and was planning on leaving the next morning by boat with some other travelers I'd met here. The Fijians—Laudi and his cousins and a few aunts and uncles—were down here giving us a farewell party. I hardly knew Laudi then. None of us did. He was shy and I often saw him sitting alone by the water on a rock, lost in thought. His solitude intrigued me in this land where people hate being alone. Other times, I'd see him taking care of his little teasing cousins, tossing them in the air, holding their hands on walks down the road, or splashing them in the water. Laudi and his male cousins, whom I called the Quiet Cousins because they spoke and sang with such soft voices, had sung for us almost every night but we knew little about them. The men sang beautifully into that night while the moon rose through the trees. Laudi's cousins were teasing Laudi, and I suspected it had something to do with me. Earlier in the day, Laudi had brought a horse down to the campground and each of us had taken a turn riding it along the beach. When it was my turn, the horse walked along the beach for less than a minute before deciding to turn and walk directly into the ocean. I didn't mind. I love the ocean too. I figured the horse liked the feel of cool water on her legs and belly and I sat on her for a long time while she stood still and gazed pensively out at the sea's horizon. After a while, drenched by the sun, I thought I would go back to shore. I tried to turn the horse around but she refused to move. I tried everything. Back on the beach, the Fijians and campers seemed to think this amusing, my attempts at moving a sea-loving horse, and they shouted out a list of useless advice. My horse was mesmerized by the sea and nothing I did to move her had any effect.

Finally Laudi waded out. I watched his bare chest gleaming in the sun as he neared me and thought of a scene out of twenty old corny movies: man rescues stranded woman on a horse. Not that I was truly stranded; I could have simply gotten off, left the horse in her trance in the water, and come back to shore on my own. This way was more interesting. Laudi hoisted himself up on the horse to sit in front of me, clicked his teeth and kicked at the horse. "I already tried that," I said. The horse paid no attention to Laudi either. She remained motionless, transfixed, eyes on the horizon. So there sat the two of us, Laudi and I, near strangers, on a horse that did nothing but stare at the sea. So that's what we did too. We stared at the sea. Every passing moment, with the two of us sitting so closely together on the horse, swelled with intensity. I think he felt the same way I did, although neither of us spoke. Finally someone shouted from shore, "What you two doing out there?" A Giant Aunt called out, "That horse smart. That horse knows what it's doing," and we could hear laughter thunder out of her body like a slow-moving storm. Laudi laughed and shouted something in Fijian back to her but that only made it worse. The cousins, aunts, uncles, children, and campers on the shore teased us without mercy. Fijians love to tease.

"They're just jealous," said Laudi. "They'd love to be out here too. Why would anyone want to be anyplace else?" And he was right. I felt like staying forever.

"Well, I'm having a hell of a good time," I said.

I was. It was the horse who eventually got tired of the whole thing. That night when Laudi sat across from me at the farewell party, with his teasing, not-so-quiet cousins, he

smiled my way as he sang, and I knew he was singing for me
and the horse and for our time watching the sea. I also knew
I couldn't leave on the boat the next day. It was too late. My
heart had melted.

"Where have you been tonight?" asks Laudi when he stops
singing, startling me out of my reminiscence.

"Oh, walking on the beach, watching fireflies. How
about you?"

"Up the hill, helping Uncle Voulu."

"Oh really? You haven't been down here on the beach?"

"No, why?"

"Haven't you been talking to Vaneesa? You two must
have a lot to talk about."

"No, haven't seen her since dinner."

Haven't seen her since dinner.

My earlier elation vaporizes like a genie diving back in
his bottle. The world has just become heavier, I think, as I sit
on the bench, burying my feet in the cool sand. I need a
clear view of his words which have come tumbling into the
darkness. So Laudi, too, tears pieces away from the truth.
People say what is easiest to say. Whether it's true or not is
irrelevant. I'm lost in a world of lies.

A world of lies. I visited that world once before, the
world of lies. In a place called Fez.

CARPET FEVER

*My guidebook to Morocco warned me: Under no circumstances
enter the walled city of Fez alone. Even the best sense of direction cannot unravel the maze of twisting lanes and dark alleys in the largest,
most confusing and possibly most perilous medina in the world.*

NOT TO WORRY. I had found a traveling companion just
days before, in a large Austrian goatherd named Rolf. His
most alluring quality was his maleness. My guidebook also
warned of the dangers of women traveling alone in North
Africa. I was thrilled with my find. Morocco could now
reveal its secrets in a safe, relaxed manner. Or so I thought.

We fled the crammed cross-country bus, with our dusty
luggage strapped on top, for the bustling fury of Fez. Or did
we just get off in the Middle Ages? Swarthy men in tur-
bans, robes, and pointed slippers stared at us while women
hiding behind voluminous robes darted their eyes down to
the red dirt roads. Snake charmers and dancing girls shaking

tambourines tried to lure us into seedy underground dark places that cast red-lantern shadows and smacked of nineteenth-century opium dens. And everywhere, from places unseen, came the frantic cry of frenzied music, as if orchestrating the temper of this most bewildering and misunderstood Islamic city.

At Fez's tourist bureau we inquired about a hotel recommended by another traveler. "Oh, that hotel burnt down last week," the woman in the tourist office said with a little too much intensity. "Try this hotel across the street instead." She pointed to a building that was trying to heave in on itself, that could have used a good torching like the other one. We were tired. We checked in.

Within five minutes after we'd collapsed into our room, a young man named Najib knocked and entered to explain he was the hotel's official tour guide. He wore the Moroccan man's robe, the *jellaba*, and when he took down its hood to uncover his head and smile, I was struck by how immediately familiar his manner was, as if he'd known hundreds like us before. He spoke to us knowing exactly what to say, knowing what we'd say to him, with none of the usual reservation among strangers, especially those hailing from such different worlds. He was good with people, perhaps too good.

He told us that Rolf and I were his "special guests" and he'd be honored to give us a free tour of the medieval maze of the old town, the *medina,* the next day. His brown eyes held a hint of the glint that travels in so many Moroccan men's eyes, revealing a playful boyishness, curious, a little naughty, but harmless.

The man was a charm infiltrator. He cast a spell so personable it pushed aside any skepticism we had about entering the *medina* with a guide. Horror tales and travelers' myths about Moroccan guides abounded. Everyone had some sort of story. The most popular story was of unsuspecting visitors hiring a guide to show them through the complex alleys only to be led to a point of no return, unless they could buy their way out. But Najib wouldn't do that. Najib was different. Besides, only those born in Fez, the oldest, most brilliantly secretive imperial city in Morocco, can find their way around it. And this man worked right at our hotel, a hotel recommended by a tourist agency. How could we go wrong? We agreed to leave for our tour the next morning at eight o'clock.

Inside Fez's ancient walls, lusty passageways unravelled before us, seducing our every sense. Each twist and turn in the maze carried us deeper into Morocco: lush smells of fresh mint, spices and cooking kebabs, ornate patterns and colored tiles, hidden palaces, and mosques filled with men beseeching Allah at the prayer call. Children with enormous soulful eyes and tattered little robes ran after us while old men, who probably weren't that old at all, rode by on mules to herd their goats. We saw withered women with long hennaed pink hair and tattooed foreheads, Berber women. This was a country of rich human texture, where people had stories written across their faces.

One man wanted to buy me from my father for fifty camels. When I told him my father probably wouldn't want fifty camels, the man seemed puzzled until he concluded that one hundred camels should be sufficient. I told him his camels would be confused in Canada, just as my father would be confused by them, and I was a lousy cook anyway.

The casbah was crammed and frenzied, full of sights, sounds, and smells I'd never known. Men in the open market urgently advertised goods of every description, while others quietly embroidered caftans inside their ancient shops. Some of the ninth-century streets were only a meter and a half wide. We pushed through thick multitudes of heated crowds, dodging donkeys, chickens, other guides and pushcarts, into the midst of a loud chaos that raved and laughed, both excited and excitable. How, I wondered, was all this passion born?

We wandered through all of this for much of the day, until Najib announced it was time to visit Fez's famous government-run carpet factory cooperative—the cheapest carpets in all of Morocco, and non-profit, no less.

How's that again? Did he just say carpet factory?

"But we don't want to buy any carpets."

Najib assured us we wouldn't have to.

"It's only a tour, my friends. Just looking."

JUST LOOKING! Did he really just speak those two words that alert all travelers they are now walking into enemy hustle territory? Scam Street? Rue de Rip-Off? No, not Najib.

We were wimps. We surrendered. A little factory tour would be harmless. After all, Najib had been so polite and generous all day. He had even refused to take the guide's commission when I'd bought a pair of embroidered leather boots. We would stroll into the carpet joint, just looking, without abandoning our travel-wise senses, our rip-off radar.

That's when things began to change.

Once we were inside the carpet warehouse, the toothless smile of an elderly man named Mohamid greeted us at the door. He ushered me alone into a room filled with a stunning array of brightly colored hand-woven rugs. Mint tea thrust into my hands, I was told to relax on the couch and await the arrival of another man named Mohamid who apparently spoke mastered English. Someone led Rolf into another room where a third man called Mohamid would "entertain" him in German.

As I sipped my mint tea I resolved not to buy carpets. I didn't want any. How would they fit into my backpack anyway? Besides, almost a year of traveling had left me nearly broke.

When the English-speaking Mohamid cha-cha'd into the room with all the dramatics of an overacted stage play and poured me a second glass of mint tea, I was ready to tell him not to launch into any sales pitches. I never got the chance. Mohamid #2's penetrating eyes just inches from my face and his buttery voice telling me tales of nomads weaving these carpet designs in the Sahara seemed to be exorcising my once-wary sensibilities.

"Here, Mademoiselle, have some more mint tea." Forty-five minutes may have passed, but I can't be sure, of Mohamid waving his body back and forth, his eyes never averting from mine. I sat transfixed, hypnotized, moving in time to his rhythm. Pots of mint tea kept coming from other rooms while Mohamid entranced me with carpet yarns.

At some point, I recall babbling, "Carpets, carpets, yes, I want carpets…carpets…" I remember rising off the couch to choose my treasured rugs, surprisingly dizzy, led by the warm, strong hand of Mohamid. My head swam as I selected not one but four carpets, close to a thousand dollars each. They would be flown safely back to my home in Canada, he told me. I don't even remember bargaining with the man, a custom I'd taken for granted from other travels and from my previous weeks in Morocco. My credit card passed from my hands into his and I distinctly remember looking down as if in slow motion at this transaction. I remember signing papers. I remember the blur of textiles dancing around the room, little woven camels and desert tents, red and gold patterns zigzagging in and out of my expanding head until I hopped aboard those zigzags back into the swirling carpeted desert where the sun melts reason away. I remember it all as one recalls a dream. But this was no dream.

My desert trip inside carpet-land ended abruptly when Rolf, my trusty companion, burst into that hazy unscrupulous room to ask, "Laurie, did you just buy six carpets?"

"No, actually I bought four carpets. They told me you bought six."

"I bought five," beamed Rolf, a little wild-eyed and unsteady.

That's when our guide Najib and all three Mohamids whisked us out and on our way as if the Mohamids suddenly remembered they were expecting important company for dinner. They never let up on their graciousness; they really did seem to like us, even when we landed back out onto the street, a little dazed. But they had been so polite.

Najib told us to follow him to his aunt's house where women would serve us a traditional Moroccan couscous dinner. We had to run to keep pace with the man.

Somehow the maze of alleyways felt different from before. Incredibly, daylight had bailed out on us and the dark nightlife had taken on a sinister glow. How long had we been in that place? Two hours? Three? As we flew through the streets bumping into the animated crowds, chasing an unmistakably distraught Najib, an impenetrable fog seemed to be besieging me, whirling up from the streets, blurring my sight, confusing my way. My head began to bang.

"STOP!" I shrieked out, surprising all of us. I knew something felt terribly wrong. I wanted everything to slow down, especially time.

"No, we must hurry," pleaded Najib. "My aunt waits for us." What was the panic when he'd been so relaxed before?

"Rolf, what just happened back there? I know we've just bought carpets but...why?"

Najib cut into our conversation to divert our attention to a fruit stand selling fresh dates. Najib was becoming annoying.

We entered a darkened little house and climbed a narrow staircase that twisted up and up until we reached the roof. A woman who held a scarf over her face, covering all but her black eyes, served us couscous on that dark roof, then disappeared like a shrouded whisper without saying a word. The fog had crawled up into my head. As in a dream when one is paralyzed, I couldn't find my voice to question Najib through all that haze. He was our friend, wasn't he? How could I be so distrusting?

Finally I broke through. "Najib, I want to go back to the carpet place." His face hardened. His smile skipped town.

"Impossible. I don't know the way back."

That's when the haze cleared. What a pathetic lie. A tour guide, having lived in Fez all his life, trying to tell us he didn't know the way back? Were all the lies told to us that day so transparent? This was a world of lies. I felt sick on several levels.

After my turn at high-pressure badgering, I eventually convinced Najib to take us back to the carpet joint. I thought I'd try their technique: I lied. Rolf proved useless in this endeavor, as he still appeared stupefied with carpet fever. Perhaps he'd guzzled more mint tea than I had. Or perhaps his Mohamid's occult powers, or whatever they were, had been even stronger than those of my Mohamid.

In any case, I had to go back and I'd do or say almost anything to retrieve that lost time. And my lost money.

Najib and his friends' skills in lying were superb but their proficiency in detecting other people's lies was lousy. Maybe they weren't accustomed to Western visitors trying it out on them, thinking they held a patent on lying. My first lie was telling Najib I'd left my camera at the carpet shop. A flimsy lie, since I didn't have a camera, but the wizard of deceit went for it.

Upon our unexpected return at the carpet factory (government-run cooperative, cheapest carpets in the country, non-profit and famous) Mohamid #1 (the older, toothless one) didn't seem nearly as pleased to see us as the first time. In fact, he flailed his arms around as he and Najib battled it out in raspy Arabic. Evidently it was against the rules to bring customers back. Evidently Mohamid #1 had undergone a personality change.

I interrupted. "You're a liar. These carpets aren't worth these prices. You don't really fly them all over the world. What was in that mint tea anyway?" The words flooded out of my mouth without my permission but I couldn't stop. Rolf, Najib, Mohamid #1, and now Mohamids #2 and #3 gaped at me as if I had renounced my sanity. And my manners.

"Laurie, you're insulting them," said Rolf out of the side of his mouth.

"Yes, Mademoiselle. Listen to your friend. Rolf, don't allow her to talk this way. You offend me, Mademoiselle. How can you say these things when we are all good friends here?"

I could see straight through his sleazy charm this time. I could also see he was nervous.

"Okay," I said, "prove you're a government-run co-operative."

"Uh...no...the papers, they are locked away in the safe...yes, the safe."

Aha, Mohamid #1 was breaking down.

"I want my money back."

"No, that's impossible, Mademoiselle. The money is all put away into the computer. It is too late."

"That was a fake name I used on everything I signed," I lied. "I'll tell the police this." With my mention of the word *police*, all three Mohamids paled.

Something interesting was happening whenever I said "police," so I kept throwing it in. Rolf twisted his face in confusion. He wasn't catching on at all.

Mohamid #2 disappeared and returned with everything I'd signed, most importantly my credit card receipt. The three of them looked everything over and whispered in a corner, as if it was all so top secret, as if we could understand Arabic anyway. Where was *60 Minutes* when the world needed it?

"Let me see that," I said as I walked over to the Mohamids. They were nervous as they handed me the papers, the fools. When I had all the papers I'd signed in my hand, there was nothing to do but rip the papers up and throw the pieces on the floor. I enjoyed that, so I smiled at them. I thought they might start screaming or chase after me around the warehouse, but they didn't. They didn't blink either; they were in shock. But after a full minute passed as we all stared at each other, they did something I'll never forget. They smiled back at me. They even laughed. Then all of us laughed for the whole pie-in-the-sky world that was completely mad, misbehaved, unfettered and needed a padded cell. Except for Rolf. Rolf didn't laugh. A desperate believer, he remained confused yet carpet-steadfast. A stubborn goatherd, he'd heard the calling for carpets.

I like to think carpet scamming was the one crime the Mohamids had in them; they were pretty good at it too. I didn't hate them either. In a twisted sort of way, I liked them more now, having seen something dark and essential of their world and their natures.

I once read that a similar thing happened to Marco Polo in Fez seven hundred years ago. His head had also been dunked into a stupor so disorienting he had laid out big bucks to buy rugs. It's a time-honored tradition, this curious form of carpet salesmanship, passed down expertly through the generations, and I felt rather privileged joining the ranks.

Now, several years later, I still get letters from one of those Mohamids, although I'm not sure which of the three he is. I still get the occasional Christmas card from Rolf too. "Dear Laurie," he writes, "I still wait for my carpets to arrive...."

CHAPTER EIGHT

I LIE IN MY TENT in the early morning hours, drifting in and out of sleep, listening for the Giant Aunts to make their pilgrimage into the sea. I've been watching them all week. But it must be too late this morning because already the new day is ripening into the color of pink seashells. The Giant Aunts must have come and gone while I dreamt of water. At the precise line between day and night they fall flat back on the sea, shatter it like glass, and lie there wide open and vulnerable to the night, protected by the day. It makes me think of Canada, at the time when the darkest, saddest part of winter breaks through into spring. It's like crossing the Continental Divide of the seasons. Everybody knows the day winter finally leaves and spring comes, just as the aunts know the secret lying between night and day. Borderlines of nature. I like to be there for the crossing, for the privileged moment when summer plunges into winter like a knife, cuts off even the memories of cold and dark. I like to watch the Giant

Aunts sink into dawn, blasting the water like trumpets griev-
ing for the dead. In those seconds that the world gives way,
some mystery occurs. I never want to solve it.

Oh God. I'm spinning out of orbit.

A scratching on my tent jolts me. I open the flap and see
Vaneesa's face inches from mine—like the dark night on the
beach when I was invisible. In the light, though, there are no
secrets. Supposedly.

She wants to go swimming. After days of acting mean she
wants to go swimming. But Fijians don't swim; they bathe,
or they spear-fish. They don't swim. They think I'm crazy
for swimming.

Vaneesa has mauve lips like cushions. I watch the velvet
sounds fall out of her lips when she speaks. She has milk-
chocolate eyes that tip up at the ends, eyelashes so heavy they
weigh down her eyelids, like wet feathers.

We run out into the water, dive in. Something else
about Vaneesa: her curved thighs remind me of polished
antique wood.

"Do you love Laudi?" she says.

How refreshingly direct. How un-Fijian. She asks this
with her head remarkably erect out of the water, eyes on
the horizon.

"Yes, I think so. But we're from different planets." Five
minutes go by, more than that of water time, and her body
glides like a sea creature through the waves. She draws closer,
brushes against my arm and says: "Can I visit you sometime?"

"Where? On my planet?"

"Yes."

"Of course."

Vaneesa is a woman disappointed by love. This makes us friends. Sometimes one thing in common is all it takes.

One man used up her whole life. I find this extreme but understand what she means. He invaded all her hopeful spaces, her vacancies that dream of how things should be rather than how they are. She says she can no longer think a clear thought without a vision of him. He follows her mind wherever she goes. I say to her: How is it that some people keep living inside us even when they're no longer welcome guests? She says love kills in the end.

I like Vaneesa.

Days Later

Vaneesa and I are telling each other stories of our lives. Each of us listens with desperate attention. We've been swimming, cooking, and exploring the bush. We go spear-fishing at night but don't even try to capture fish. Instead, we watch the zillions of glowing phosphorescent stars come at us through the night sea. As we swim out further, it doesn't get blacker and darker, but lighter and lighter. When we cut deeper into the water, side by side through the glittering onslaught, I know she feels the same as I do. We are explorers through time and space following an ancient beckoning of fallen stars.

Kalisi tells me not to trust Vaneesa. I tell Kalisi that Vaneesa is wonderful, just misunderstood. Vaneesa is content to sail her own private seas. She states how she feels. This doesn't go over well in a place where everything said is vague and nothing is direct.

AT THE BEACH

Fiji always feels like a Sunday afternoon. Nobody hurries. The whole family is down at the beach today, a Wednesday. They made a *lovo* so everyone is stuffed full of food, fried things and kava, in a state of dazed confusion. Kalisi and some of her female cousins and I have been gathering *tavewa* nuts, discussing the sad state of affairs between the sexes. When the subject of men arises, Kalisi continues to wave her hand and say "No time." Mara, a sweet and soft-spoken cousin, whispers to me that her husband beats her every month, and also once when she was pregnant. Her sister Luscia says, "My husband is wonderful. He finally put the little marbles in." Everyone squeals with laughter.

"The what?"

"You know, the little marbles men put into their *bothis*" (penises).

"Marbles? What do you mean, marbles? How does that work?"

"Canadian men don't do that?"

"No. Tell me about the marbles. It sounds bizarre, kinky; it sounds painful."

"No, not painful. It's ohhhh…"—Luscia's body shivers—"it makes everything fine, really fine. It's adding what nature forgot to add."

"How does it work?"

"They get their brother or cousin to cut the very thin outer layer of skin from the upper top end of their *bothi*, closest to their body. They make a little cut with a sharp razor."

"Razor?!"

"Razor. Then they put in these little tiny marbles, two or three. When it heals, the little marbles stay up there. They make things right for the woman. They touch and rub on the right place for us," giggles Luscia. The other women nod and agree.

"Oh my God. Yes, I can see what you mean. They really do that? Are you kidding me?"

"It's true. Half of those men sitting over there on the beach have little marbles. All their wives are happy."

On the other side of the beach is the circle of men, Laudi and his cousins becoming semi-comatose on kava. I try to imagine which of them have little marbles in their *bothis*. Every day in this country, something new amazes me. Wild things happen that I'll never understand or truly fathom. Hardly a day passes that I don't awaken with a feeling of disorientation, astounded and delirious at finding myself in the most improbable situations. I'll have to investigate the marble implants further. I'm never sure which stories are true and which are invented for amusement. I hope this one is true.

The men have just returned from a two-day wild boar hunt. They chase down little bristled black pigs, move in for the kill with spears, and return home, triumphant. When the women welcome the men back and build fires for the feast, some fossilized part of my brain stirs in recognition and I'm ecstatic. I feel a cusping of time when the world cracks open, just for an instant, and all that has happened in the centuries past pours into now.

On the shoreline the children splash in the water like dolphins. Fijian children are the happiest children I've seen. All their lives are spent outside, playing, singing and doing chores. They always want me to play with them and I always do. Being in love with someone can be heavenly but hellish as well. There's often tension, heartbreak, agitation, and loss of freedom. Playing with little children is none of these. Nothing is expected from me but to giggle in tickle fights. We watch them shining in the sun, squealing at the simplicity of their lives.

Coming through the trees towards us is Vaneesa balancing something on her head. Kalisi and her cousins switch from English to Fijian so I don't know what hateful things they're saying about her. They think I'm naïve and silly for befriending Laudi's ex-girlfriend. That she's fascinating and fun is immaterial.

"You all gonna be sick from eating those things," says Vaneesa as she strides by. A minute later, when she's past us and is walking her long legs along the shore, we hear her laugh, a single and outrageous burst of open-and-shut passion. Out loud and by herself.

I've been watching Uma this morning. I love watching her. Life flows in this woman. Nature is full and mysterious in her.

She keeps the fire alive all day, caring for it as if it's her first-born son. To let it die out would be unthinkable when there's always cassava to roast and people wanting tea. People get thirsty in this heat, and from the English colonizers they learned to quench their thirst with black tea. Cool sweet water sits high in the trees inside the soft white flesh of green coconuts, like a secret prize, yet people guzzle hot tea from tea cups, flap themselves with woven fans and say "Isa, hot day." Coconuts crash, full and forgotten, to the ground where the fire burns.

As Uma shows me how to weave a fan under a tree, she asks if I'll ever marry. People are concerned with these matters here. A single woman exploring the world on her own makes no sense in their world. I tell her yes, maybe someday I'll find the right person to marry.

"Plenty men in the world for you. You're too picky," she laughs. "You gonna wait and be loved in heaven. The spirits will love you then." She continues to weave her fan for a while and then without looking up says, "The spirits love you now."

Vaneesa and I are collecting enormous prawns out of the sea

to cook in coconut cream. We're experimenting with a new recipe. A new recipe is unheard of here, where people have eaten the same few things forever. I think I'm getting fat. The Giant Aunts will be pleased.

We're swimming out further than we should. Every day we seem to extend the limit of what is accepted. The Giant Aunts hate it, or they pretend to. We're excellent fodder for gossip, but we seem to be upsetting an unspoken status quo. The Giant Aunts whisper terrible things to me about Vaneesa. Quite possibly they whisper terrible things to Vaneesa about me. How am I to know what lies hidden behind these smiles? The worst is when they talk about us in my presence. They speak quickly so I can't catch the meaning but I watch their faces. I watch them shake their heads in disapproval when they say Vaneesa's name. They pick lice out of each other's hair and do a "Tsk, tsk" with their tongue and teeth. They're mean then. Their conversation is like a sacrificial slow roasting.

Vaneesa's arms glide over the emerald waves while the peach-burned sky holds up the world. She has the same zest and affection for life on earth that I do. I see it in her eyes when she watches the water all around us. Her eyes grow big enough to reflect the whole ocean, as if she can't believe this green liquid substance is actually suspending us. Something private and primitive and gently disquieting is at work when we swim away from shore, and the further out we get the more powerful it becomes. What we left behind us, the nasty gossiping tongues, the silly men, the rules—it all falls away. Only our bodies moving inside the sea remain. That anything else matters is absurd. I come from the middle of a continent, landlocked, and although I've always loved the water, it must be different for Vaneesa, who was raised by the sea. One can't live by the sea her whole life and keep it out of her veins. From the very beginning it must creep in slowly like the night tides and never leave. Even in a desert, a sea girl remembers the call of the waves.

Days ease by like wine down the throat: a gentle slide into oblivion. It could be a Tuesday, it could be a Friday, it could be summer somewhere else; it's always summer here. Summer must have moved in one day and decided to stay for good.

    I'm carrying an armful of supplies from the shop today. The road is wet and muddy from last night's rain, which is a good thing. It means dust won't fly in my face if the bus passes. The air feels cleaner after the rain, cooler even, as if it's kissing my skin. Everything is vibrant, fresh and alive. Everything that flies by is fat and heavy, full of flamboyant color and song. A shrieking miracle of birds rainbows the sky for a hectic minute, then disappears. Above most of the road, the treetops touch each other in a canopy of tropical shade. I can't think of anywhere else I'd rather be. All day long, I've been singing Judy Garland songs. I look at the sea.

The glistening green and blue patchwork quilt on the water, and the parrots arguing in the trees above, pump me full of happiness and I can't hold the world close enough. I remember a time when I wasn't here, but that time seems impossible. When I dreamt of coming to the South Pacific I was walking along a country road in the dead of winter. The sky was slate-grey and my hands were frozen. I wanted to go to a place far away where the light was white, like the sun, so bright it would burn through into my dreams. Where I was, the light wasn't bright enough for a bat's funeral.

Coming towards me I see two people walking together, a man and woman. How odd. From my favorite part of the road, beyond the curve and coming down the hill, I see who they are: Vaneesa and Vix. I've never seen Vix walking with anyone, especially a woman, especially Vaneesa. But I know it's Vix. Already I can see the unusual lurid glow in the balls of his eyes. It's as if a wild animal hides somewhere inside him, a mad dog that could tear out of his skin at any time, rip us all to shreds. People see it there in his eyes. He can't keep this wild part of him a secret. (I believe he has no control over this matter.) The whole village knows, speaks of it in hushed tones, tries to avoid the eyes when passing him on the road. He himself, I often think, is ashamed of his beast within.

Yet here he is walking with Vaneesa and they're getting closer. They're watching me as they talk, whispering out of the sides of their mouths. They're laughing. Vix never laughs. No, I can't be seeing this right because Vaneesa is my friend.

It must be a trick of light. The road seems to falter beneath me as we draw closer. "*Bula,*" I say and smile.

Nothing.

They say nothing. They simply walk on. I walk on too, until my heart starts to pound out of my chest at this rupture of faith. I slow down. What's happening to me? Why is this affecting me so? Something just happened back there that should never have happened, something dark and still, like the feeling before a tornado. The road looks different now, deranged, shut in by a dark tangled mass of bush. The ocean's lively patchwork is gone, covered over by a black sheet hurled up from the depths. I can't see anything clearly but this: the image of their faces when they passed, faces so subversive it makes me fear for my life.

I pass the house of musical children but don't stop to visit. I was told not to visit again and suddenly I take this seriously. I know this makes no sense. The children wave and call my name but I keep walking, trying to smile back at them. Their delight in chasing each other around the house amazes me when a few minutes ago it would have seemed perfectly natural. I envy them their fresh skin, skin with little knowledge of the world underneath it yet, with their bodies still unaware and their hearts still unstirred and intact.

Vaneesa, what happened to you? Who are you? I now believe it's impossible to enter the true feelings of these people. All this time there have been thorns hidden in the folds of my happiness that I never dreamt were there.

★

In the west the sun crushes orange velvet into the blue sea, a heartbreaking encounter, then scratches blood across the sky.

Like the sun, I would also like to quit the day. In the last light I'm reading a book under the trees, still a little devastated. The Big Dipper will be rising up over the water soon. Upside down. Everything is upside down here, the stars, my life. I turn around to catch something said behind my back but it's too late and a smile swipes the place of a whisper. I hear lies spoken in the night. Do I imagine these things? I never know what's really going on. Why can't they say what they mean and mean what they say? Is everything a lie? I scan the sky for answers. Where is the Southern Cross anyway? Maybe its stars don't exist. Maybe the Southern Cross, too, is a lie.

I hear my name. She practically sings my name. I look up to watch Vaneesa skipping towards me. She's back from the road and Vix. "Want to swim?" she says. The words settle like nuclear dust.

"No thanks."

Her face takes on a hurt look, like a child about to cry. Then it hardens to a degree I find alarming. Finally, her face empties of all expression. She swings her hips around and walks away.

Where in the contours of the human mind does deception stake its place?

Who can solve her inner mysteries? Did she hire her own personal designer at birth?—slightly twisted, original, wholly lacking in taste?

Get me out of here. It's time to build the campfire.

The campers and I are discussing places that have turned us upside down and inside out, shook us up. I enjoy a good shakeup now and then. When your world is toppled over, you must build it back up, but build it differently than before, inventing new interpretations. In this way, you never stop creating yourself. Shastri tells us about almost dying of three different diseases in India. Some villagers took him in and saved his life. I think back to a place that had my head reeling, that stole up on me like a sneak thief in the dark. I never knew what to expect in Malaysia. In the end, I was only beginning to understand.

MALAYSIA MALAISE

ASIA. EVEN THE WORD *Asia* sounded mystifying and strangely haunting. I might name a child Asia. Certainly a cat. During my last week in Australia, before flying to Malaysia, Asia had taken up exclusive occupancy in my mind. Friends took me to a Malaysian restaurant in Brisbane the night before my flight. We ate spicy noodles with peanut sauce, *gado-gado* and *satay*. Halfway through the meal I said it aloud, to test its authenticity, to secure its place in my universe. "Asia. Tomorrow I go to Asia." "Yes," they said as they coughed and choked, their eyes reflecting the watery light in mine. "Asia." Red chilies blazed trails from our taste buds to our toes. Conversation ended there.

I expected to love Asia immediately. But high expectations are always folly. We forget that.

After a late-night landing in Kuala Lumpur (meaning Muddy River Mouth), Malaysia's capital, I stood in line under blazing fluorescent lights for the obligatory two-hour customs and immigration ritual. On the walls of this stifling hot and hectic airport were warnings—something about drugs found in baggage and getting hanged for it. Would that be a public hanging? I wondered. The long flight had exhausted me. The long flight during which I'd caused a kerfuffle.

The kerfuffle: the airline people had mistakenly stuck me in the midst of the smoking section. I don't smoke. I detest smoke. As we rolled up into the stratosphere, a little red smoking light came on, setting off a chain reaction of ignited cigarettes all around me. Nausea. As if flying itself isn't nauseating enough. Eight hours is a long time to hold one's breath. After the first hour I knew I could endure it no longer. I walked up towards the front of the airplane, to the head of the non-smoking section, and I leaned against the wall. I was happy there. I wasn't hurting anybody. Then a flight attendant came on the scene. "What are you doing up here?" she asked me.

"Breathing."

She ordered me back to my toxic place at the back of the plane, as if I were a naughty schoolgirl.

"Sorry. But I won't go back there."

"You have to go back there. You can't stand up here. It's against regulations."

"I don't care. I won't go back. Can't I sit somewhere else?"

"No. This flight is full."

By this time we had an audience in the non-smoking

section. Through the curtain ahead of me I could see that the flight was not full. The first-class section was nearly empty. The first-class section with its reclining lounge chairs, its clinking champagne glasses and its puffy pillows.

"I see lots of empty seats up there." I pointed to the luxury section.

"No. You can't go up there."

"Sorry, but I'm going up there."

What could she do when the audience of passengers clapped for me? I took my luxury seat and settled back to dream of Asia. They refused to feed me their exotic Asian cuisine but I cared not. There would be plenty of that where I was going. A heavy-set man in a business suit across the aisle shook my hand to congratulate me. I thought he might offer a victory cigar.

After the officials had thoroughly searched my bags I headed out into the heavy night air of Kuala Lumpur to find a cab. Taxi drivers roared up with flung-open doors, ready to shuffle me in. The pushiest man won. I let him win.

"Where to?"

"Chinatown." The cheap hotel district, my guidebook had told me.

Chinatowns always bustle and hum with life but since this was Chinese New Year the bustling and humming had sped up to an elevated throbbing. Every guest house, hostel, and hotel was full. Finally we found a place. The taxi driver grabbed my backpack and carried it up to my room.

A light bulb dangled from a cord over the bed in the closet-sized room. City sounds of horns and drunks rose up from the streets through the open window.

"Good room," said the taxi driver. He threw my backpack to the floor and bounced himself onto the bed. "Good bed too." Clearly, this was a man of scant intelligence.

"What are you doing?!"

"I'm tired; I need to relax. Busy night."

"What?"

"Just an hour."

"What?!" He kicked off his shoes. "This is ridiculous. Get out."

"Driving a taxi makes me tired. I hate my job."

"Interesting. Now go away."

"Why?"

"I'm going to scream."

"No, don't. It's late. You'll wake people up."

"That's the idea."

"Okay, half an hour. Wake me up."

"IT'S THREE IN THE MORNING, IT'S NINETY DEGREES, I HAVE JET LAG. ALL I WANT TO DO IS SLEEP FOR TWELVE HOURS AND I HAVE A TAXI DRIVER IN MY BED IN A SEEDY HOTEL. PLEASE GET THE HELL OUT OF HERE. NOW!" I said this loudly.

"You crazy foreigners. I never understand any of you."

He tied his shoes back on and left.

After ten hours of sleep I jumped out of bed ready to begin

loving Asia. The day before didn't count. Tioman Island was my destination—an island off the southeast coast of Malaysia, an island of paradise, people said. I planned to meet my friend Charlie from Canada there.

Dirty exhaust fumes streamed blue hazy streaks out of every moving vehicle in Kuala Lumpur. I tried to ignore it. I was on my way to paradise. The sun roasted every person on the streets, both living and dying, as I searched for the train station. But that didn't matter either. Soon I'd be swimming in the ocean. Soon I'd be watching ruby-tinted sunsets in an evening breeze.

A large map on the train station's wall clearly marked the train routes and roads for the entire country. It looked as if I could take the train south to a place called Gemas and from there take a bus straight east to the coast, to the port city where I'd catch the boat for Tioman Island. Simple. I found the station's information desk where I'd ask to make sure. A sign proclaiming "I speak English" sat in front of a veiled woman at the counter.

"Hello, I'm going to Tioman Island."

"Oh, it's beautiful there."

"Could you tell me if I can take a bus from Gemas to get to the coast?"

She narrowed her eyes and thought for a second.

"Yes," she smiled and nodded her head. "Yes, you can."

I believed her. Why wouldn't I? She worked at an information desk for tourists. She said yes. How was I to know

I'd entered a land where people say yes if they think you want to hear yes, even if yes is not the answer? I bought my train ticket for Gemas. I bought a third-class seat. I wasn't fussy. I wanted to love the country and its people. I wanted to live, breathe and feel Asia. All of it.

And I did feel all of it on the train ride. All the overhead fans were broken but a hot breeze from the open window blew the sweat off me. Only when the train made its stops at the villages every ten minutes did the real wall of heat come crashing down. I tried to sit perfectly still. Every movement of muscle dripped like heavy hot metal. Even blinking my eyes drained something from me. Across the aisle two men wore long woolen robes and little hats. The women with them wore long polyester robes and veils, with wool sweaters. The temperature was close to a hundred degrees. It was painful to watch them in those clothes. For the entire journey the men read the Koran and twice they bowed on their seats and prayed towards Mecca. The women watched the scenery. We passed by luscious green coconut palms and banana trees leaning out of rubble and shantytowns. Flowers, not prejudice, grow out of every kind of shackled impoverishment. The train jerked its way along through rainforest and garbage at a jogger's pace, allowing the land to be close and immediate, not detached pictures whizzing by. I could feel it, touch it. I stuck my head right out the window to catch a breeze, to be part of the place. A sprinkle of water from somewhere outside hit my face and cooled me. I love Asia, I thought. I've touched it already.

Half an hour later I took a walk up into the next train car. I watched a mother hold her naked little boy up to the open window so he could take a pee. ON MY SIDE OF THE TRAIN. I made for the nearest sink to wash my face. Like a mantra I made myself say it again over and over. I love Asia. I love Asia.

Every time the train stopped, people from the villages would load on and fly through the carriages selling nourishment to passengers—bottled water, rice snacks, bananas, candy, patties. Patties. I was hungry, so when the man selling patties came by I asked him if there was meat in the patty he held out to me. He narrowed his eyes and thought for a second just the way the woman at the information desk had. "Yes," he said. "Yes, there's meat in it."

"Oh, no thank you then." I didn't want meat in my patty.

"No meat in the patty," he said as he pushed the same patty closer to my face. And smiled.

Asia. It's full of mystery, I realized. Only by biting into it would I begin to make sense of the place.

At last we reached Gemas, the town where I would catch the bus to the coast for the boat to Tioman Island, to paradise. I was on my way. I was almost there.

I walked along the dirt road away from the train stop with the awkward feeling that I was being watched by an entire town. Had Gemasians never seen a foreigner before? I saw a man skewering chicken kebabs over a barbecue pit in a little outdoor shack. "Best Muslim Restaurant in the World" read the sign above him. He waved me over as he pointed up at his sign.

"Bus? Bus in Gemas?" laughed the man. He continued to laugh for an inappropriate amount of time. Rather rude. I could see that this one-horse town might not have its own bus station but surely a bus would pass through it. The woman at the information desk back at the train station had said so. I would ask someone more polite, someone with more knowledge of his town.

I continued along the dirt road. Nobody seemed the least bit reluctant to stare openly at me. A pack of big-toothed dogs ran up to me and barked, groups of teenage boys heckled shyly and attempted whistling noises, and a small child started to cry when she saw me and hid her face into her mother's robe. Then I reached the end of the dirt road, the end of Gemas.

I hadn't seen a bus, nor had I seen anything resembling bus paraphernalia.

The man who ran the world's best Muslim restaurant was right. The woman at the tourist information desk was wrong. I was a wandering alien at the end of a place called Gemas.

I asked a few more people about the bus, not wanting to give up on the idea entirely. I must have been pronouncing the Malay word for bus correctly because whenever I said it, people would shake their heads, or giggle.

I realized I would have to wait for the train to come through again the next day to take it further south until I reached a city with a bus. Until then I'd explore Gemas, although I'd seen most of it already. A smiling Chinese man approached me and touched my sleeve.

"Where you stay?"

I told him I didn't know, since I hadn't noticed any hotels or guest houses.

"No hotels in Gemas. You stay at my house. My wife good cook. Come." He took my sleeve again and dragged me along.

I was being taken care of. It felt good. Gemas's hard uninviting edge softened and I no longer cared about the townspeople's alien-sighting. The smiling Chinese man, whose name I repeated to myself many times so I'd remember it, showed me up a staircase above a little fruit market. We walked along the balcony to a door. Before opening the door he paused and I thought I heard him sigh. "My family," he said.

On the other side of the door was a circus. At least eight children chased one another around the room. Three women in the kitchen appeared to be at war with each other as pots boiled over and rice steamed hot vapors into an already humid space. One woman waved a cleaver through the air. At a table two men smoked cigarettes as they argued over a board game they were playing. An old woman sat on the floor smiling, serene and oblivious.

My smiling Chinese man yelled something out into the chaos. It took him a few tries before they heard him. Then the noise stopped. So did the various disputes around the room as everyone looked at me. The woman with the cleaver, who acted like his wife, said something to him in a shrill voice and so began a conversation in Chinese that I imagined must have gone like this:

"Who's that woman with you?"

"She's a lost foreign woman."

"Why is she here?"

"She looked helpless and pathetic out on the street."

"But why is she here?"

"No place to stay."

"Why did you bring her here?"

"Because I'm a smiling happy man with a beautiful loving family who takes pity on the downcast and wretched."

"Where will she sleep?"

"In bed with the children." He pointed to a mattress on the floor that the kids were bouncing on.

"Get her out of here!" She flung her arm out at the dirt road.

I don't have to be here right now, I reflected. I could be back home in Canada, sitting in a pub by a fireplace with snow falling outside, talking to friends. I wouldn't begrudge winter. Really I wouldn't.

Another woman in the kitchen joined in. Something close to a smile crossed her lips as she looked at me. Maybe

she was the man's sister, another smiler in a family of smil-
ers, Good Samaritans.

"I'll take in the poor pathetic creature," she seemed to
say. "She can come to my house." The woman walked over
and took my arm. The man shrugged. Incredibly, he was
still smiling.

So after leaving and thanking the wife for playing such a
small and passing role in my life, I followed the sister back
out to the dirt road that was Gemas. Non-stop she talked,
and very excitedly. She seemed to have a lot to tell me, not
that I could understand a word of it. Apparently, life in
Gemas was quite outrageous.

Her house was somewhat calmer but not exceedingly so.
I shared a bed with two kids rather than eight, and the men
playing the board game in her house were far more pleasant
and hardly argued at all. On their floor also sat a smiling and
peaceful old woman.

I hoped to sleep well that night. I didn't mind the kids
rolling around, kicking and tickling each other. It made me
happy. It wasn't the persistent barking of a dog all night
long that kept me awake, nor was it the stagnating heat, lack
of air, or lack of space in the bed. Something else kept me
awake, something that made those things seem like quiet
little daisies in a meadow. This was something that disturbed me deeply. At first I thought mosquitoes were
attacking me, the silent variety that doesn't buzz. But we lay
under a mosquito net so that didn't make sense. Still, they

felt like mosquito bites. All night long, inconsiderate insects chewed on me. Bedbugs, the most unpleasant life-forms I've ever encountered. Every time they nailed me I slapped myself silly—an exercise in futility; the bedbugs didn't care. I think I finally slept for five minutes at seven in the morning, out of sheer exhaustion, just before the sister woke us up for breakfast.

When the sister looked at me, her face twisted into an expression that suggested she had just eaten rotting food. She didn't look good. I thought maybe she'd had an unfortunate night too but then she pointed at my face and put her hand up to her mouth. The kids did the same thing. It made me self-conscious. One of the men found a hand mirror in a drawer and held it in front of me. He kept his distance, as if suddenly wary of this stranger in his house, as if the stranger might be contaminated. I looked into the mirror and didn't recognize myself. During the night I'd apparently been punched out, beaten to a pulp, had engaged in guerrilla warfare and inner-city skirmishes, or so the mirror and the family seemed to be indicating. My face did feel miserably itchy and swollen. One of my eyes was almost completely clamped shut under a ballooning eyelid. The rest of my face had been raided, sieged upon. Damn little bugs. They're invisible. How could something so minuscule and insignificant wreak such havoc?

After drinking tea but not eating breakfast (swollen face, couldn't chew) with the lovely family, I thanked them kindly and got the hell away from there. Back on the dirt road, the Gemasians now not only stared, but winced and openly gaped in horror when they saw me. Hey, it doesn't mean I'm not a nice person, I wanted to say. When I passed the Best Muslim Restaurant in the World the man was still there skewering his chicken over the fire pit. He waved me over and pointed up at his sign—just in case I hadn't noticed it yet, just to be sure I realized the prestigious rank of his establishment. I sat down on the wooden bench beside him at his barbecue. It was a one-bench kind of restaurant but that didn't mean it couldn't have the world's best food. Small can be good. I'd have to wait five hours for the train so I decided to write letters to tell friends what a wonderful time I was having. Later, when my face was feeling better, I ordered lunch. The chicken *satays* were delicious, spicy, with peanut sauce. But then he prepared for me an assortment of his specialties. I love almost all food. I'm experimental. I didn't want it to be so, but aside from the *satays,* the Best Muslim Restaurant in the World had the Worst Food I've Ever Tasted. I'm not even sure what most of it was. A neon red sauce covered a suspicious, sausage-shaped piece of meat with a limp jellied consistency that left me wondering where and what it had been in its lifetime. A question recurred with disturbing regularity: had it always been that limp? Two hours after eating it I was sick. Asia's fascinating, I wrote my friends. Truly.

As the train pulled out of Gemas I was tempted to wave

good-bye to that town but thought better of it. I was trying to keep a low profile. I started to sleep on the train in an attempt to restore some vital part of myself I feared must have gotten lost somewhere, maybe on my flight to this continent. I also thought sleep might prevent more bad things from happening. But then it hit me: if I'm truly under a curse, sleep can't save me. Worse, it could hurt me. People get robbed while asleep on trains. I wondered how my friend Charlie was faring on his way to Tioman Island. Surely he was going through the same passage to hell that I was. That would only be right.

I sat motionless on the train with my one remaining open eye aimed straight ahead of me, stealing only occasional furtive glances out the window. I couldn't take any more chances.

In the city of Keluang the bus I needed was easy to find. Nothing bad happened. As I boarded, I thought the curse must have passed. I must have slipped through some sort of dark and hideous continental crack, victim of an ancient initiation rite. Now, surely, I had emerged relatively unscathed on the other side. I even got a window seat.

I wouldn't have thought it possible but the sun beat down more intensely and the air was engorged with even higher humidity than the day before. A profoundly large Indian woman in a draping polyester sari took the seat beside me. We smiled at each other and I didn't mind that even before the bus began its journey I could feel the heat radiating off her leg and spreading onto mine. Bus seats are small in Asia because Asian people are usually small. But not always. A river of sweat began to flow between us and the polyester made a marvelous dam. But I would ignore what was happening down there. The curse had passed. Paradise was coming.

The rough road twisted and turned in on itself over bumps, hills and potholes, jolting us up, down and around like cheap thrill-seekers on a roller coaster. The bus driver's only concession to safe driving was to honk at every curve and he truly seemed to enjoy his reckless driving at jet-engine speed. One of those male things, I suppose. We almost hit a little man in a straw hat riding a bicycle on the edge of a town. As the bus roared by, the bicycle, loaded down with basketfuls of food, crashed straight into a thicket of shrubs lining a ditch. People on the bus laughed. As the bus swung and heaved, so did the motions of human stomachs. Luckily my stomach had already decided to disgorge the goat dick laced in red sauce, or whatever it was, so I wasn't worried about getting sick. My leggy bus mate, on the other hand, wasn't doing so well. I thought she might be sick at any moment. To get some fresh air, I opened the window, thinking we would all feel better with a breeze. Already people behind us were throwing up— a terrible sound. For some reason everyone kept the windows closed. It didn't make sense, especially in such unreasonable heat. As soon as I opened the window the woman next to me reached over and slammed it shut. Then she shook her head at me disapprovingly. Was I violating some secret fresh-air code? Did these people want to be sick? We careened up and down over hills, swerving and sweating, with more people retching—the majority of the bus passengers, it seemed to me. And as if things weren't nauseating enough, a smell of diesel fuel permeated the air.

Then it happened. The woman next to me, my leg-sweating partner, threw up.

It was a strange and terrible moment, far too intimate, yet disgusting also. Remarkably, she seemed unperturbed about what she had done. She held the vomit there, safely and neatly, in the lap of her sari. Polyester was a good fashion choice for her after all, the material having extremely small pores for liquid to pass through. I was thankful to polyester just then, never having been a fan of it before.

Now I had every right to open the window. To jump out, if nothing else. Besides, how could she reach out to close it again now that both her hands were occupied in subduing the contents of her stomach?

I set my gaze out the window for the next three hours, only once casting my open eye down to snatch a glance. Just morbid curiosity. Her rejected lunch still lay there intact, her leg now permanently cemented to mine. She had fallen asleep with her hands still in their rightful stabilizing position. As I watched rain forests zooming past I knew the worst part wasn't the rank smell rising up from the depths of the woman's sari, nor was it the pools of vomit awash on the bus floor. Nor the heat, nor my queasy insides. The worst part was the curse, still with me after all. Never before one to believe in superstition—although I do have Irish roots—I was forced into re-evaluation.

The next bus, the one that would take me to the coast, was packed so full of passengers both sitting and standing I realized there would never be room for me. Heads and arms that wouldn't fit inside jutted out the windows. At least this meant they believed in the open-window policy. The people on the bus seemed jubilant about their congested conditions and they waved me on to come join them. I only made it as far as the second boarding step but evidently this was good enough. Off we went. I liked where I stood, out there on the step grabbing on to a pole, just a foot from the open road. It was strategic. If vomiting sessions began on this bus it would be easy to bail out. And with the bus as crammed as it was, vomiting sessions would not be a pretty sight.

Hanging out the door was fun. The curse gods couldn't get me out there. Too risky for them. But then we reached the coast where the monsoon, in its final days, had been pounding rain down onto muddy wet roads. I adopted the muddy wet look myself. Nobody threw up near me, though. That was something.

Since Chinese New Year celebrations still raged on in the fishing village of Mersing, finding lodgings took me two hours. I finally found an unadvertised room for the night above a friendly Chinese restaurant. The shower down the hall was broken and the restaurant owners seemed particularly apologetic about this, forcing me to conclude that my face and hair must have looked a filthy and sorry sight. I would try the low-profile strategy again and avoid going downstairs when they were serving dinner to patrons. Out in the rain I walked down to the docks to look at boat schedules for Tioman Island. One of the fishermen told me very few boats had been venturing out due to storms and I might have to wait a few days until the sea calmed. I hated the thought of waiting. Rough seas or not, it was dangerous not to leave as soon as possible. I was driven by a feeling that the curse couldn't touch me once I reached an island of paradise. Paradise wouldn't allow it. On arrival I'd be decontaminated, exorcised, sprayed free of the vile thing.

A Malay fisherman who introduced himself as Sanny told me he would be going to sea, to Tioman Island, in his little fishing boat the next day, no matter the weather. I liked Sanny immediately. Right then and there I paid him for the voyage. Things were looking up. I explored the nightlife of Mersing and found the entire town to be in a festive mood. A fireworks display I watched from an outdoor café awed the crowd and didn't come close to setting me ablaze. I wanted to skip for joy back to my room. Nothing had gone wrong for four hours.

Then came the fifth hour. Minutes after getting into bed it started happening again. I didn't want to believe it at first, but that was blatant denial. The bedbugs were back. How was it possible for them to find any place left on my body to gorge on after their evil cousins' knockout binge back in Gemas? I rolled down in defeat onto the floor to attempt sleep there. Surely bedbugs couldn't find me on a floor.

As I lay on the floor laced with cockroaches—preferable to bedbugs by far—a new theory struck me: there had been a travel-lore mix-up. The Open Road, the exhilaration of moving on each day, the journey itself—being flung out and cast adrift through time and space, colliding with new, strange lives and lands, always the wayfarer down the road—this was always supposed to be the good part, not the destination. But this didn't seem to be working for me anymore. The poets, the explorers, the hard-core travelers, the Beatniks—all those who praised the song of the open road were full of crap. I turned against them all that night. The cockroaches agreed.

The clapping of thunder and heavy rain woke me up the next morning, setting off fears about the day's voyage to paradise, fears that the voyage might not happen. But I had faith in Fisherman Sanny. I had seen a crazed light in his eyes.

Down at the dock that morning, I saw the crazy Irishman again, the same crazy Irishman I had seen so many times in Golden Bay. I'm not sure if he recognized me, but there was no mistaking him. He wore a yellow raincoat and rubber hat. He also was waiting for a boat to Tioman Island.

"Hey you, have you touched the core of your sorrow?" he called out to me from a dock as rain pelted down on both of us.

"Actually, yes, I have," I yelled back at him.

My already-soaking backpack and soaking self loaded into Sanny's rickety paint-peeled boat along with Sanny, his fishing crew, at least ten locals and seven other travelers, including the crazy Irishman. Other fishermen at the dock shook their heads at us. We cared not. Through the hazy stream of drizzle I looked at my fellow boat-mates and felt instant affinity for them. It felt good to be in the company of other people, people as undaunted as myself. Intrepid dissenters, various lunatics.

I sat talking to two English women as we leaned against the back wall of the boat holding a plastic tent tarp over us in an unsuccessful attempt to stay dry. Every oncoming wave sent our little vessel bolting straight up to the sky and then crashing down again, lashing everyone on the boat with salt water followed by a rain-water rinse. Even Sanny said he'd never seen rougher seas. He loved it, lived for it, I could tell.

Water, water everywhere. Four and a half hours of it. People started getting sick. Fortunately, on a boat, unlike a bus, a vomiting person has an obvious receptacle. The sea doesn't care.

All around us we watched people retching over the sides. The few of us who remained unmoved tried squeezing our eyes closed to shut everything out—the storm, the stomach-dropping churning of the boat, the nausea, the sight of the sick. It only made it worse. The sea forced us to be part of it all. We had to watch. Then I was the only one left. First one then the other English woman surrendered and crawled over to offer her breakfast to the sea. But I had to hold on. I noticed Sanny wasn't sick either. We shared something in common, he and I. Sanny must have known about the curse gods.

The storm continued to toss the boat around as if it were the depraved sea's dispensable toy. Hot and heavy bolts of wet rage pelted down on us in surges of anger that had smashed away ordinary rain. I sat staring out at the violent sea. I couldn't feel anything. In the past three days I'd seen more vomit than is necessary to see in a lifetime. My face had been sunburnt, muddied, stormed on, rained at, peed upon, and torpedoed by hostile invisible bugs. My stomach had been assaulted by undercooked and dubious genitalia from the animal world. I'd been misled by a woman who had told me yes. Why was I here? Where was I going? I couldn't remember. Something about paradise. What was that?

Then a voice spoke to me from the thunderclouds.

Maybe I'd gone mad or maybe it was the curse gods apologizing, trying to say it was all a mistake. They didn't mean it. I wasn't supposed to have slipped through the trapdoor into Dante's Inferno. Things would be better now.

"There are great days coming to live and die for," said the voice.

The clouds parted company to make way for the sun. I could see land. Tioman Island. My last meal wouldn't be rotting carp. I wouldn't die a horrible death at sea. I would know paradise.

I love Asia, I said to the sea. I do.

I knew I'd reached the right place. The tilted hand-painted sign at the end of the dock told me so. "WELCOM TO PAR-ADISS," it said. I laughed aloud at life's great cosmic joke. Then I walked the shores of paradiss with a broken sandal, a dirt-streaked and insect-ravaged face, muddy hair, and a soaking wet, torn, filthy cotton dress. I walked the shores of paradise in bliss.

Until I came to a sight disturbing to my eye.

I saw a man lying in a hammock under a tree by the water, being served a pina colada by two beautiful Malay women. This wasn't right. He looked untarnished, far too content, completely unaffected by the sinister dabbling of dark forces into innocent lives. He looked familiar. He looked like my friend Charlie. Yes, it was he.

"Hey Laur, is that you? Come on over, life's great."

I wanted his hammock to give way and break. Where were my curse gods when I needed them?

CHAPTER NINE

Would a traveler go back at the end of a trip and do it all over again? Relive all the hassles, the heat, the misadventures?

Yes. Usually, anyway. If only for the rare moments that are travel, that make it vital. Even if those moments take forever to come, they're worth the wait. They're the same reasons that keep us alive. Wouldn't most people go back and be a kid again, go through all the hurts, bruises and misunderstandings of growing up, relive everything, just to be able to smell spring the way we did when we were ten?

OKAY, NOW WHAT? I'm tangled in a world I've helped tangle. I still can't leave this place, however. I get so lost in their world but when I'm down here on the beach I have myself back. Instead of gorging on heavy coconut-laden feasts of fat, I eat the fruit from the trees. I swim. I talk to the other travelers. They tell me of places they've come from and I remember the world. I realize I can be part of that world again, anytime, if I want to. I don't have to stay. It's often unbearable with the

heat and flies, the lack of communication, the male chauvinism, the same food all the time, Vix and Vaneesa. The lies. I
miss independence, solitude, individual thinking—all foreign
concepts here. But then I hear them sing outside my tent at
night. Their voices lure like the sirens and I fall into the music
like falling into the ocean. I can't imagine leaving. I'd be crazy
to leave. This place lays me down flat, holds me to its moist
earth. To stay deepens my life.

Vix and Vaneesa have been friends with each other all
along, secretly. What kind of friends I can't imagine. And I've
learned this: both of them are vipers, sucking what they need
from other people. They have a common goal: that I leave.
Vaneesa wants me to leave because she wants Laudi back.
She wants me out of the way. Just this morning she told me
I didn't belong here. She snarled when she spoke. And Vix
hates me. I don't know why. Probably because he knows I
don't trust him. It's not that I've had the guts to confront
him, ever, on anything. Maybe I looked at him the wrong
way over the turtle stew.

Laudi, Uma, Kalisi, and the others are wonderful to me.
They say forget the evil ways of Vix and Vaneesa. They tell
me not to worry. But they give in to Vix every day. They
never stand up to him or tell him what they think of his
behavior. Last night, Vix was in a drunken rage, shouting
from up on the hill down to all of us on the beach. He
screamed for us to stop the music. Acoustic guitar music
barely makes its way to the road. It doesn't rise up the hill.

But the cousins stopped playing. They simply unstrapped their guitars and walked away. I couldn't believe it. Words of protest got caught deep in my throat and stayed there.

Maybe it's easier this way, to give in, to conform, to slide peacefully into communal waters. But if nobody says anything, we become our lowest common denominator, all covered with the same slime. We can't get out. We don't even try. Vix's demons intermingle with our own and we don't see them slip in.

As for Vaneesa, I'm left parched. All that remains is nostalgia for a thing of beauty. I'm left wondering how some people can inhabit their lives with such contradictions. Only when Laudi holds me in his arms at night does everything fall back into its proper place.

Vix and Vaneesa: I leave the two of you alone to your destiny.

Today at school another teacher, an Indian woman, shares her curry with me for lunch. She tells me secrets of the school. As if I need to hear more secrets. I'm so swollen with people's secrets I could give birth to a secret child. Her eyes are polished jewels that shimmer when she speaks. Such scandals! No, really? Oh, that's awful. She touches my arm and tells me, Yes, it's all true. Her hands are soft and warm. I marvel not at the sordid school politics but at the curious human bonds created out of gossip.

Laudi comes to meet me when I walk home. Even far

down the road I know it's Laudi by his walk. All Fijians walk slowly—this is the tropics—but I've actually seen Laudi zigzag along the road, as if the road itself were life, and life could be stretched out into blissful eternity. Clarence McQuiggle should come to Fiji and meet Laudi. This is something I truly value about Laudi: he's never in a rush to Make Time. Making Time is especially absurd here, where people have walked and hummed, fished, sung, laughed, and played the same way for generations. Where would they hurry to? They're happy. They're happy as they are. I can hear Laudi singing. How sweet of him to meet me on the road like this. Just watching him sway and smile makes me forget the gossip and deception of this island. We run towards one another with our arms flung out, but pass each other and continue to run with open arms until each of us is well down the road, alone. Then we turn around, run back, and get it right this time. I don't know how this game started, but Laudi finds it hilarious. I guess I do too.

"Laudi, I've been meaning to ask you, is it true about the marbles?"

"Marbles?"

"I heard that men slit little marbles into the skin of their *bothis*. It sounds wild. Is it true?"

"Oh, that. Did Kalisi tell you that? It's true. But I've never actually seen it. We talk about marbles a lot, but I've never seen anyone with them. My brother has marbles. At least, he says he does."

"Why don't you have them?"

"Are you joking? Have some guy cut me open with a dirty razor and stick marbles inside my *bothi* so they can roll around wherever they feel like rolling?... Should I get some?"

"Why not? It doesn't sound that bad."

I still can't be sure of this questionable sex-enhancement practice. Fiji is a book of tall tales. When I was growing up, I knew a girl my age down the street who tangled herself in a daily web of outrageous lies. She couldn't remember the details of the lies told the day before, nor to whom she had said exactly what. Every week she sank deeper into a dark pool of deceit. She would do well here. She would fit in.

I must ask Uma about the marbles. She'll tell me the truth.

As we continue our walk, Laudi recites the words to a new song he just wrote, but stops halfway through to ask, "What's that sticking out of your sandal?" All week, my sandal has squeaked when I walk, driving me crazy, so I solved the problem this morning by sticking a good-sized leaf on the sandal's sole.

"It's a leaf. What does it look like?"

"I know it's a leaf, but why is it in your shoe?"

"You're joking, right? You don't know? It's for good luck. To ward off evil spirits. Don't you ever wear a leaf in your shoe when you wear shoes?"

"No. I didn't know. Is that Canadian?"

"It's everywhere. Everyone has to stick a leaf in."

Laudi tears a leaf from a plant and places it carefully

between his foot and his flip-flop. We walk the rest of the way home singing his new song.

When I get back I walk into Nana's house to help cook dinner. Three of the aunts are inside peeling cassava, and as I sit down on the floor with them they start laughing at me, shaking their heads in disapproval. What have I done now? Am I sitting the wrong way? It could be any of a hundred different things I've said or done today. Couldn't be that leaf thing, though. It's too soon for that. "What? What?" I say. They laugh harder. They laugh for reasons that are worlds beyond my understanding.

I don't mind, really. I like laughing. But as they continue to laugh I look out the window at the sea and wonder whether I belong in a blue-green world. I'm adapted to other shades and hues of the earth, like white and grey, sometimes pine green. Maybe this world of aquamarine fairyland colors is just a funnier place.

ANOTHER HOT DAY, ANOTHER HOT WEEK
My whole life comes back to me when I travel. When I'm on a trip, even my dreams are filled with people and events I haven't thought about in years. I dream of childhood friends who come knocking at my back door to ask me to come out and play—as if they've traveled miles across oceans and years to see me again. Traveling flushes everything out: every conversation I've ever had, every romance,

every fight with my sister as a kid, neighborhood battles, nicky-nicky nine doors, endless summer days of baseball, truth or dare, tree forts, jumping in musty maple leaf piles, surviving years of high school, and the years that followed, when life really began to reveal itself. It all gurgles up from the recesses of my mind.

I dream and dream all night until the roosters sound off at dawn. The Giant Aunts call out: *Cana, cana,* eat, eat, and my dreams fly off on their own into unexplored territory. They drift away, fleeing the pancakes and the heat. Dreams never die just because the dreamer has to wake up.

The Giant Aunts tell me at breakfast that I can't go swimming anymore. They tell me there are sharks out there. If there are sharks, why didn't they tell me this a month ago? Have they seen sharks recently? Nobody answers my questions. I need to swim. Without water, I drown in this place.

After lunch I gather everyone's dishes but Nana stops me as if I'm too fragile or weak even to wash dishes. I wish they would allow me to do more things to help. Nana lost track of her age at seventy and still scurries around as if she's twenty-five. She's small and active, with tiny bones that jut out under the edges of her soft, leathered skin. From dawn until dusk she seems to be everywhere at once. She shoos me off to a mat on the floor of a back room, tells me to nap. I don't want to nap. But I've been ordered.

I lie on the mat fanning away flies, trying to remember

what month it is, trying to remember a time when there must have been many things I could do.

Things I miss about home:
- my family and friends
- cream cheese, not that I ever ate it that much, but knowing I could if I wanted to
- snow—not for its coldness, but for the way it softens the hard edges of the world
- the English language
- the change of seasons and what lies between them
- dancing
- guys who aren't macho
- not being an alien
- libraries and bookstores
- movies
- riding my bike

Things I don't miss:
- traffic
- minus twenty degrees not including wind chill
- scraping snow off windshields on dark grey mornings
- shopping malls, not that I ever go to them, but knowing they're out there
- strip malls, same as above
- alarm clocks
- television
- junk mail

As I lie staring at the ceiling, my mind reels back over images of this country until it encounters something I'd nearly forgotten: a memory of two days in Fiji that remains separate and distinct from other memories I've gathered here. I want to hold on to this memory because thinking of it fills me with pleasure and warmth, like a child clutching a doll.

I don't know why those two days touched me so much at the time. They were very simple really and may not have seemed extraordinary to anyone else. Yet when I close my eyes I see them in the smallest detail, even now, almost a year later.

In the final days of my first time in Fiji, Laudi and I had left Taveuni together by boat for Viti Levu, Fiji's main island. I was on my way to New Zealand and Laudi planned to work in Suva for six months as a tour guide on a boat. We had a week to travel and visit some of Laudi's relatives before my flight to Auckland. One of Laudi's brothers, Jone, who was living on an island called Wakaya, suggested we visit an aunt and uncle of theirs who lived in the countryside between Suva and Nadi. Laudi had met these relatives when he was twelve years old, but couldn't remember their faces. "They live right beside a river," Jone told us, "in a big house." I asked Jone if we could go swimming there and he said, "Yes, in a giant swimming hole, with a waterfall." Was it near the ocean? asked Laudi. "Right beside the ocean," answered his brother. "You can fish there, swim in big waves, too."

It was late afternoon when Laudi and I got off the bus in

the flat land of sugar cane near Sigatoka. We were dusty and parched. The air is so hot and dry on that part of Viti Levu you can feel it pump all the way down into your lungs and stay there. I missed the moist dewy air of Taveuni; the garden island, they call it. Viti Levu holds its own fascination, however. Viti Levu is harder to crack. The earth isn't soft and moist and dark, like Taveuni's, but tough and leathered, sun-baked. The people of Viti Levu are different also.

The bus driver let us off in what looked like the scorched center of the earth, the empty spread of a yellowed map. Fields of sugar cane and empty countryside stretched as far into the distance as the curvature of the earth allowed us to see. I felt as if we were in Africa, not on a little island in the middle of a big sea. We walked along a road for almost an hour while the wind swirled up dirt from the ground into our eyes. We could taste the wind. Sweeping through the sugar cane, the wind sucked dry its sweetness. Eventually, we came to the only house in the vicinity, the house that had to belong to Laudi's aunt and uncle, according to our directions. Yet no river was in sight, no ocean, and there were certainly no waterfalls.

"Is this the place?"

"Has to be."

"At least your brother has the directions right, anyway. Are you sure it's okay just to show up like this?"

"Of course; they're my family. Fijians are like that. We just show up. They don't have a phone anyway."

The little house stood far back off the main road. Something about the place made it seem desperately alone in the world. We walked along the narrow red dirt road leading up to the front door and noticed the corrugated roof needed fixing. The shutters of all the windows were tightly closed, as was the door. Two tall and very old palm trees, one on each side, swayed over the house. No other trees were in sight. "Maybe nobody lives here anymore," I said. "The world is full of abandoned places."

"No, this is the place. My brother said it was this road."

"You're forgetting your brother's sense of accuracy is flawed."

"He has an imagination."

"His imagination is large."

"He's Fijian."

"I forgot. Doesn't look like they have any neighbors out here. Is it just the two of them?"

"They have a daughter."

When we were halfway up the smaller road, the front door of the house flew open and crashed against the outer frame. Standing behind the door stood a substantial, solid woman, who looked as if she had been standing there on guard all day. She didn't say anything and neither did we. With her hands on her hips, she watched us walk up the road. Her hair was white and thick and round, like drifts of snow enveloping her determined face. The wind didn't blow through her hair, not at all, although I could see the branches of the trees blowing above the woman, and could feel the wind on my back.

"*Bula, bula,* Auntie Ivy." Laudi waved at her and said something to identify himself. I waved also but didn't say anything. I smiled, feeling awkward, as if we were intruding. Laudi had tried to tell me this was a curious North American affliction, always feeling as if we were imposing. Visiting isn't imposing, he had said. Visiting is what people do every day.

The woman maintained her defensive football stance, and then suddenly bellowed out, "Laudi! Laudi! *Bula, bula, mai, mai*" (come, come). She called to someone in the house. I immediately felt relieved. Suddenly, she seemed thrilled at seeing outsiders walking up her road.

When we reached the house, Auntie Ivy hugged and kissed us as if we were her long-lost children. She took our hands to lead us inside.

Unlike most Fijian houses I'd seen, which are minimalist in the extreme, this house was crammed with furniture and overflowing bookshelves, which spilled books and newspapers onto the floor. Auntie Ivy kicked away piles of papers as she led us into the main room. "Laudi, you're big now. You were just a run-around little boy last time. Nobody told me you have a wife."

"She's not my wife. She's from Canada."

"Canada? She looks Irish. Look at her hair."

She took my face into her hands and rubbed my cheeks

vigorously. Perhaps she thought this is what one does to people with red hair. I didn't mind her erasing the outer layers
of my face; eccentric people can get away with these sorts of
things. I looked at her cheerfully etched face nestled deeply
inside the cotton-batting helmet of hair and couldn't help
smiling at her. This woman's face was constructed for love.
"You marry Laudi. He's a good boy, used to like fixing
radios. Smarter than most. Bush Boy, I used to call him."

A man appeared out of another room carrying a newspaper under his arm. His hair had receded as far back as it could
reach, setting off his important eyes magnified behind a pair of
glasses. Few Fijians wear glasses. I immediately recognized his
gentle nature, which many men of his age come to possess.
He seemed somewhat confused by our presence. Eventually,
he walked over with his arm extended to shake our hands.

"*Bula, bula,* welcome. How long can you stay?"

After Laudi, Aunt Ivy, and Uncle Desmond had
exchanged sufficient Fijian pleasantries, Aunt Ivy said, "You
two are filthy. Go have a bath."

I instantly felt at home. Out the back window Aunt Ivy
called, "Kiki, Kiki, come. Take your cousin and his wife to
the bath."

"Laudi, remember our daughter, Kiki?" asked Uncle
Desmond.

"I remember a girl older than me. She sang to herself."

"She likes to sing."

Aunt Ivy shook her head and said, "Oh, you two go out

back there and get her. She's shy of strangers. We don't get many around here. You're the first in so long. Kiki will take you to the bath. You have to walk a little to get there. Follow the sugar-cane tracks. Takes about half an hour. Take some towels."

Laudi and I walked into the field behind the house to find Kiki. Wild grasses swayed freely in the wind, grasses as tall as we were, tall enough to get lost in. We didn't see anybody. "Kiki? Kiki?" called out Laudi. Nobody answered. "Kiki, Kiki." We walked through the golden wind-rustled vegetation until we heard a humming noise that sounded like a high-pitched mourning dove.

We found her sitting in the grass, a little girl with bony shoulders and twiggy limbs. She rocked back and forth, hugging her legs. Her eyes followed the swaying motions of the grass and she didn't look up when we approached. She hummed to herself, lost in some sort of whimsical childlike trance.

"*Bula*, Kiki," said Laudi.

"*Buuuulaaa,*" she said pensively, still not looking at us, her eyes fastened to the grass as if she were communicating with fairies of the wild rather than with people. She had a singsong voice.

"I'm Laudi, your cousin. We played together when we were kids. This is Laurie. Can you show us the bath?"

In time, she turned her little face up from her grass-gazing to look at us. When she smiled, I saw she was missing a front tooth. Her tiny features were squashed into the center of her face, features that amazed me. She had a face not made for beauty, but for something else. Something about her suggested wisdom and sweet simplicity. She reminded me of a porcelain doll. Her eyes were round and staring and her hair shot up to the sky in excitement. If I hadn't known she was at least twenty-seven years old, I would have wagered she was no more than twelve.

Since she didn't stand up, we sat down with her in the grass. Instinctively, we sat on either side of her, as if we knew she somehow needed protecting. I can see why she liked that secluded golden place sheltered from the wind. The place was private and smelled like dry husks of summer heat. Maybe she had a phobia of people. Maybe the harsher, louder world had such an impact on her that she found it happier to stay hidden in the grass.

I think she came to feel comfortable with us in her secret place, because without looking at me, she took my hand in hers and squeezed it tight; then she swayed my hand back and forth with hers. She squeezed and tugged and swung my hand until I was eight years old again. Her humming gave over to laughing, quiet laughing at first, until she convulsed with hilarity. Laudi and I laughed with her. The sky was losing light as the three of us sat inside the tall grass laughing at nothing specific, or at everything specific. We laughed at the eternal human joke, the joke that everyone who passes through life eventually laughs at.

After a time, Kiki jumped up and said, "Bath."

We followed Kiki along the little red dirt road behind her house until the road reached a set of narrow-gauge train tracks, tracks used to transport sugar-cane carts from the fields into town. They reminded me of a train toyland. Kiki hummed softly to herself as we walked along the tracks beside the flatlands of sugar cane on the way to the bath, whatever the bath was. In the western sky, deep lavender settled over the sugar cane. Rising towards the center of the sky, the lavender merged with pure night.

The bath turned out to be a hand pump in a cane clearing. Beside the pump sat a battered bucket. "You go first," I said to Laudi. Laudi tore off his shirt and started pumping the handle. When water rushed out of the pump and into the bucket, Kiki squealed. The squeal was more animal-like than human, which I found fascinating. Enough light was left in the sky for us to see Laudi splash water over himself. His back looked muscular and sinewy and gleamed wet in the falling dark. His back was a thing of earthly lusty beauty. Kiki, too, must have been moved by Laudi's back. She squealed again, louder this time. She squealed so much I wondered what the matter was. Perhaps she had never seen a half-naked man before. Laudi looked at me as if to say "Why is she doing that?" I didn't have a reasonable answer, but could only guess she squealed from the unfathomable joy she found in being so close to this human bathing event.

When it was my turn to bathe, Kiki didn't squeal. She giggled.

Laudi and I slept on the back porch on a bed that Aunt Ivy made up for us. All night long as the stars crescendoed across the sky, we listened to a strange crying sound coming from the tall blowing grass, a high-pitched humming kind of noise. Kiki lay sleeping inside the house. The sound in the field could only have been one thing: Kiki's grassy hiding place was calling her to come out and play.

The next morning I discovered how the family household operated. Uncle Desmond happily filled us in on the details. For the past twenty-eight years, Aunt Ivy has woken every morning at four o'clock (except on Sundays, when she sleeps until six) so she can prepare breakfast, lunch, and sometimes dinner, for her husband and Kiki. She washes dishes, clothes, and sheets before taking the early bus into Sigatoka to work nine hours at the MH department store. When she comes home at the end of the day, she cooks again.

"And what do you do while she's away?" I asked him.

"Oh, a little vegetable gardening. I take a nap."

Uncle Desmond didn't seem to find this routine odd in the least. He settled down in a big chair and sighed before reading something aloud from the *Fiji Times*, an article on the imminent introduction of television to Fiji. The coming of television to Fiji alarmed me as much as the outrageous inequity of labor between Aunt Ivy and Uncle Desmond.

I looked for Kiki after breakfast. I knew where to find her. When I reached the hiding place, she grabbed my hand and yanked me down into the grass with her. Her eyes were full of little-girl excitement as she held my hand. She filled her lungs with air, puffed up her cheeks, and began blowing on the grass. The wind wasn't strong that day; the grass was still. Perhaps she thought she needed to do the work of the wind. Clearly, the swaying of the grass was important to her. On her hands and knees, she crawled like a cat through the field, blowing at the grass. She turned around and looked at me significantly. I assumed she wanted me to blow on the grass with her. What the hell, I thought. I can do that.

After we had crawled and blown a good distance through the grass, she stood up and led me to the edge of a sugar-cane field. Between the rows we began to walk. We walked a long time, deeper and deeper into the crop. The cane was well over our heads, thick and green and overbearingly alive. Kiki turned to look at me and I saw a sharp joy rush into her eyes. She started to run. Back and forth between the rows, she laughed, ran and skipped in the tall plants, often turning around to see if I was still behind her. Occasionally, she would rip some cane off a branch and gnaw on it, which explained her missing tooth. Eventually, we reached a spot where Kiki stopped. She plunked herself down on the ground and didn't look at me as she caught her breath. Then she began to sing. I noticed then for the first time what a stirring and lovely voice she had. No words came out of her songs, only sounds, but the sounds seemed to imitate those in the natural world around her, like the melodic wind in the reeds of grass. The cane seemed to move in time to her inner rhythm and something golden seemed to fall from the sky, something lighter and cooler than sunlight. This was Kiki's life, and her life amazed me. In her own elaborate fantasy world, Kiki was alone in the sweet stillness of the land, communing with the things that grew out of the ground, and with the wind that blew into her voice.

Laudi and I cooked dinner that evening. Kiki helped peel cassava and Uncle Desmond read us more articles from the *Fiji Times* as we chopped onions. The Fijian Rugby Team would compete in the World Cup. Australia was determined to get rid of the Queen on its currency. "It's about time," said Uncle Desmond. "We shipped that woman off long ago."

When Aunt Ivy arrived home, we all ate together at a table. We didn't eat on the floor. This family didn't seem to adhere to many of the traditional Fijian customs. We even discussed different things from what I was used to discussing at Fijian meals. We talked about the failing economies of New Zealand and Canada, the overuse of pesticides, and the racial prejudice of many native Fijians against the Indian population. We didn't gossip; nobody lived nearby to gossip about, and even if they had, I doubt we would have gossiped about them. This family wasn't the gossiping sort. Uncle Desmond opened up the back door while we ate, so Kiki and the rest of us could enjoy the back field breeze. I think her parents understood about the grass fairies, and what Kiki did in the sugar cane. They had no other children. The three of them were alone in the world, full of desperate and loving concern for each other.

When it was time for Laudi and me to leave the next day, Kiki walked us back along the narrow red dirt road. When we reached the larger road, she stopped abruptly. Suddenly she looked like a frightened kitten afraid to take another step. She put her lined little hand in mine and swung it gently back and forth. When she smiled I saw her delicate mouth and missing front tooth and knew I would never see her again. We kissed her good-bye and walked away, turning often to wave back at her. Every time I turned around, I saw her arm waving across the sky at us. As she became smaller and smaller in the distance, a tiny figure with a swaying arm, the thought struck me that she might never in her life go beyond that red dirt road.

The Road stretched out before us, the Road that would lead us back into the larger, noisier, less enchanted world. I wanted to preserve that instant of time, the instant when a sweet Fijian man held my hand as we walked by fields of sugar cane in the sun, while behind us, a wise woman who loved tall grass waved good-bye.

PITCH-BLACK, VERY LATE

Everyone has gone to bed. I walk through the woods over the rippled sand to get some water, and, from the road, I hear high-pitched squeals, followed by a series of crashes through branches, then footsteps.

"Allo? Allo?" calls a voice out of the dark. The voice is nearby, a French accent, and belongs to a woman. It's too dark to see even a silhouette.

"Allo," I say. "Where are you?"

"I'm here, I think, but I don't know where here is." She laughs and her laugh is like starlight and fills the night. I like her already.

"You're at a campground on the beach. Buvu Beach. Where did you come from?"

"Oh, this family on the road, beautiful family. They invited me to eat with them when I passed on my bicycle. I came on the boat today and oooh, I felt so sick. The boat and waves and my stomach…"

"I know. I was the same. What's your name?"

"Genevieve, and you?"

Into blackness we talk while setting up her tent. We talk deep into the night of our travels, adventures and loves. Travelers sometimes pour their hearts out to each other, as if we're each other's angels. We say, Of course you're crazy to be roaming the world alone; I'm doing the same thing.

Do you ever think we should be settling down? Should we try to stay in one place for a while? Get married, acquire furniture?

No.

Me neither.

Silly thought.

I own a bookshelf, two bikes, a bunch of clothes and a bunch of books.

Me too, and a coffee maker.

What about a man? Shouldn't we find one of those?

I've had plenty of those.

Me too. Always fun.

Always fun, fascinating.

I like to find the ones I know I can't stay with.

Of course, the ones entirely unsuitable.

Safer that way.

Then we can leave, go exploring again, see more of the world. We have to go.

This is our natural state, to be wandering explorers, seekers of life.

We're born alone, we die alone.

We're explorers.

This is our destiny.

Our hearts are pure and free.

And wild.

We're weird.

Probably.

Underneath a temple of trees in the night's most quiet moments we come to an understanding. We know it must be similar to quotes and phrases we've read countless times in poems and on tea packages, but it seems significant nonetheless: everyone eventually must choose her road. You either stay on the road that's comfortable and safe but limiting, or you break out on the other road, the unknown road, and follow your deepest inner longing. This one isn't an easy road, but it's your own, the one you know you have to take in the end.

Genevieve and I learn in the dark everything about each other except our faces, hair, even skin color. These things don't matter because we're the same inside. Only in the morning will we see what the other looks like.

Thank God she's arrived. She brings back the gypsy soul in me.

Genevieve is circling the world on her bicycle. She left her home in France five years ago and still has years and countries of roads and lives to see before returning, if she ever does return. The Giant Aunts ask her if she's married and she answers yes, to her bicycle. She doesn't trudge and sweat over hills in the heat like the Germans, she says. She takes slow breezy rides down country lanes, stops often, and stays in villages for months at a time. She pedaled through every country but one in the Middle East. At the border of Pakistan and India she was terrorized by border guards who took her passport away for two frozen nights that refused to end. From north to south India she journeyed through waves of heat and spice and color. She attended week-long weddings. In Mongolia she rode the only road through the far-reaching steppes. For an entire winter she stayed with a Mongolian family and ate greasy boiled mutton and yak. She loved their ruddy-faced children. In China and Taiwan she learned from Buddhists how to sit still and meditate. She watches her breath for hours at a time while the outer world falls away like layers of an onion. In Tokyo, she set up her tent in downtown city parks, taught French, and played her guitar in subway stations. The Japanese loved her, threw coins for her music, and laughed. The Japanese authorities wanted to kick her out unless she sang Edith Piaf songs; then they begged her to stay.

We'll tell stories tonight. I can feel it already. With Genevieve here, everyone is reinvigorated. She's tuning her guitar in the kitchen hut while Laudi's cousins watch her, fascinated. Laudi is pounding kava. Ana, Yurgen, and I are building the fire. Some of the Giant Aunts are here tonight with their children for the music, which is rare. When Auntie Sala drags a piece of driftwood over to the fire, I notice something sticking out of her flip-flop. "What's that in your shoe, Sala?"

"It's a leaf. For good luck." Her little son is also sporting a good-luck leaf in his sandal.

What have I done?

We lie on the sand for hours under the stars, singing Fijian love songs with Laudi and his cousins—we've learned the words—and listening to Genevieve's incredible travel tales. Enormous sand crabs investigate our hair while we lie on the beach. They don't bite; they're just exploring (being from another planet, they're curious) and after a while we allow them into our nests of sea-salted hair without even flinching. Under the musical spell the children's eyelids grow heavy on rose-petal cheeks and they fall asleep in their parents' laps. I love how the men here are just as affectionate with the children as the mothers are. Some of the kids stay awake, listening to the stories of us *kavalangis* (foreigners; literally, those from another island). Their eyes grow wide at the stories and I wonder if they'll remember these nights years from now, as we will.

We're adults for so much more time than we're children, yet childhood takes up so much of our lives, of who we are. Travel has the same effect. Not only does time stretch out when we travel, like a curvy road into the unknown, but travel takes up so much space in our lives, as if, like childhood, travel is the one overriding factor that colors our lives more richly than anything else. The world in bright crayon. I think of Morocco, the vast endless desert colors of Morocco. I remember the desert dwellers, and as I look into the fire, I recall Moroccan carpets...again.

A CARPET ENCOUNTER
OF ANOTHER KIND

I MUST HAVE SOME SORT of carpet karma with Morocco.

Several years after the carpet scam in Fez, I returned to Morocco for two months and had another carpet encounter. This one was a long time coming and of a different kind.

While visiting a friend in Madrid where the winter is almost as unfriendly as in Canada (no central heating in Spain) I thought I'd sneak down to Morocco for a while. Morocco would be warmer and cheaper than Spain, and the off-season meant few tourists. Morocco has a bad reputation amongst travelers but that's part of its allure. This time I'd be less silly.

To cross the Strait of Gibraltar towards Morocco is to leave behind many things. Jittery nerves, for instance. And quirky western notions about the way things ought to be. Crossing the Strait of Gibraltar is to sail in storied waters. Here is where Europe meets Africa, where Christianity meets Islam, where the Atlantic meets the Mediterranean, and where I met an American named Fred.

Fred, whom I guessed to be older than my father, told me on the boat that Spain didn't grab him, mainly because the Spanish don't speak American. Morocco sounded more interesting. He didn't know a thing about the place, he said, but had seen *Casablanca* several times. He asked me who I thought he looked like and when I guessed Ernest Hemingway he said, "Bingo! Smart gal." Very amusing he was for the short voyage but I didn't want him hanging around when we arrived at Tangier. I could see already that his southern drawl at a hundred decibels and his ignorance of cultures other than American would announce to everyone that he was an easy target for all sales pitches.

I planned on getting a train immediately and heading thirty miles down the coast to the little town of Asilah, avoiding the expected onslaught of guides at the Tangier port as much as possible. I tried to tell Fred, also known as Ernie, that we'd be swarmed by guides the minute we landed. He said he had a sure-fire way of preventing this. I was dubious.

Within ten seconds of walking down a ramp into Tangier we were bombarded by hustlers. First a tall man, snake-skinned in social graces and sporting an unconvincing "official guide" badge pinned to his *jellaba,* declared: "Stop. I'll take you where you want to go." As we tried to wave him off, another fell upon us. Then another. That's when Fred tested what he called his "mosquito repellent." He stood in front of all the guides and, striking a righteous pose, crossed himself and said, "Bless you, my sons." They scattered. Maybe Fred wasn't so bad after all.

On the train ride down to Asilah, I sat with my head and folded arms halfway out the window so I could take in the country again. Fred rattled off his life story the whole way. "All through the fifties I tried to meet Marilyn Monroe. She never answered a single letter I sent her. They wouldn't let her, those bastards." I didn't try to make sense of Fred. His angst-ridden life drifted out the window like a stream of cigar smoke. The train moved through the land slowly, just as I like it. We passed surprisingly green hills scattered with shepherds herding their sheep, children who waved at us and fetched water from wells, veiled women in colored robes who strolled along village roads, ancient red clay houses with tiny windows concealing mysteries of family life, camels in contempt of the world kneeling on the beach, and donkeys looking small and burdened in the fields. It was replenishing to be back in Morocco.

Asilah, a small fishing village along a white sweep of Atlantic Ocean shore, is over two thousand years old. Fred and I were the only passengers to get off the train there. The train actually stopped outside of town. Ahead of us lay a twenty-minute walk along a grassy path beside the ocean. Fred dragged along behind him an overstuffed suitcase on wheels, which toppled over every five seconds. The suitcase would have done better in airports. The walk made Fred irritable, and a little man from Asilah, who had been enterprising enough to come out and meet any suckers getting off the train and follow along behind to try to get us to stay at his house, go to his brother's restaurant, buy leather, exchange money and, finally, buy hashish, didn't help things. Fred kept trying to tell the man to go away in Spanish. Fred didn't believe me that France, not Spain, had most recently colonized Morocco. Fred said he could only say one thing in French but it should work. In a brazen and slow, twanged American accent, loud enough for the approaching town to hear, Fred aimed this at the little guy: "NE TOUCH-AYE PAW ME!"

An eerie light settled over the ocean where a half moon hung in the sky. The air was moist and cool. Waves pounded ashore. The annoying little man who had been loudly rebuked spat at our feet to show how he felt about us—just in case we weren't sure. As Fred lifted his suitcase back up on its wheels, he looked up at the night sky, watched the little man running off, and said, "Well, this has got to be *the* wildest and strangest thing that's ever happened to me on this planet. And I'm a sixty-nine-year-old man." I had to laugh because I'm sure that for Fred, so drenched in the American way, this was true.

By the time we reached the first building in town, Fred was in culture shock and his feet hurt. The first building in town just happened to be Asilah's only fancy hotel. The hotel overlooked the ocean. Fred headed straight for the front door. Asilah's other places to stay were cheap and Spartan, called "bottom end" places in my guidebook. I was headed for one of those. Fred said he would pay the difference if I stayed at the fancy hotel too because he didn't want to be alone in a country "where ya can't trust anybody and don't understand their genie languages." I weighed the options. It's true, Fred was annoying, but he was also kind. Besides, night was approaching and the thought of an obvious outsider and single woman in an Arabic country traipsing around to hunt down a place to stay didn't appeal to me. Not on my first night. The cost of staying in a fancy hotel for one night would be to endure blaring cultural insensitivity and possible snoring. Clarence McQuiggle came to mind. Still, I decided to take Fred up on his offer. The fancy hotel had hot showers.

Fred and I ate dinner together that night at a restaurant in town. Fred didn't have a clue about anything on the menu. The words *couscous* and *tajine* nearly scared him out of the place, and when I jokingly mentioned something about camel stew, he paled. The restaurant was crowded with people who sat at tables placed closely together, as is often the case in non-western restaurants. In a voice loud enough to be heard in his home town of Atlanta, Georgia, Fred said, "Ya know, I bet these here people don't even KNOW how to make a good steak in a country like this."

It's true what they say about some American tourists.

After dinner I wanted to go for a walk around town. Night life always throbs in countries where passion is conducted by hot evening air instead of being killed by television. Excitement hovers over crowds of people strolling the streets and talking in outdoor cafés.

In the case of Morocco, crowds of people mean crowds of men. Women aren't seen at night. They stay hidden in their homes, tending to domestic chores and talking amongst themselves. Even in the daytime women are rarely seen in cafés. Cafés are for men. In small Moroccan towns, respectable women don't go out at night. It just isn't done.

Fred tagged along for the walk. I thought walking would be better than going back to the hotel right away to listen to him one-on-one. But then he pointed at some ornamental lights hanging from buildings. Clearly, their function was to celebrate an upcoming Islamic festival. Fred thought they were Christmas decorations. "What do you think their Santa Claus looks like here? Do you think these people even know that he has a white beard and a big belly?"

Fred is a lawyer. This concerns me.

The next morning Fred shook me awake to get out of my bed at seven o'clock. I never get out of bed at seven o'clock. The only thing that got me out of bed at seven o'clock that morning was the happy realization that in a few hours I could escape from Fred.

We drank mint tea in the morning sun at one of the cafés in the town square. I had told Fred the night before that I planned on going deep into Morocco for at least a month and a half, way down south to the Sahara Desert. I was sure Fred wouldn't be interested in this, and, the night before, this was true. He had even said he was just dying to get back "stateside, and real fast too." The next morning, however, he lay back a little too far in his chair at the café, his closed eyes aimed into the sun, and called out to the waiter to bring some more mint tea. This behavior worried me. Where had his paranoia gone? He appeared fully cured of his culture shock, relaxed into the country, basking in its warmth and intrigue. I'd seen this kind of thing before but never had I seen it come on so suddenly. Fred sat bathed in weary airs of self-importance—a nasty affliction affecting some ex-pats who have spent too long in a foreign country and think they own the place. But Fred hadn't even been in the country twenty-four hours. Already he thought he was sultan of the people.

"Ya know what, gal? The Sahara Desert does sound like a fiiine place. Always wanted to ride me a camel. Do the Bob Hope and Bing thing."

Yikes.

We crossed the road to cash traveler's checks in the bank. This is where I made my escape. Inside the bank a long line of people—locals as well as a smattering of foreigners and a few backpackers—waited their turn. The bank bustled and hummed as if the people inside were excited about the day, as if life was fun, as if the world were doing a jig outside the bank waiting for them to hurry and finish their money dealings and get on with the essential nature of their lives. We joined the back of the line.

"Why aren't those charts up there in American dollars? Where's the Yank dollar?" called out Fred at maximum volume. The people in line at the bank turned around to look. So did the bank tellers. People like to attach a face to the voice when the voice resembles a sonic boom. I whispered back at him, so he'd understand, so he'd shut up. He didn't get it.

"Can't understand how these people live like this." He said this at maximum volume too. I wanted the floor to open up beneath me so I could disappear. Better yet, I wanted the floor to open up beneath Fred. I decided to ignore him. Maybe they'd think he was talking to himself.

"Well, Laur, what should our plan of aaaction be todaaaay?" Fred said that so loudly, even the bank manager came out from behind a closed door to get a look.

"Gee, I don't know, Fred. I was thinking getting kidnapped into the white slave trade might be appealing."

I had to get away. Condemning glares were all over the place. In front of us stood a family of blond backpackers. When the whole family turned around to stare I gave them my very best *I'm not really with this guy* plea-for-understanding look. The look has something to do with a notion of bewildered alarm in the eyes. They understood at once.

The little girl of the blonde family spoke in an unabashed Aussie accent, "Where ya headed?"

"I'm headed south. How about you?"

"So are we." She looked up at Fred, who was playing with a calculator, mumbling to himself. "You with him?"

"No, well, kind of. We just met yesterday. He wants to come to the Sahara Desert with me."

She must have caught the signal of flickering panic in my eyes because she said, "Oh, it's dangerous down there. They'll steal from ya blind down there, hey."

I knew this wasn't true. I knew she knew it wasn't true. A nine-year-old Australian stranger had taken upon her slight shoulders the task of rescuing me from further humiliations associated with this Ernest Hemingway impostor, or from the marginally brighter prospects of delving into the seamy underworld of white slave trading. She raised one eyebrow over a knowing eye at me, a secret sign, possibly of an Australian variety, and I responded in kind.

"What do you mean, dangerous?" belted out Fred.

"I mean bloody scary."

"You been there yourself, kid?"

"Don't have to go to know."

I privately thanked the outback god of Australian witticism for sending this child my way. "It takes forever to get there too," I added, "days and days on rickety buses, trains, maybe camels."

"Bloody hot down there too, I reckon," said the Australian prodigy.

"Hadn't figured on that either," said Fred. "Well, now, I

don't know…ummm…Laurie, would you mind if I did not accompany you down there into the dezzz-ert? I can't say I relish the thought of my suitcase getting all that saaand in it."

Ahh, the taste of freedom. It's as good as they say.

"Oh, that's okay. I like traveling on my own. You're right about the sand."

"Thing is, I just can't make up my mind." Fred was wavering.

"The bloody heat," piped up the little Aussie prophet.

"The rickety buses, the danger, the messy sand." Something close to pleading had taken over my voice. Was I overstepping the borderline out of Canadian politeness?

"Fred, I really think I should go on my own. I think it's best."

There was a pause, an overfed moment of silence in the Asilah bank. The bank manager froze. The small and blond Australian who pretended to be a mere mortal earthling squeezed her little eyes shut. Then Fred spoke.

"Okey dokey, gal. Have fun."

That's it? That's all I had to say all along? I think the good witch of the north forgot to tell me that.

I'd made my escape. The Australian family adopted me as one of their disciples of the small and blond pretend-little-girl called Trudy. We'd all head deeper into Morocco together, forging a new religion, one based on dissuading loud tourists from seeking the Sahara.

I soon learned this was a false religion, if such a term can

be used. This religion had holes, was hypocritical. The
Australian family was a family of surfers, and surfing is a religion in Australia. The family of blond Australians whose
smallest had rescued me in the Asilah bank had surfboards
waiting for them outside the bank that day. Even my small
mentor was a surfy. The two men—and let me say now that
Australian men think they as a species are the world's spe-
cialty on toast—were on a quest for the "choicest" surf to be
found on the Atlantic coast. Morocco's people and their
ancient culture, the stunning landscape, the history and
architecture of the country were as dull to them as a flat day
on the ocean. Slow day on the swell. Surfing was Life.

A couple of days later the surfers and I left Asilah and
boarded a train headed south, bound for Rabat. Apparently
Rabat, Morocco's capital city, had swell, which is surf talk for
big waves. Swell aside, I liked the surfers.

The last thing I did in Asilah was fall in love with the
bank teller who cashed my traveler's checks. His name was
Aziz and he was suave. Such flirtatious banking behavior isn't
natural where I come from. It's not politically correct. Or it's
forgotten. Our encounter lasted only five minutes; we pretended we were banking. Back outside, I told Jan, the
Australian, to go in and cash some of her checks. She said she
didn't need any more money just then but I told her she
should do it anyway. You never know when you'll find
another bank. Oh, and be sure to go to the last teller on the
left. She returned in a few minutes and thanked me for the

excellent advice. Then her body collapsed onto the bench beside me as she regained her breath. "Ever think we're missing out on something?" We caught up with the others at the train station, each of us lifted by the stirrings and complexities of the world, each of us smiling. It was time to leave Asilah and I wondered why.

In Rabat, while the others surfed in polluted waters and Jan haggled and dodged her way through the market, I made friends with our young hotel clerk, Hamid, who practiced his English on me. Hamid told me a story. In Saudi Arabia he had worked for two years in a glass factory, and for his first eight months in the country, he never saw a woman. "As if they had all died from the world," he said. Occasionally he would catch glimpses on the street of what he knew must be a woman enclosed in a black shroud with her head and face concealed. One day in the glass factory, a young woman came in by herself. Hamid couldn't believe it. While showing her some glasses, he whispered that he'd like to talk to her. She told him it was forbidden but she'd do it anyway. She was nineteen and married to a man forty years older, a man she loathed. Her life was wretched, he learned from her, but no different from any of her sisters' lives. Hamid's manner was gentle and kind and I could see how she would have fallen in love with him. They had an affair. She always switched taxis at least four times on her way to meet him in case someone suspected her. If caught, she would have been stoned to death. Hamid would have been sacked from his job at the glass factory. "They're backward there," he said, "not like in Morocco where we're liberal. Women's robes don't hide their faces in Morocco, and some women in big cities, like Rabat, even wear the jeans, like in your country."

Hamid took me on a long walk that evening through Rabat's old town of mazed alleys. I ate dinner with his family in their house of small whitewashed, rounded rooms somewhere inside that labyrinth, although I could never find it again. Arabic pop music fizzed out of a radio in their courtyard. His four sisters and a couple of cousins who had been hanging laundry on the roof greeted us and kissed me, held my hands and became my instant friends. No men materialized until mealtime. The women, who had prepared and served the food, ate their meal in the kitchen, after the men had finished. On the kitchen floor we sat and asked each other a hundred questions, and laughed—a laugh born from the uneasy surprise of peeping into each other's worlds. Later, Hamid and I ran off to a nightclub packed with people and life and live Arabic music. A big man with a moustache did amazing things with a tambourine as he strolled around the patio, singing for us in an operatic voice. The moon lit up a mosque. When I got back to the hotel I tiptoed into the room I shared with the four Australians as the first morning prayer call boomed out into the early dawn.

Before I fell asleep I thought about the woman in Saudi Arabia whose life was so devoid of all things good that she risked what life she had to feel love. I found it incredible she was alive and thinking somewhere in this same world, breathing the same air, under the same moon and desert sky. I realized that life seeks out its own mysteries, intricate and chaotic.

At the Rabat train station that morning, the train conductors turfed the Australians and me off the train to Marrakech because of a rule: no surfboards. I think they invented the rule when they saw us coming but I couldn't blame them. The Australians' surfboards had already crashed into more Moroccan heads than I cared to count. "Bloody nuisance these boards are, hey," said little Trudy. We took a bus instead. The surfboards could ride on top.

A Moroccan bus journey is an odyssey. No one should leave the world without having known it. Even before the bus leaves, the show begins.

As we sat cramped in our broken assigned seats awaiting departure from the dirty transport central, an entourage of people fitting every conceivable description from a nineteenth-century sideshow boarded the front door of the bus, one at a time, to make presentations to the passengers. The first man was about three feet tall, a beggar with no legs whose hands were plunged into red high-heeled shoes to push himself along the aisle. The shoes looked brand-new and shiny but the rest of the man was tattered and worn. His high-pitched voice penetrated the bus and I wanted to understand Arabic, to hear his story. The man stopped for what seemed an eternity beside my seat, directing his pleas at me. I put some coins into the cup held around his neck even though the woman across the aisle shook her finger at me as she held her scarf up over her face, covering all but her black-penciled eyelids. I wondered where the man slept at night, who his mother was, and how he had come by those shoes.

He made his way down the aisle towards the back door of the bus, still giving his speech as if it was a tired daily ritual. Something made me turn around for a second, maybe to see if others were giving him money, to see how he was making out. That's when I saw Shane, the twenty-year-old surfy who traveled with the Australian family, get out of his seat behind me to head to the bus's back door to buy almond cookies from a woman outside. Shane paused when he got to the little man with red shoes for hands. Narrow aisle. The surfy was stuck. Surely he'll turn around and go back to his seat, I thought. Or wait. He's only buying almond cookies, for God's sake. But no. Shane hoisted himself up and over the little man by using the backs of the chairs for support. Leap-frog adaptation. To this day I wish I had never turned around to see that.

After the beggars came the salesmen flogging their wares. That was the order of things and it seemed fair. One man stood at the front of the bus talking at us for ten minutes as he held up a brown glass bottle and caressed it. Magic oil. The man after him was especially clever because he handed out little pamphlets about his product for people to read. Luvley's Beauty Cream. The beauty cream salesman's skin was as weathered as cracked tundra. He didn't sell any. He made a point, however, of recovering his pamphlets to use on the next bus, which I thought was a good idea.

On the bus ride southwest from Marrakech I watched packs of camels standing absolutely still in the desert, as if waiting for something profound and momentous to occur. They waited patiently, all facing the same way, staring at a deprived vastness from where change would surely come. Cacti took human forms. Lonely palm trees stretched up like spires to reach for the blue in the sky, leaving the thankless ground far below—any escape from the desert was reasonable. Nomads swaddled in ingenious twists and folds of material waved at the bus, fast and metallic, as it interrupted the language of the desert. Ancient men rode donkeys. Where they could have been coming from or going to, I had no clue. All that lay in the distance were the snow-peaked Atlas Mountains.

The crazy bus driver never slowed down, not even when we whirled up into the mountain passes. We barreled along in his indestructible 1950s-mobile, listening to loud Arabic tapes belting out of the speakers while passengers clapped and sang to the music. A grotesquely large full moon hoisted itself up over the foothills as the sun fell away ahead of us. The world around us was suspended in orange light, spacious light, a light of sensation I never imagined existed.

My favorite part of the ride was going through a little
Berber village in the High Atlas Mountains on the remote
Tizi-n-Test Pass, one of the highest passes in Morocco. It
felt like a drive through the past. Dusk had fallen and a
herd of livestock had gone on strike in the middle of the
dirt road in front of us. From the bus window I watched
people go about their lives as I imagined they would have
a thousand years ago. Nothing was modern. Wraps, shawls,
long robes, and hoods hid faces, body shapes, ages, and
lives. I watched ragged barefoot boys sneak pears out of a
wheelbarrow pushed by a withered man. Donkeys seemed
the preferred mode of transport, our bus clearly a big and
silly nuisance to goats and people both. I thought how
strange and how obvious that this place, too, is part of
the world.

I stayed with the Australians for another week. We rented
a small house in Tarhazoute, a fishing village on the coast of
southern Morocco owned by a man named Mohamid Ali.
Mohamid Ali didn't box and the Aussies' antics of trying to
mime the sport of boxing for him only confused the issue
further and demonstrated that Westerners really are crazy.
While the Aussie men and little Trudy cruised the waves, or
whatever they called it, Jan and I made friends with the
locals, read books, and swam. I wanted to absorb the sun's
heat deep into my bones to store it for the coming Canadian
winter. I like to believe things work this way. We lived off
almonds, fresh dates I never knew could be so juicy, and

mandarins. A big bag of mandarins cost fifty cents. I must have eaten twenty a day.

One day I gained a newfound respect for Shane, or for surfing anyway, because he explained surfing's lure to me. If I hadn't seen Shane hopscotch over the red-shoe man on the bus that day, I might have thought the world's oceans had splashed Shane with some form of Zen surfer wisdom. He said when a surfer is enclosed in a tube of water, it gets almost completely dark inside. The Green Room, they call it. He looks ahead, sees the opening of light at the other end and yells out "Whoooa!" The yelling of "Whoooa!" is essential. "I reckon just at that moment," said Shane, "that's life."

After that I had to try surfing for myself. It was life, after all. I hit rocks, people laughed, I got salt water up my nose. Never saw the light.

On another day, Jan and I took a bus south, into the city of Agadir. I bought a piece of pottery from a man in the marketplace. He wrapped and boxed the item for me. Later, when I happened to open it to show Jan, I realized the salesman had pulled a switch and given me a cracked version of the pottery I had chosen. From past experience, I knew he would vehemently deny any accusation, so when I went back to his shop, I used the "There's been a funny little mistake; I'll save your face, you shady rascal" tactic. That worked. He gave me the original one and invited us for tea.

The day's heat nearly melted us. We were exhausted and dusty and couldn't wait to get back to our village. For close to an hour, we stood at the wrong bus stop in the sun, inhaling diesel fumes in front of an outdoor café whose clientele called out "Hey baby!" every three minutes. Finally we found the right bus back home. On that bus I remembered why I travel.

The bus was jammed and excited. At first, we couldn't even get a seat. The energy generated by the people on the local bus that day should have been poured into the fuel tank. We wondered if a big holiday was starting so I asked the woman next to me what the excitement was all about and she told me it was because it was seven o'clock. Her English stopped there, so I never found out the significance of the seven o'clock celebration but it must be big, I thought. Only later did it occur to me she was probably telling me the time.

The bus pulled onto the road beside the shore just after the sun had dropped into the sea and we all became doused in an orange-purple glow. Perhaps it was the radiant glow of the sun on our skin, or the way the sun suspended itself in our eyes, or perhaps it was the luminous green of the sea; some commanding and influential force caused the mystery to occur. All I know for sure is that somewhere at the front of the bus, someone began to clap, although I barely noticed it at first over the rest of the commotion. But then the clapping got a little louder, then a little faster as it made its way back through the bus like a slow-burning fuse. Then someone started singing. Then someone else. The woman beside me broke into song, made me think I was living in a musical. Little girls with incredibly long eyelashes who stood in the aisle let loose their vocals, and so did the three old men across from us who had been expressionless before that. Soon everyone on the entire bus was clapping and singing as if we had caught on fire. It was that high and frenzied Arabic rhythmic beat—a varied rhythm, overlapping and jiving and alive, all building up and up to an intricate and profound glorious song. But it was more than just a song, more awesome than a symphony. Somehow the bus had hurtled into another dimension. By giving ourselves over to the rhythm we were generating, to our deeply buried tribal bones, we had lost our individual selves and had, much more powerfully, dissolved into one supreme and extraordinary single entity. We were simultaneously delirious, exultant, long-lost friends from a long-ago journey. I couldn't stop smiling. I turned around at the sound of a tambourine shaker but couldn't see beyond the beaming smile of the sweet old man in the seat behind me. A wild-looking man with long hair danced up and down the aisle, begging, doing a kind of jig. "He's a glue sniffer," someone shouted. He had glazed eyes, crazed, and people clapped and sang for him and his dance. It didn't matter then, at that moment, that people led hard lives. This was something grand and untarnished, as if we were striving for something beyond our meager lives, striving for something mystical and divine. Everyone on the local bus was blissfully happy that day, at that time, and that, I remembered, is why I travel.

Seven o'clock has never been the same since.

It was time for me to hit the road. I said good-bye to the Australians and headed inland. The sea was sublime but I wanted desert.

By the time I got to the street counter that was the Agadir bus station to catch the bus east, a man told me I had just missed it by five minutes. Then another man flailed his arms and said the bus left three hours ago. The next man I asked said there was no bus at all going east that day. Maybe try tomorrow. Diverging opinions on these things are understandable. I've even come to accept the "I don't know so I'll make something up" cultural phenomenon. BUT THOSE MEN I ASKED ALL WORKED AT THE BUS STATION.

I stayed that night in a run-down hotel just a block up the road from the bus counter. That way I wouldn't miss the bus the next morning. I made lots of friends that night. The road beat with vitality: people, shops, cafés, live music. The next morning everyone on the road seemed to know I had missed the bus to Ouarzzazate the day before and everyone seemed to want to help me not miss it that morning. I was the only foreigner around and my catching a bus seemed the event of the day. The hotel clerk, Hassan, knocked on my door even before the sun rose. "Mademoiselle, let me in. I tell you about the bus." I even found a collection of people downstairs in the hotel lobby waiting to direct me to the exact place where I should stand to catch the bus. After drinking tea with them, of course.

From the bus window I waved good-bye to the people who lived their lives out on that road. They waved back. I traveled by bus for days and days after that, further and deeper into a country that bewitched me. For days and days I never saw another foreign traveler. First the rich green valleys of mandarin groves passed by, then red clay villages that looked like sand castles, and the Sahara Desert with sand, sand sculptured by the wind into overwhelming cliffs and sensuous curves that stretched into the sky. Valleys lay far in the distance as vast and red as the Grand Canyon. There were palm trees, nomads living in tents, and more camels. Higher still we traveled into mountains with roads of hairpin curves and no other traffic, just the raging bus in pursuit of expansiveness. Conversations with the people I met always sounded the same, with the same questions asked about each other's lives, always in broken French. The few words of Arabic and Berber I learned were never enough for real conversation so I remained alien to a land I wanted to understand. Southern Morocco, unlike the north, is relaxed, and I never felt scared despite being the only woman on the bus most of the time. The bus drivers always wanted me to sit in the front seat so they could watch over me and ward off aggressors, but to me the land felt gentle, populated with gentle people. I was glad of the first seat for a larger picture of the grace of things out the front window. Everything I saw was new to me so time took on its childhood-wonder dimension where days feel like weeks and single moments last forever. I lived to encounter people whose lives would never again cross mine, to be absurdly unfamiliar with everything around me, to bump into a passage of life with an entirely different musical score. On those days, I never fell from my heights of exhilaration. It was like falling in love.

Late one afternoon the sky rolled over to burnt pink, and, from the bus window, I looked out to see a picture that has never left my head. I saw a girl in the desert who wore a bright red robe that flowed behind her in the wind as she walked by her house. Her skin was smooth and she was pretty, probably fifteen or so but I'll never know. Just as I'll never know anything of her life, where she was going, what she does every morning, whom she loves. Her house was made of the same sand on which she walked barefoot and stood alone, far away from everything, just a single sand castle dwelling in the desert. The splash of red from her robe that smacked against the endless stark, rolling sand-hills burst open the world.

I crash-landed upon scenes of human beauty like that every day. Once the bus stopped to pick up two very old men on the road. No settlement of any kind was visible anywhere, not for fifty miles. They both carried wooden staffs and wore burlap capes. The men stood for a long time before getting on the bus, and I watched their soft, leathered skin and ancient kind eyes, dark eye rims. Were they wary of the bus? They've just walked out of the Bible, I thought. They boarded and stood at the front, beside me, for twenty minutes as we drove along. Then they clapped their hands to indicate they wanted to disembark. I watched them walk away, seemingly into nowhere, not even a path to follow, just the desert. I watched them wander towards the hills until I couldn't see them anymore.

Often the bus would be halted by a herd of sheep on the road and often the sheepherders were young boys. They would always smile up at the bus and wave at me, and for an instant it would feel as if our souls collided. Their eyes were deep brown and immense and sometimes I wanted to get off the bus and go with them into their lives.

I stayed in all kinds of places at night, in oasis settlements, solitary mountain towns built out of red earth walls, blank spots on the map, whatever I could find. One night I stayed in a room in a guest house in the center of a noisy little town. The desert, so empty and dry, makes one desperately thirsty not only for water, but for people. I hadn't had a real conversation with anyone for so long that I think I must have forgotten how. A mirror hung in the room and it shocked me to look into it. I hadn't seen myself in a mirror since I'd left the village on the coast.

Who is this person in the mirror and why are her eyes so wild? I'm so far away from home, from my country, from everything I know. I'm trying to figure out if this brings me closer to myself or further away, because it's just me out here. No familiar culture to protect me, to fit into, to hide behind, to define me. We wear our culture like a blanket, but out of the blanket, who are we really? This purity of distance I've craved for a long time, for its outer limits, for its recklessness. I am a foreign country.

My bus rides through southern Morocco haunted me. The desert offers few distractions. It offers open space. The mind unravels, stretches out along the curves of sand for miles, for hours, until finally it breaks on a single fig tree in the distance, a rock, a sand dune formation. These catches of the desert are necessary. They prevent the mind from entering infinity. Sometimes I wanted the desert to keep spreading until it took over my mind. I craved the vast uncluttered sands, free of chatter, car fumes and memory.

After many days I finally touched down on the human world again. Night had fallen by the time I got off the bus in a village in the Draa Valley. I was deep in southern Morocco, near Algeria, and had seen no other foreign traveler for over a week. I must have looked forlorn. The place didn't seem large enough for any kind of hotel or guest house and the air was cold. That's when a woman approached and held my hand. All I knew of her lay in her eyes. The rest of her lay under a veil. "Fatima," she said. Her smile warmed my entire body. She had been waiting for her younger brother to get off the bus and the three of us walked back to their home which lay on the outskirts of a town that was already the outskirts of the world. Their home sat on the edge of the desert.

The air inside the house was as frigid as the air outside, yet the family seemed to burn with a loving warmth. The sister led me to the family room where her mother sat bundled in blankets against the wall. The mother's chin was tattooed with a green design in the Berber style, and around her head she wore a kerchief which covered most of her long silver hair. She worked a little wooden contraption that spun wool to make carpets. When I entered, she patted a cushion next to her for me to sit down on, as if she'd been expecting me. Her jewelled eyes sank into mine as she held my face. Her hands were hot. In thirty seconds she managed to bring me back to humanity. Two other brothers and a little girl appeared. The oldest brother, Houssien, was tall, probably twenty-five, and the middle brother, Omar, spoke some English because he'd once worked at a hotel in a city. He translated. The sister brought us too-sweet coffee and a big bowl of a salty grain saturated in buttermilk from goats. The food was the best I'd eaten in days. They told me their father, who was in another room, wanted to meet me, which made me a little nervous, but he was just as lovely as the others. I felt so grateful and happy that I must have said the Arabic word for thank you, *shukran*, forty times.

When we'd laughed and smiled at each other enough it was time for bed. Fatima showed me to a room that whipped cold air at us when she opened the door. The room had no roof, no furniture, just a few carpets and inhuman sounds erupting from the dark. Against the shine of the oil lamp I saw a woman eroded by a century of sun and wind, wrapped in blankets in the corner talking to herself, wavering back and forth. "Oh, my grand-aunt, old woman," said Fatima as if she'd forgotten the woman would be there. Fatima's mother followed us in and indicated for me to lie down on the edge of a thick rug, which struck me as strange but I did it anyway. She kept shooing me over to the very edge and I thought maybe everyone slept together and I was making room for us all.

But then she rolled me up in it. The little sister was rolled up in the rug next to me, and, in the carpet above my head, they rolled up the old woman, who never stopped talking to herself. I couldn't see her, of course. My arms were fastened tightly against my legs with no room for maneuvering. I landed upright on my back at the end of the roll, thank God. The mother and Fatima kissed us good night and left the room as if they had just performed the most ordinary act in the world. Carpet jailers.

Several questions came to my mind as I lay straitjacketed inside the carpet looking up at the open sky. First of all, who rolls up the roller? Does she do it herself? And if so, I'd really like to see that. What if there's a fire? And most importantly, what if I have to go to the bathroom?

The next morning when they came to unroll me for breakfast they said they had to talk to me, "most significantly."

They had looked up the word in an Arabic-English dictionary. Would I marry Houssien, their oldest son? They said they'd give me a little time to think about it—half an hour or so. In the meantime, Fatima mixed up a green paste of henna and applied it to my hands in swirly designs which would turn a rusty color and last for weeks. She taught me the Arabic word for sister-in-law. My bus was due to leave at noon. The youngest son went off to check on the bus schedule because they thought I was wrong about the time. He returned saying the bus had already left. I was suspicious but my hands weren't yet dry of the henna concoction and Fatima wanted to show me how to make flatbread and the mother kept kissing me and telling her son to tell me how much she wanted me in her family. I stayed another night.

That was the night Omar introduced me to his friend's motorcycle. I was reluctant to try it at first, never having driven one myself before, but I knew I had to go. Under a desert moon on an empty road he explained the choke and the brakes. Not very well, either. Then I was off. Omar yelled something as I sped away but I didn't catch it. The road was straight and I kept looking up at the pearly moon's familiar face to ensure I hadn't shed the earth and landed in another galaxy. The moon is good for that sort of thing—much better than the stars. The moon lets you know you're just fine down there on Planet Earth. I didn't go far, but far enough to know I had to try it again someday. That night still exists somewhere, the night I felt myself sear across the warm desert night like a comet, wild and free.

Another night in the rug, most uncomfortable. More questions: if I married their son, would they roll us both up in the same carpet simultaneously? Wouldn't that make things a little cramped? How would sex work inside a carpet? How is a family's hospitality so consuming that I find myself held captive by a rug in a roofless room under the stars of the Sahara each night and sleep to the babbles of an ancient aunt who is also carpet encased? And, just what is it with me and Moroccan carpets anyway?

I unravelled early the next day so I'd be sure to catch the bus. The family understood, I think, why I couldn't marry their son. At first, explaining was confusing because the translation kept misfiring until finally I told them I was like a gypsy and had to keep traveling. They got that. We took pictures which I promised to send and I gave Fatima my earrings and the youngest son a bright green t-shirt he liked that said "Canadian Women Take Back the Night." Somewhere in the desert of southern Morocco lives a ten-year-old feminist revolutionary boy. I'm still waiting to hear about riots he's instigated.

I didn't have much time left before I had to get back to Spain, then back to Canada. I didn't want to leave. I'd become addicted to my daily bus journeys through the country, bumping down the road, soaking up the land. No bus ever rattled down the road the same way. Each day's venture roused new thrills, and, without fail, no matter how insubstantial a place felt to me on arrival, by the time I left I always found myself waving good-bye from the bus window to my new friends, astounded at the ease of their kindness.

One day I found myself in the north again. The cities of northern Morocco feel stirred up, agitated, prone to flare-ups, like a glass toy that's a calm little village until shaken into a snowstorm. To be shaken by Morocco is expected; it's not knowing exactly how one will be shaken that unnerves the most. Occasionally other travelers would pass by, or, rather, run by, with a flock of guides and merchants on their heels. The travelers I met had only fled across the north, mainly in the State of Panic, usually just for a few days, and their frazzled nerves radiated out of their bodies in all directions, including Mecca. They were victims of the great Moroccan chase of harassment. The south's secret of relative serenity had magically blessed me with a protective shield that made me invincible to most of this. An inner calm kept me from standing too close to the verge of the northern neurosis.

In this light-hearted state of being, I struck up a conversation with a Scottish backpacker one day on a train out of Meknes. We talked about Morocco, not surprisingly. I told him about the rug scam with all the Mohamids and the Austrian goatherd in the carpet factory. I chuckled when I told him, thinking it amusing, years later. But as I recounted my tale I noticed the Scotsman had gone from an off-white

to a green to an unpleasant shade of grey. Motion sickness?
I asked.

"Fez, you said that happened in Fez?"

"Fez."

"Drugged? You're sure?"

"Dolloped into the mint tea, no less."

"And your friend never got his carpets?"

"Never got his carpets. Unless they arrived since I last
heard from him. Where are you going?"

I didn't see him after that but I suspect, sickness permit-
ting, he was going back to Fez.

One day was all I had left of Morocco. The boat would
leave Tangier for Spain the next day but I didn't want to go
near that infernal city until a minute before the boat
launched. Tangier and single travelers don't mix well, unless
you want to live out a Mad Max movie. That inner-calm
thing wouldn't work there. The calm would abandon its
inner and run for its outer the minute the first pack of
Tangier hustlers circled its prey. I searched my map for a
place to spend a peaceful last night. It didn't look good. But
then, suddenly, like a long-forgotten friend, in small letters
on the edge of the map, with that pretty name that no two
people pronounced the same way, lay my peaceful last night.
Asilah. Village of the white sand beach, quiet walkways, old
town ramparts, even a palace. Oh yes, and a bank teller.

What was his name again? It felt like six months since I'd
been in the Asilah bank. Six months of travel time was six

weeks of real time. (Traveling is a little secret on how to make your life last longer.) Only two more people stood ahead of me in line at the bank and I realized his name had long since left me. He still looked as if he had walked out of a 1940s Hollywood movie playing the swarthy mysterious foreigner, dashing and handsome. Even his white suit fit the part.

"Ah, Jean, *bonjour*," he said through a lit-up face when I reached his counter. "I can't believe it, you have come back. I am surprised by this." I was surprised by this too. He remembered my name—okay, my middle name, which he must have read on my passport six weeks earlier and taken for my first name, but what a memory. He pronounced it with a French accent.

Since I was leaving the country the next day I didn't need to cash any more traveler's checks so I invented a banking question, something about changing currency back to Spanish pesetas. He replied by saying we should have dinner together.

When Aziz and I met that evening at the town-square café, the same café where Fred had decided Morocco suited him, I discovered Aziz, unlike Fred, was a clever man. I liked him. Not only was he intelligent, he had imagination. He was a bizarre being, an original face. Why not, I thought, I've tried ordinary humans. Aziz told me he had studied philosophy and drama at university in Paris where he'd been rained on for four years—except for Sunday afternoons when he did theatre in the park. Always days of the sun, he said. He was thirty years old and had written a book on cross-cultural communication. Before he said things, he would pause, as if he wanted to get the translation exactly right, as if the moment hung on each thought. He had soft brown eyes and a large-muscled frame. We had two thus-far lifetimes and the rest of the universe to talk about. We were so taken with each other, we barely noticed when a crowd gathered around on the street to watch us. Asilah is a small town. Aziz came up with an idea.

"Jean (still in French accent), we go off to Tangier tonight. Tangier is my home, not Asilah. Tangier is full of the life."

I loved the way he spoke.

Off to Tangier (full of the life) we raced far too fast in his car along the coast, singing show tunes as I watched stars out the window and considered contemplating whether or not this man, myself, the whole bargain-basement, mercurial world were completely mad. Decided it was irrelevant.

It looked as if a bomb had dropped on the Tangier suburb where Aziz lived with his family. We walked up and down steep narrow passages where construction workers had left vast gaping wounds in the middle of roads, making driving impossible. Row houses and top-heavy apartment buildings groaned in depression onto the lifeless cobbled streets below. Nothing broke free from a voracious film of dust. Where were the people? Where were the children? Not even a skittish cat to feel sorry for. Crumbled, everything felt crumbled and darkly futuristic. But this was not an impoverished neighborhood. This was no shantytown where people lived in cardboard boxes beside garbage dumps. Squalor didn't suck lives dry here. Something else did. Compared to the other homes I'd visited in Morocco, Aziz's house felt palatial, despite the deceptive exterior. The house was tall and slim, like a square rocket with various forms of human activity on each floor. On the first level, five women laid themselves out on fat sequined cushions in an airy room lined with low sofas and ornately tiled walls, voluptuous rugs. Lounging women. Women lounging in floating incense. I've entered the inside of a genie bottle, I thought. Curved lamps diffused soft light on silk pillows in the corner. Aziz's two sisters, cousin, aunt and mother, in that order, shook their thermal hands with mine and sat me down on the divan. Aziz disappeared on his motorbike—"to discover the wine bottle shop." Clearly he stood out of his realm in this women's world.

For the next half-hour the women drilled me—my entire life history was offered naked for inspection. Ruthless loungers, they showed no mercy. No one has ever displayed such an insatiable interest in the exact birth dates and ages of my family—not even my own family. They wanted to know my family's names (ooh, so funny-sounding), my religion (ooh, no religion? ooh, tsk tsk), my work (ooh, teaching, ooh), my education, my marital status (why not yet?), how I met Aziz (ooh, so funny, the bank? so romantic), my favorite foods, boyfriends (in between what right now? dysfunctional relationships? ooh), what I did on the way to school when I was twelve, the names of every movie I'd ever seen and did I take the popcorn with the movie (lots of butter or little? ooh). Could I sew, cook, and clean? What was my shoe size?

I discovered these women lived out most of their lives in this insular room. Kept women. No wonder they tried to swallow up the events of my life like starved animals. What a waste and how criminally sad, I thought. Half the population, completely disregarded, their minds censured, their souls censored.

After the inquisition and a lively discussion amongst themselves in Arabic, they announced it: You can marry Aziz.

I hadn't realized I'd been considering it. Luckily, Aziz reappeared just in time. "Come, Jean, we go off into the night."

Honest, he said that, he really did.

Tangier, full of secret corruptions, notorious for espionage and intrigue, once-decadent city of hedonists, writers, freebooters, artists, philosophers, Beat poets, exiles, and spies—where had they all gone?

This is how I remember that night with Aziz in Tangier: a whirlwind night of crazed dashing. We dashed all over the place, from nightclub to disco, to nightclub, to some lookout point, back to another nightclub. Finally, we ended up at a belly dance club.

The belly dance club reminded me of an underground cave with hidden chambers. I could hardly see through the darkness, through the curling smoke of cigarettes, hashish, incense, and something sweet and sickly rising from the pipes of men huddled in corners. Dimly lit red lanterns glowed on the skin of belly dancers. In transparent muslins studded with gold beads they swung their jellied hips in hypnotic dance. As if in a trance, they moved in time to the throaty voices of men on stage who brought their rhythms and drums to frantic climaxes. A midget got up to sing. Everyone knew him. People cheered. "He's famous," said Aziz.

Aziz clapped and sang to the music from our table. I watched Aziz, so full of charisma and beauty. But I didn't like him anymore.

Perhaps it was the pompous attitude that gradually transformed into chauvinism that got me. Or perhaps it was because he treated me as something less significant than a weak appendage. Perhaps it was the leering that gave way to glaring because I refused to play my proper role. Perhaps it was because he assumed we would sleep together. Everything was heinously wrong. Clearly, this was a B movie he was charming his way through and I was about to walk out of it. There in the belly dance joint, an abrupt desire to be out of the clamor and away from Aziz seized me and I had to follow. So I broke away into a city of shadows and disfiguring nastiness around every corner. I broke away weightless. Eventually, I found my way back to Aziz's house and slept on the divan with the company of women. I was happy there.

To cross the Strait of Gibraltar towards Spain is to leave behind many things. A country with a multiple personality disorder, for instance. A country with a chink in its psyche. A country that lives in capital letters. Morocco is a country that suffers from a nefarious belief in total suppression of female power. Morocco is also a country bursting at the seams with passion and radiance. Aldous Huxley said that to travel is to discover that everyone is wrong about other countries. But Morocco is everything that anyone has ever said about it. Its ugly side of the vile imbalance defying natural laws, where women are repressed to their very marrow, is soothed by its secrets—by people clapping and singing on a local bus, by a desert girl in a bright red robe whose face sits in stillness and light. A face where all the world's poetry lies.

Customs officials stamped my passport in and out of Morocco with ink so faint it's barely perceptible. How inappropriate for a country that has branded my soul.

CHAPTER TEN

LAST NIGHT WE TOLD STORIES of journeys that continue inside us long after we've come home, of places that have taken up residence under our skin. Genevieve told us about riding her bike through China and getting held up by two teenagers at knife-point until some peasants happened by to stop them. She stayed and farmed with the peasants for a month. We stayed up till four. I told them about my last trip to Morocco, even the part about Aziz. I haven't thought about Aziz in ages. I wonder now about my impulse that was so compelling it carried me away from someone so full of life, so soaked in passion. An impulse stronger than that for love. Aldous Huxley said that love is the primary and fundamental cosmic fact. I usually think that's the one truth ever spoken, but it wasn't true that night in Tangier. My impulse to be rid of Aziz had nothing to do with love.

Dawn filters through the folds of the mosquito net, a ghostly pale orange light at first, then golden as the sun rises. Just outside the window a frangipani bush bursts upwards out of the earth without shame, throws off scent into the room, drooping like ripe fruit that begs to be picked. Fijians never seem to have screens on their windows, and often mosquitoes pour into the rooms. While this can be bothersome, today I prefer to view the world without a smeared glass or screen. Flowers so female in shape and smell and texture flaunt themselves everywhere. Velvet petals holding sunsets inside them will shout their color in the heat of the day, then pale with the evening. Egg-shaped buds open into deliciously round cream-yellow bundles with tips that blush pink. The scent of white lilies, trumpet flowers, jasmine and red powder-puffs intoxicates. Flowers swirl off bushes and trees, drip their sweetness to the ground like syrup.

I once read that Henry David Thoreau, on his deathbed, asked to be lifted up to the window so he could catch a glimpse of one last spring. He would have loved this profusion.

On the ceiling a fluorescent green gecko remains motionless upside down, content to absorb the morning offerings of scents and awakening beauty. The gecko may stay that way for hours. Most extraordinary are its claws. The claws look like actual hands with soft green fingers, little pads I'd love to touch.

Laudi and I are looking after Nana's house because she has gone off to visit relatives on another island. She is still terribly sad about losing her husband and seems to be adrift in an engulfing sorrow.

Already this morning a Giant Aunt is sunning her mats on the grass. I see her from my window. This is something I don't understand. The mats here are full of dust. I'm not the only one who sneezes almost every time I sit down. But instead of beating the mats with a stick or shaking them to get rid of the dust, they lay them on the ground in the sun. That's it. They let the mats sun themselves. Then they take them back inside their houses to be sneezed on all day. Crazy.

But nothing can disturb me today, certainly not dusty mats. Everything this morning is so heartbreakingly gorgeous, draped in mauve and indigo shadows, with a faint touch of a silky breeze. The breeze brings smells of the ocean.

With nobody else here this morning, we can eat what we want. "Mango! We can eat mangoes this morning," I say more to myself than to Laudi. Fruit doesn't excite him as it does me. Books don't excite him either, which drives me crazy, although I keep this to myself. "And pineapple. Let's go pick a pineapple; they're growing right outside the door. We can drink coconut water. Show me how to climb that coconut tree outside." Laudi throws his head back to laugh the same way Uma does. Heartily.

"I've never seen a woman climb a coconut tree. No, wait. I have. There was a crazy cousin of mine living here, Livi. She could climb a coconut tree. But she took off for Australia. Never heard about her again."

"I wish I could have met her."

"No, she was crazy. Really."

"Why? Because she liked to climb trees?"

"She liked to ride motorcycles. That was her dream. She drank kava too. A lot. My aunts drove her away."

"Poor thing. I'm glad she got away. I hope she found what she was looking for in Australia, a motorcycle, some freedom. She wouldn't be considered crazy where I'm from, you know."

"I know. You're all crazy there."

Instead of arguing, I sprinkle salt on the flesh of a giant, sun-warmed avocado and spread it on a tea biscuit. They would laugh at us, the Giant Aunts, if they saw us eating this way. Where's the tea and sugar? they would demand. Where's the fried cassava, the fried taro, the fried bread-fruit, the pancakes? Where's the coconut oil? Don't you want to be fat? I'd almost forgotten what it feels like to be in control, to eat what I feel like eating, to sleep when I feel like sleeping.

As we eat, Laudi does a remarkably accurate imitation of one of his Giant Aunts. His eyes grow wider and wider as he eats, just the way her eyes do. "Oh, oh," he groans, bathed in delight at the food he's devouring. We laugh, but I know he respects his aunt immensely.

Little children are chasing each other around the house, squealing. The morning sun is ripening. Today I'm filled to the brim with happiness and will ignore all things I don't like.

Today I love Laudi for his sweetness alone. On this island of lies, that seems enough for now.

Perhaps that makes me the biggest liar of all.

Genevieve, Laudi, and I are off on an adventure today. We take the bus north to Bouma Falls where we swim until we're waterlogged in the cool green pool fed by a high waterfall. As we emerge, a young Fijian woman is wading by herself in the shallow part of the pool. She splashes us and giggles. She giggles for so long I realize there's something strange about her. At first I think she is a teenager but when I look closer I see she is much older than that. Her hair streams wild in all directions and something about her posture suggests she has carried her body for a long time. Yet her face is childlike. We try to talk to her but she doesn't seem to listen, as if she's in a trance, buried inside her own private bliss. Her eyes gaze straight through us as she continues to splash us and laugh. She reminds me of Kiki, Kiki of the Tall Grass. When we dry ourselves, Laudi tells us that a coconut crashed on this woman's head when she was sixteen. The whole island knows the tragic story. Apparently she had been very bright and had stood first in her class. Now she's simple and no longer speaks, only giggles. How would her life have been if it weren't for the falling coconut? Does she remember her old life? I smile at her, watch her stare zombie-like into her past. She seems happy, at peace. Who knows what mysteries are hidden in the heart?

We hike along a trail that leads upwards, to more water-falls. The bush creates an unbelievable tapestry of colors, shapes and textures as we tramp over wet soil beside lush ferns and coconut palms. The ground becomes damp, dank, like volcanic ash. Sun melts us like butter. Birds high in the temple of trees are louder here than lower down and they're saturated blue, the color of the sea. The jungle world presses down on our backs and we become dazed with heat and heavy moisture. Swooning, we feel like dropping to the ground. Dropping to the ground would be like sleeping in a tangle of seaweed at the bottom of the sea.

We walk higher and higher, far off the main trail, on to smaller paths where we have to bushwhack.

Then we see it. Suddenly, naked land lies before us like a bludgeoned battlefield, a black and exposed coffin of the earth. A clear-cut. Trees have been ripped from the ground. The scene before us looks like a black-and-white picture of post-war Europe, decimated by a bomb, smoldering and pitiful. It feels like a knife in our chests, as if something has been allowed to happen that should never have happened. I'm shocked to find this here. Laudi tells us a Japanese company bought this land and the Fijian president was happy to sell it. "We're hurtling into your century. How can we stop it? And listen to this: the International Date Line crosses this island, so Taveuni will be the first place in the world to be in the twenty-first century. Think of that." I look at the gigantic bleeding grave in the ground and feel sick.

We can't escape life's dark edges, I realize. We can't skirt catastrophe, even high in an island forest.

Back at sea level, Laudi goes off to play soccer and drink kava for his manly ritual, and Genevieve and I take the bus further along the road until it ends. We try to find someone with a boat to take us to the waterfall we've heard about on the far side of the island. The waterfall, it is said, plunges thousands of feet into the ocean. But nobody will take us. Not today. It's not safe today. Nobody gives us any clear explanations. Hurricane season is coming, one man mumbles.

Sunset

I hear Shastri, the Spanish-Indian pretend Sikh, and Yurgen the Eccentric Romanian arguing on the beach. This should be good. The other campers and I often debate which of the two is more arrogant. Shastri, the anthropology Ph.D. student, is just twenty-five years old but he says everything with the air of a sixty-year-old professor. Yurgen is esoteric and anti-academic. He's still experimenting with kava, and I've noticed he's given up painting. I walk into the kitchen hut to hear Shastri's theory of humans: "I've been all over the world, I've studied tribes and lived with different people from every continent and obscure island you can think of. I've read hundreds of books on ancient and modern civilizations. Do you know what I've finally realized?"

"That you know nothing," Yurgen says defiantly.

"No. I've come to the conclusion that all people

everywhere, in the whole world, are pathetic. Look at these Fijians. They destroy their rainforest for money. The Japanese make throw-away chopsticks for their fast-food joints from the wood. Americans shoot each other at the drop of a hat. Pathetic, everywhere, pathetic."

"Yes, it gets how-you-say pathetic on this realm of existence. You should try other realms," suggests Yurgen.

A F T E R   D A R K

Genevieve, Laudi, Pita, Uma, Kalisi, little Kura, and I are on Nana's porch. We lie back and watch shooting stars slice the sky like glowing arrows. It must be a meteor shower tonight. I tell them that Ralph Waldo Emerson wrote that if the sky were to open up just once every thousand years to reveal the stars, we'd believe in heaven.

"But we already believe in heaven," says Uma.

"Yes, but he's saying what if we only saw the stars once in our lives or maybe only heard about them because the sky opened up just once in a thousand years? Just one night? It would be this great event."

"But we see the stars every night. That's silly," she says. Uma disappears into the dark to her house and comes back with her cherished cassette deck with its new batteries. She plays a tape of Fijian music. Uma begins to dance.

"Uma, I've never seen you dance before!"

"Come, come dance with me. I'm shimmering."

We dance on the porch, all of us, under stars that have

shown themselves every night since the beginning of time. Even little Kura dances because she's four and Fijian and in love with life. We dance as the stars sail across the sky, as the tide settles in below us, as the night passes in a million small villages around the world. Then Pita turns the music down. "Shhh. Listen," he says. We stop dancing. Down the hill a man screams like a hyena.

"What's he saying?" asks Genevieve.

"He wants us to stop dancing."

"This is so much bullshit," she says. "Why do we stop dancing because of this? Why does Vix have this problem?" Laudi and Uma stare at each other, mumble words I can't catch.

"Long time ago," says Uma, "evil spirits crawled into Vix. They never crawled out."

"What?"

"Laudi tell you story. I take Kura to bed." Uma goes off again into the dark towards her house, protecting her daughter from the knowledge of terrible things.

"One night a long time ago, when I was a teenager, Vix was possessed by something. We think it was the demon who lives in the rocks, but we didn't know that then. Vix started throwing things everywhere; he screamed at everybody who came close, ran after his wife with a knife. He wasn't drunk. He didn't even drink back then. Nobody could control him. Nobody knew what was happening. This white foam came out of his mouth and we thought he was sick from something he'd eaten. He was doing this with his stomach." Laudi clutches his stomach, as if in agony. "But nobody could get near him. He sounded like an animal. We couldn't understand what he was trying to say. It was a nightmare for all of us. Finally he ran up into the plantation and was gone all night. We could hear him screaming the whole time. He shouted evil things, how he hated all of us, even the children. He came back down in the morning with blood-red eyes. He was wrapped in a blanket and wouldn't look at anybody, just stared at nothing. The dogs growled at him like they wanted to tear him apart. You know these dogs; they never growl at anybody. Finally we sent for a medicine man from the village. This man knows how to get the *tevoro* out of people, the evil spirit. He took Vix inside Nana's house and we don't know what they did in there. When Vix came back outside, he was crying, like a baby girl. It was over."

Vix has stopped shouting from the beach below. Everything's quiet. I can feel my eyes are wide with something—surprise, fear, perhaps sadness. I always thought Vix must own a strange history. "But Vix is still bad," says Laudi. "He's been bad since that night."

"Maybe he was hit by a coconut," I say. But I don't believe it. I believe the story.

Genevieve and I cannot even contemplate sleep after Laudi's story. We stay outside talking and telling stories on the porch. We can't seem to rip the darkness from our souls, not after hearing Laudi's story of Vix. She tells me about a ghost she met on the River Ganges. I tell her about the time I thought I met the Devil. We stay up all night, until the sun rises, until all remains of darkness and devils have fled.

THE DEVIL AND HARE KRISHNA

BY THE TIME I LEFT THAILAND and returned to Malaysia after three months in Asia, one month in Australia, three months in New Zealand, two months in Fiji, and six weeks traveling west across the States from Ontario to Hawaii, travel had begun to wear me down. The Road's soft green moss and feathery fractured light had receded. Now the Road clawed up at me with jagged edges. I'd been gone a long time, gone from where, I couldn't say anymore. I wanted to go to a place where I could stay, to a solid place that would wrap itself around me like a well-worn jacket. I knew Fiji was that place. I had to find a way back to Taveuni, reverse my journey, retrace my sodden steps, do what wanderers rarely do: return.

I would need another teaching job. A flight to Fiji would be expensive, even from southeast Asia, cheap-flight center of the world. I decided to go to Georgetown on the island of Penang, Malaysia's chief port city and old colonial center for artists, dissidents, intellectuals, and dreamers. From the ferry I squinted at the glare of Penang's tall buildings of gilded glass. Cities are selfish, greedy, reckless, hard-boiled, dirty, and they don't give a damn. But I needed a city. Penang would help me return to Fiji. With Fiji's silky sunsets and easy smiles idling in the back of my mind, enduring another city would be a cinch.

A cinch.

The first person I met in Penang was the Devil. The Devil just happens to be a taxi driver, among other things. He also wears polyester hip-huggers, red flip-flops, and a half-unbuttoned shirt exposing two gold chains dangling low on his chest.

Nonetheless, I never would have imagined the Devil could display such concern for anyone other than himself. Actually, I would never have imagined the Devil existed at all, but there he stood, waiting for me at the ferry dock, happy to make my acquaintance. He had taken English lessons. I could tell.

"Where did you learn such excellent English?" I asked, not yet knowing whom I was addressing.

"International English School, in big ta-wa building."

"Tower building? Do you think they need teachers? I'm an English teacher."

"Yes, need teachers. Need you."

I tossed my backpack into his cab and off we sped in the direction of the big ta-wa building to find me a job.

Arriving in Malaysia was much easier the second time. It just takes practice.

Except we weren't going to a big tower building.

As we drove through the city, the Devil asked me all kinds of questions about my travels and about me. He seemed to know the right questions to ask. Not everyone does. After twenty minutes we reached a building on the outskirts of town, but it wasn't tall. It was long and snaky, flat, with slits for windows.

"What is this place?" I asked him.

"Just to look he-ah first. Maybe you want work he-ah instead teach English. Pay betta this place."

I noticed his English had deteriorated.

"But what is it?"

"Come hinside."

On most days of our lives, even while traveling, we follow fairly predictable paths, not in a ho-hum way, but thoughtfully, with intent. We're happy, or as happy as the next person claims to be, but then without warning we fall off the path. We find ourselves in another world, an underworld existing alongside our happy-go-lucky world of relative normalcy. We don't know our way around down there because it's dark and frightening and new, although it's always been there…waiting.

It was difficult to see anything once the doors closed behind us even though daylight still polished and graced the world outside. Dark ruby lights revealed figures casting shadows onto a plush red rug. Women, or possibly just girls, were harnessed into leather miniskirts, low-cut Lycra tops and pink pumps as they lounged on bar stools and couches and sipped bright red drinks from tall glasses with straws, like Barbie dolls, Barbie dolls gone wrong. They glared at me. Heavy rouge and gummy neon lipstick concealed their ages, and their souls. Men with facial scars and sleeveless black t-shirts stood on guard, crossed-armed. They glared also. This was the first room in what appeared to be a long line of rooms. A waiting room. Twice, from a room beyond, screams broke out into this vile deposit of lethargy and seemed to charge the air with perverse expectations. Then the feeling would die.

I considered the fact that I'd entered a brothel. Either that or the movie set of a cheap porno flick. Or possibly hell itself.

"What are we doing here?" I asked as I stood gawking, although I knew the answer.

"You can work he-ah. Good job. Good pay. Own-ah good friend to me."

This was a ghastly thought. I wanted out, although secretly the place fascinated me. Who were all these women? Where did they come from? Why were they here? The creepy blackness of the place began to seep into my skin. He stood blocking the doorway.

"I'm leaving," I told him.

He aimed his dreadful face at me and released his horrific smile and that's when I understood his true identity for the first time. "No, you no leaving."

"Yes, actually I am." And I did, once I barged past him and out the door. But that was only the beginning of the Devil in Penang. And my dark underworld.

I tried to erase the underworld from my mind as I asked someone directions to the center of the city. After three months in Asia, I'd learned how to ask questions. Rather than pointing in a specific direction and saying "Is this the way to town?"—which inevitably leads to a yes answer even if it's the wrong way (because they don't want to disappoint the person asking and make her look foolish)—I would say, "How do I get to the town?"

Nearby, I found a discount travel agency where I checked on fares to Fiji. The fares didn't look good. Everything in the city was more expensive than I expected. In the travel shop I met a Portuguese traveler named January who told me about a place where travelers could stay free. The place even had a beautiful garden AND free food. What's the catch? I asked him.

"It's a Hare Krishna temple," he said, embarrassed, "but it does not mean you have to be one, a Hare Krishna follower, not necessary. I'm not one and I am there now three weeks. They don't care."

He didn't have a long draping orange robe and a shaved head and I saw no sign that he'd been bestowing flowers on strangers at street corners. No vacant glassy overjoyed look in the eyes either. He looked ordinary enough, for a traveler.

"Are you saying it's a non-pushy Hare Krishna temple?"

"That is what I say to you. It's very good place. Ten travelers are there now, none of us Hare Krishna converted people."

I thought it wouldn't hurt to take a look. My first impression of the temple was that of old-world elegance gone awry. A mass of tangled thorny trees hid most of the building from the road as if keeping the temple a secret. Behind a tall black iron gate, I could see stone-carved Hindu statues meditating beside a fountain pool. A small Indian woman in a sari smiled at us as she tended a garden of flowering trees and curvy vines. "Hare Krishna," she said, bowing in our direction.

Inside the temple, recorded music of harps and flutes floated into the downstairs lounge. January led me up the stairs to the women's dorm and there I met Katja, from Yugoslavia, who gave me the lowdown on the place. Katja had been staying at the temple for over a month because she was studying tai chi somewhere nearby. She told me four women travelers staying in the dorm at that time were wonderful and I'd like them all. "Oh, and Margaret lives here too. She's Hare Krishna. Margaret's bossy. And screwy." I liked the way Katja pronounced *screwy* in her Yugoslavian accent. In fact, I liked everything about the Hare Krishna temple. It felt homey.

Then I met Margaret. Margaret looked to be in her mid-forties and she reminded me of a great blue heron. Her tall, shockingly thin body with its crudely cropped hair on top and far-away lost eyes behind magnified glasses gave her that hungry water-bird quality. Something vaguely icy about her chilled the dorm room when she swept through it. "Hare Krishna," she said when she stalked by me. She said this as if by command rather than in spiritual greeting. She told me that to stay at the temple I would have to work an hour each day performing some duty, and I would be expected to attend the nightly meetings after dinner to discuss spiritual matters. There was also the morning ritual. She didn't elaborate on the morning ritual. I asked if I could work in the kitchen and she handed me a broom to sweep the dorm and said I could. Margaret and I would be bunk mates, an intimidating thought, so I figured breaking the ice might be wise. She told me she grew up in a small Bible-belt town in Missouri where she married young and had three children and never left the state until she was thirty-five. Then one day she found herself in Hare Krishna's main temple in West Virginia. Everything changed for Margaret after that. She did whatever her guru told her to do. She left her husband and three kids and came all the way to Asia, to the Penang temple—to do exactly what, I hadn't figured out yet. Was she happy? This was no longer a relevant question. She couldn't remember happiness back in Missouri, only a lot of laundry, long and nerve-shattering drives to little-league games and a husband who liked beer better than he liked her. At the temple she felt a calm and cooling flow wash away her old life.

We ate a delicious vegetarian Indian dinner that evening as we sat circled on the wooden floor of the dining room. I met the other authentic Hare Krishna followers, and all the rest— the travelers. I had more in common with the travelers.

That night, five of the travelers and I went out on the town. I found my new friends to be a happy collection of eccentrics, which suited me just fine. Christof, a twenty-year-old Berliner, had just spent a year traveling through China. Christof was an eager intellectual, witty, and he made me laugh. Kirstina from Denmark had arrived from a Buddhist temple in Thailand where she had spent a year meditating in silence. Penang was her vacation for conversation. We talked about traveling, as travelers always do, and they told me about an eccentric traveler who had just left the temple. "A weird Irish guy" was how Katja described him.

"Did he yell out 'Hey you!' all the time, and then give you a corny piece of his philosophy?"

"He did that all the time. That's all he did. Nobody could ever talk to him. In the middle of a meal when everyone was quietly eating, he would shout out, 'Hey, we're all in this together, we're all wandering rootless nomads.' Or else he would just shout at one of us. He would say, 'Hey you, do you risk looking like a fool for love?' Something like that.

Then he would go back to eating and not look at anybody. You know him?"

"I can't shake him. He's everywhere. But I'm glad. I like his corny pieces of philosophy."

The six of us found an old colonial hotel filled with students and foreigners drinking and dancing under a high ceiling and chandeliers. Malaysia's racial mix of Muslim Malays, Chinese, and Indians seemed to work well in Penang, especially in this nightclub where everyone laughed and intermingled. Music from every part of the world blared out of the speakers and our little group danced for hours. I noticed a table of Penang university students sitting beside the dance floor. They were laughing at us. The students seemed particularly amused by Christof, who was a fabulous and expressive dancer. When a slow and hard-to-dance-to song came on, Christof began to perform tai chi-like movements as if every note of the music commanded a different muscle in his body. He closed his eyes in ecstasy. This was too much for the students at the table; clearly they had never seen the like of it and a couple of them snapped pictures. Then one of the students, an especially bold and inebriated one, came up to join us. The student had horn-rimmed glasses and stood right beside Christof, studying him. Then the student too began to dance. Soon he was imitating Christof's every move, and by the end of the night, the student danced as beautifully as Christof. As he was leaving he shook all of our hands, told us we had changed his life, then turned around to fall flat on his face. In a graceful, expressive way, of course.

By the time we left it was after three in the morning. The curfew to be back at the Hare Krishna temple was ten in the evening. Hare Krishnas believe the body and spirit are at war, all desires of the body are bad, and going out dancing is just plain evil. We had to sneak in over an iron gate and tiptoe upstairs past a snoring Margaret.

It was probably four in the morning when I fell asleep. I hadn't even begun to dream when I was awakened by an annoying clanging from downstairs, followed by the rude deployment of far-too-bright fluorescent lights in our dorm. Margaret's doing. "Get up, all of you, and come downstairs," she said. I guessed this was the morning ritual I'd heard about and I seriously thought about ignoring it. At five o'clock, my personal morning ritual has always been sleep. Margaret must have sensed my less-than-enthusiastic devotion to her religion because she poked me in the stomach with a long twiggy finger and told me to be downstairs in two minutes. Were we living like medieval Catholic monks here? After some groggy reflection, I considered going downstairs after one hour of sleep a relatively small price to pay for free room and board. Besides, I might finally figure out what Hare Krishna people actually do other than stroll airports. The secret study of Margaret was alone worth the price of a night's sleep. I dragged myself down there with the others.

What I found downstairs at five in the morning at

Penang's Hare Krishna temple were twenty people circled on the floor banging on pots, pans, and little tin drums as they chanted the Hare Krishna chant over and over for exactly one hour. The real Hare Krishna people, orange-robed and baldheaded, chanted and swayed with love and vigour in their hearts, while the rest of us just clanged a lit-tle on the pots and pans to keep from nodding off. After the hour of clanging, all of the travelers ran back upstairs to sleep until noon. That part surprised me more than anything: they let us go back to sleep, to deprogram. If they really wanted to brainwash us, surely this wasn't the way.

That day I found my job teaching English. Not in a big ta-wa building either. I met an English woman who was shopping in the textile market downtown for batik material to take back home. She told me she had just quit her teach-ing job at an adult language school and would introduce me to the school's director. After taking a cab back to the tem-ple to change my clothes and retrieve my resume and cer-tificates from my backpack, I hurried to meet her and off we went to the school. The director said I could start teaching the next afternoon.

I arrived back at the temple that evening in time for my kitchen duty, where I was taught how to make *rotis* from a sweet saried woman from India who chanted the H.K. song the entire time. I didn't mind, though. She had a nice voice. Besides, I found it rather soothing and pleasant after the har-ried and noisy city.

Most of my students at the English school were busi-nessmen intent on getting only the gist of the language to carry them through business deals, which seemed like a sign of linguistic decline. My few female students were usually too shy to speak. As in Japan, many Malaysian women are trained to be subservient and to coddle their men. They aren't expected to have opinions of their own. But after class, after the men left, the same women would let loose, giggle shyly and then laugh wildly, as they told me the most astonishing things. That was my favorite part of teaching there. Conversations with the women always stopped just short of feminism, which some of them considered danger-ous. They liked hearing about my life, however, and always asked me plenty of questions, especially the old standard: "Why aren't you married yet?" I would tell them marriage sounded like too much work and they would laugh and agree with me. Often they would express candid opinions in English that they would probably never say in their own language. I learned a lot from those women.

The men in the classes often puzzled me. Many Asian men think of Western women as not quite real, a little barbaric and aggressive, certainly sexually permissive and possibly alien. One man in a conversational class asked me, quite seriously, "Please tell, in your cold country, is it warmer for white women to do things upside down?"

The days flew by like golden butterflies: up at five to bang on pots and then back to bed to restore my head, then off to teach for six hours before my dash back to roll rotis, followed by extraordinary Indian cuisine and long talks with the travelers, sometimes meditation and tai chi lessons next door, then off to the nightclubs to dance, later to sneak in and be scolded by Margaret, and, finally, sleep until the clanging commenced. Days of noisy joy.

Then one day I saw the Devil again. I was looking over lychees in the market after school when it happened. His nasal, churlish voice had branded itself into my skull and there was no mistaking it. As I squeezed fruit for freshness he spoke into my ear from behind, which made me wince, gave me goose bumps. "My friend, you want job now? Good pay. You like it there. Come back." I squeezed too hard and squashed something, some innocent piece of fruit; juice squirted all over my hand and I ran away. "Come back, lady. I give you the job." I could hear his raspy voice calling after me for three blocks before I lost him in a crowd of teenagers gawking at bootleg CDs from a street stall.

The Devil figured out where I worked and, eventually, where I lived. Not that it could have been too difficult for him to track me down. He was the Devil, after all. Or so I made myself believe. Ordinary humans didn't move through the world the way he did. In the streets I'd see a multitude of confused souls walk by and I knew he played no part in this confusion. He carried something else inside him, something more terrifying. I saw it the first day we met. There in the tiny irises of his eyes was all the evil I had ever seen,

heard of, known. It suffocated all traces of human vulnera-
bility, wiped out the history of compassion, bloodied centuries of human weakness for love. Nothing in my life had
prepared me for such a discovery. Avoidance was crucial but,
for unknown reasons, impossible. I would see him all over
town, hear his inhuman footsteps behind me, and storm
clouds would gather in my chest in silent terror. Sometimes
I could have sworn he was just ahead of me, waiting at a café
or inside a store. He would always attempt a smile but it was
never genuine. His smile curdled blood. It lived in a viper's
den and only came out when it wanted something. "Come
take the job, lady." I would watch the ugly words fall out of
his mouth like drool. I tried to take different routes to work,
come back home through different neighborhoods. I even
stopped eating lunch at my favorite little neighborhood
restaurant which served coconut-milk fish soup. I hated him
for that.

I remember walking into a batik fabric shop one day to
have a dress made. I'd been there many times to admire and
touch delicate material that smelled like sandalwood incense,
and I liked the way the shopkeeper's eyes enlarged when he
heard gossip. The man loved to eat and his laugh was deep
and reassuring. On that day, when I turned to greet the
friendly shopkeeper, I looked straight into the face of the
Devil. There he sat behind the counter on the shopkeeper's
stool. Surely they weren't friends. The Devil parted his lips
back to show me his stained and collapsed teeth, and his

glazed eyes pierced mine too thoroughly. Across the counter, where the shopkeeper had eaten a thousand curried rotis, I felt the Devil try to X-ray my vital and most secret core. I opened my mouth to speak, to demand to know what he had done with the shopkeeper, but no words came out. I felt paralyzed as if in a nightmare, unable to move or speak. "May I help you?" he asked. I shook my head. As I flew out the door I heard him laugh and I swear the laugh came straight from the rotting depths of another world not nearly as likable as this one.

After that I tried to think only good thoughts in an attempt to keep him out of my life. I vowed to meditate in the quiet garden sanctuary at the temple. I would cleanse myself of any darkness hiding inside, darkness the Devil must have sensed. I might even pay attention at the morning rituals.

Unfortunately none of this worked, despite all the new-agey books written on this sort of thing.

The day he knocked at the Hare Krishna temple to ask for me, Margaret answered the door. I'm glad she did, too, because anyone else, blissfully unaware of the diabolical nature of the visitor, would have come and found me working in the kitchen. But Margaret told him I was "doing my service to Krishna." That sent him scurrying, perhaps akin to holding out a cross or garlic to frighten vampires. He certainly didn't try to whisk Margaret off to the big ta-wa building to convert her into a prostitute. I'm sure he could see that Margaret's soul was tied up elsewhere.

Encountering the Devil was rather amusing at first. Actually no, it was never amusing. Unsettling was more accurate. Then it became strangely alarming. For some reason I couldn't tell my friends about it. I'm not sure why. Perhaps a part of me was fascinated by what lay inside the big ta-wa building. I've always been intrigued by worlds populated by lost and dangerous souls. After weeks of teaching and banging pots every day, leading a well-ordered life, part of me wanted to step down off the path again, just for a while, and explore the darker places, the places not understood.

Unreasonable thoughts grabbed me with claws, pulled me. I followed. I found a job hostessing in a semi-sleazy nightclub. Those jobs are easy to find if you're looking for them. This was nothing like the big ta-wa building, of course, but it was part of the underworld nonetheless. Daylight couldn't reach it. Had Margaret and the other Hare Krishnas known, I would have been chased and chanted out of their temple with the musical pots and pans banging on my heels. Fortunately, Margaret and the others seemed to live in a land of air and clouds, far more serene than this one, so they never noticed my unusual hours. A second job would hasten my return to Fiji, I told myself. Hostessing paid even more than teaching and it fit into my schedule perfectly. Dancing at the colonial nightclub with my non-Hare Krishna friends would have to go, but other than that sacrifice, nothing changed. Not in the beginning.

For the first couple of weeks in the sleazy nightclub, thick layers of cigarette smoke rolled through my head like fog. Living in such a haze, I didn't have to think too much about what I was doing. My job was mindless. I made silly nonsensical chit-chat with men at their tables, heard the same questions over and over and gave different answers every time, and even poured drinks. I stopped short of lighting their cigarettes—I was only willing to go so far. It wasn't a bad job. Sometimes I even enjoyed it. I liked the other women I worked with, foreign travelers like myself who were there for the money, or a lark. We couldn't believe how much money they paid us just for showing up at the joint. We laughed at them. We thought the joke was on them.

You have to understand: we had to see it this way.

I tried to take a philosophical view of my life in Penang. Everything I did was to get back to Fiji, I reasoned, but my days were so filled, little time remained for introspection. That can be dangerous.

One day as I walked along a busy street, I realized the Hare Krishna chant had hijacked my head. It hit me that there was a good chance I'd been humming it for hours, possibly days. When I tried to turn it off, I couldn't do it. In defiance, it only got louder and more inane. I tried to hum something else to push it out—a Fijian love song, Neil Young, a show tune, Judy Garland, a Christmas carol, but Hare K. was too powerful—like a rude guest at a party who won't shut up.

Hare Krishna
Hare Krishna
Krishna Krishna
Hare Hare
Hare Rama
Hare Rama
Rama Rama
Hare Hare

It never stops. It goes on like this forever. As far as I could tell, this chant is all they do. This IS their religion.

I got a little panicky. I searched the street for a sympathetic spirit, someone to talk to, but all the faces were stark and shut down, the faces of a crowd. Hundreds of faces passed me by and I could shut none of them out. What chants played behind those faces? I wondered. It was that time of dreaded dead, hot stillness that settled every afternoon, when life hangs in heavy suspension, waits for a break. The world was too bright, too glaring in blues and whites, jerked apart by the steel grey of tall buildings. My eyes craved darkness. A naked little man passed me as I crossed a busy intersection. The tiny loincloth around his waist wasn't working for him and everything lay out there for the world to see. I kept turning around to check if I'd seen it right. A bus was stopped at the crosswalk and when I looked up I saw that the bus driver and passengers were laughing at the naked man and my reaction to him, so I smiled and laughed with them. When I turned around again to watch the little man walk away into the crowd, I realized he was not sane in any known sense of the word. But I'd forgotten what sane and normal were supposed to mean. My world was slipping into the absurd. I could feel my old self draining out of me. Further down along the street I saw the Devil waving at me through the traffic, and something happened that should have surprised the hell out of me. But it didn't surprise me, not then.

I waved back.

It was that very night that life as I'd known it stopped making sense. Later I suspected the day had been to blame because daylight isn't all innocence and yellow roses in the sun. That's how days get away with things—tricks of light. As usual that evening I went to the nightclub to hostess at nine o'clock. The first hour was dead boring, which wasn't unusual at all. I had to make small talk—minuscule talk—to a group of Japanese businessmen who could hardly speak English as I watched them try to outdrink each other. I was getting paid for this and it was turning my stomach. Over at the bar I joined my friend, Belinda, from Ireland and a German woman, Stella, who had only started working there that night. Stella was tall and busty and could shoot vodka down her throat with an ease that would have had the Russian army quaking in their boots. She was a man-hater too. She wasn't even pretending to be feminine like the rest of us. "The men in this place, they have brains like little turds; I vant to spit in their noodles, pee in their drinks." I was glad Stella was there that night because I needed to hear someone rant and rave. Her spewing venom about men might chase Hare Krishna out of my head.

"You think this is a vile place, you should see the big ta-wa building," I told her.

"De vhat? Vhat is dis?"

"It's the parking lot for hell. Makes this place look like a Doris Day bakery."

"What is this place?" asked Belinda.

"Some weird kind of brothel, really repulsive, frightening."

"Where is it?" asked Belinda.

"On the edge of town. I was only there once. When I first got here."

"Is it all one level and long?"

"Yeah, that's how I remember it. Why?"

Belinda's pretty face aged ten years right in front of us. She stood up off the bar stool and her sunken eyes looked into mine. Her eyes had black flecks I'd never noticed before.

"I was there too."

Our bodies shivered in mutual disgust, in camaraderie, like war buddies might do reminiscing about a particularly horrendous battle. I ached to ask Belinda about the Devil, to ask her if she knew him. But speak his name out loud? I hadn't said his name aloud to anyone, not even myself, except when he invaded my dreams and made them night-mares. I'd yell at him then, in my dreams, tell him to get lost, go to hell, go home. What name he chose for himself on this level of reality, I didn't know. How could I even describe him? Other than being the Devil, he was fairly nondescript, ordinary. I couldn't ask her. She would think I was crazy.

Wait, I was crazy. Krishna was seeing to that.

"How did you get there, to that place?" I could feel my pumping heart as I spoke the words.

"Oh, this disgusting taxi driver. Creepy, he was. I didn't ask him to take me there, either."

"I know."

In Belinda I had found my sympathetic spirit. Thank God, the Devil wasn't hungry for my soul alone. He was an actual breathing person, cruising the city in polyester, not an annoyance hanging out in my head along with the H.K. chant. Of course he was real. Hadn't I seen him out on the streets every day? Why hadn't I told anyone? I felt a lightness take over me, like a white soft-feathered gull sweeping up into the blue of the sky. I wasn't mad and I wasn't bad. It struck me that the weeks leading up to this moment had been a mixture of lunacy and dreams, nonsense, and chaos, all jumbled together now into a curious sensation of joy. I felt as if I'd awoken from a long disturbing sleep.

"We must go to dis place. I vant to see it," said Stella.

Stella, architect of daring ideas, Bavarian woman of vision, eager to stampede what most of us are afraid to contemplate. The world could learn much from Stella.

We took a cab there the next evening. Belinda seemed to know the way. I didn't ask her why. We were dressed to kill,

I in my black miniskirt, gold tank top, and lace-up leather sandals, Belinda in a plunged-neck sequined dress, and Stella, long and tall, in cut-off jean shorts and a t-shirt. Like falling stars we shot through the moist night toward the big ta-wa building: Belinda, for reasons she wouldn't elaborate on; Stella, presumably to bomb the place; and me, I can't be sure. It was something I had to do, something that made sense in a world where all sense had been lost.

Although I had tried to shove the big ta-wa building into the backyard of my mind, it had never really gone there, and when I saw it again, lying there in the half-light, I felt caught up in something large and intoxicating. The big ta-wa building was real and alive, bigger and more impressive than I remembered. An awakened surge I hadn't felt in weeks bolted through me, signalling a new adventure pulsing through my bloodstream. A strange wind filled my hair. I looked at my two companions as we walked to the entrance and it felt good to be caught up in this drama with others. I didn't see our shadows on the pavement and I wondered if it was true that in the dark of the night, we become our shadows.

We found the door locked and for an instant I was glad of that. My feet were getting cold. Some form of humanity, or what I hoped was humanity, was inside, however; we felt and heard it leaking out. I knew I had to go inside because as a wandering sightseer of this world I had paid my admission at birth and had long since given up my card to live by the rules. There's no need to live normally. We can chase our whims, however misguided they may be, and venture out into the amusement and mystery of the world. We're allowed.

Music that sounded as if it came from a giant tin can crawled out of the crack under the door, music for adrenaline junkies who aren't fussy about how it sounds. Deep voices and screams dominated the clamor escaping from the place and I considered turning on my quasi-high heels to run back to a safe place that would give me a peaceful easy feeling. Stella wouldn't hear of it, being from Germany and not a child of the seventies. Stella was steel wool ready to scour. At the bottom of Stella's long and bronzed muscular legs grew two significant feet sturdily wrapped in tough German sandals of unabashed comfort which she employed to kick the door. They worked well, those German sandals, because a big man opened the door immediately, a man bearing scars and tattoos. I remembered him by his feeble attempt to corral his thinning hair into a ponytail. We sat down at the bar. It was dark.

I wasn't surprised at the identity of our bartender that evening. Who else could it have been but the Devil? For half a second, his smile even looked almost authentic. Stella took him up on his offer of free drinks—she didn't know where he came from. "Hot today, no?" She commenced her chit-chatting repertoire learned the night before at her new job.

"You think this hot? Much hotter where I live." The Devil didn't really say that, but he should have. He wasn't quick enough. Instead, he just smiled, or pretended to. This is a secret: the Devil isn't that bright. But neither, apparently, was Stella. The Devil was chatting her up and she was going along with it.

Belinda nudged me. "Laur, we've got to do something. This is dreadful, this place. Why are we here? This is disgusting. This is sick and wrong."

Belinda was right. Stella was throwing back booze. Frightening people glared at us. I looked around the room and for the first time since I started working in the nightclub, the tame nightclub, I felt truly nauseated at the idea of women wooing and pampering men for money, however ancient the dynamic might be. "Shouldn't we have gone beyond this by now? How is this still happening in the late twentieth century and why are we a part of it?" I had to yell. It was loud in there. Belinda gave me a blank stare. This was no time for philosophizing.

By now, the Devil had joined Stella on our side of the bar and the two of them were playing drinking games.

"Back home, I all the time vin the games for drinking." I thought I heard some slurring in there but I couldn't be sure. Stella banged her empty glass down on the counter for another round.

Something had to be done. Things had gone too far already.

It occurred to me that I had been in a situation like this before, in another part of the underworld lit by similar dark ruby lights. A place I wanted to escape. Morocco perhaps. I wondered if there exists out there in space some sort of giant cosmic silly-putty that duplicates our awful comic ways, again and again, through the folds of time.

I still wasn't thinking clearly.

Belinda, on the other hand, apparently was, because she dumped a glass of beer on the lap of the Devil. I was impressed. And inspired. I called him a snake. That's when Stella began to laugh uncontrollably. She's under his control, his evil command, I thought. Or she's piss drunk.

"Why you do that?" demanded the Devil. "Why you hate me?"

We didn't answer. We didn't have to. A tiny woman with sparks in her eyes had arranged her body that evening to fit into a zippered vinyl contraption that set her legs free at the thighs where they could do as they pleased until they reached a pair of child-sized red spiked heels jailing her little feet. She and her outfit stormed over to us at the bar, where she flung her drink in the Devil's face. Belinda must have inspired her. The Devil's head shot back and his face dripped like melting plastic. When the tiny woman saw what she had done, she laughed along with Stella. What came out of her was more of a cackle than a laugh, which surprised me, from such a pretty little thing, possibly a mere teenager. Other women laughed also. I wondered who the Devil was. Then the music stopped.

All eyes in the room, eyes of young women, set their gaze

on us. Just moments earlier their eyes had been aloof and flooded with an apathy that knew certain experiences had isolated them from other women in the world and there was no going back to simpler times. But now these same eyes seemed to flare up, come alive with mirth and rage and youth. The Devil didn't like it. He squirmed on his bar stool.

Everything went dark after that. Someone must have killed the lights. But it didn't matter just then about the darkness, because the light I had seen in a few of the women's eyes had been overwhelming, something I needed to see. Like a camera flash, the image had impressed itself on my brain in one shining instant of intensity. I saw that life burns like fire inside these seemingly captive women and I knew they wouldn't allow the Devil their souls.

The room was dark, though, and in darkness we forget that light slants golden and cuts through fog and our hearts every morning. We forget all manner of lightness. That's how a gathering panic filled the room that night. I heard glass shattering, shouts and cries in different languages, heckling laughs. Heat seemed to rise from the floor where shards of glass lay.

"Let's get out of here," I said.

Nobody answered me.

In the blackness I made my way through the swarm of soft bodies and scent of cheap perfumes. Where had Stella and Belinda gone? I couldn't get a grasp on what was happening. The big ta-wa building was in the grip of madness, or was it always like this? It sounded as if people were throwing things, but others were laughing hysterically. Had we incited a riot? I found myself laughing inwardly for following the strange path that led me this way. But now I wanted out. I wanted my old life back. If only I could find a crack of light to escape through, I thought, then everything would be all right. But no cracks could I find. I reached out in front of me and touched skin, skin of someone who said something in an unfamiliar language, and her voice was shrill and fraught with angst. Where were my friends? Would I ever get out? What could I do?

I did the first thing that came to me, the only thing to do in a situation like that. I chanted Hare Krishna until the cows came home. Would it ward off the Devil? Would it have me committed? Would it make Margaret proud?

Krishna's powers must have finally come through for me because I suddenly found the exit door. I found Stella and Belinda too. And the Devil. They were all outside talking. Chatting, to be precise. Stella was throwing her brand of radical feminism at him and she didn't appear the least bit intoxicated. The Devil seemed to be taking it quite well. Although I was relieved to be back out into the freedom of the soft night air and a rising vanilla moon, I felt a little disappointed. How anticlimactic. I had wanted to find Stella in one of those rooms from beyond with a whip in her hand, beating the Devil silly while he cowered on his haunches and apologized for the nuisance he had been making of himself. The thought struck me that he might not be the Devil after all, but a bored man of meagre inspiration and a lousy sense of ethics. This was only a fleeting thought, however. I'm not religious but I know the Devil when I see him.

I decided to leave Penang. I said good-bye to the friends I had met throughout the city, in the market and restaurants, at the nightclub, the English language school and the Hare Krishna temple. Margaret was the last person I saw as I left the temple in the fading dusk with my backpack. She was on her way home from a day of soliciting money on a street corner and she smiled when she said good-bye. It was the first time I had seen her smile since we met. Perhaps she was happy to see me go. Or perhaps we had touched each other's lives in a way I hadn't realized.

Wanderers of the world often sweep through one another's lives and many collide. But as time passes we become familiar with the others' strange ways and notice the outer differences less and less. After layers of the heart are peeled back, none of us is really that different from anyone else.

"Hare Krishna," she called out when I walked up the road.

"Hare Krishna," I called back.

Krishna lay down and died in my head that day. He's never tried to make a comeback.

Just in time, I made it to the night ferry for the mainland. He was there at the ferry dock, of course, letting loose his smile of slime. Whether he was waiting for me or waiting for new prey, I couldn't say. A cold shudder rippled up my back as I watched him while we pulled up anchor. But I was safely away from him. I had money and my ticket for Fiji. I had Fiji in the palm of my hand and the Devil could never find such an out-of-the-way place.

Out into the velvet darkness I sailed away to disappear into a thick slice of midnight. Does the Devil have night vision? Not if you stay in the shadows.

CHAPTER ELEVEN

Stories are interlaced like reeds in a woven mat. They co-exist, become entwined in time and space. All journeys occur simultaneously and sometimes we can sense this, like looking through a peephole, or by a trick of light.

What do the stars leave in their wake when they sail through the night? An echo? Or something more, perhaps—an invisible string linking events and people together. Is this how messages are carried across the sky, from one land to the next?

SINCE TELLING THOSE STORIES with Genevieve the other night, I've been haunted. In the tent last night I woke up beside Laudi with the cold night sweats, the wrong-man sweats. I've felt this way before. I consider the man I'm with and wonder who he really is. I always vow to leave the situation as soon as I can, go back to my pure and free heart. I think, How could I have led myself this way, this far, for this long? In the days here I'm fine, happy, sometimes even ecstatic. My life is rich and full of treasures, with sunsets and the sea, strange and intriguing people, the stars and a thousand songs. Only on the rare night do I panic this way, when all is quiet except the waves of time pounding ashore. It's all right, I think, I'm young, but the waves keep pounding.

My mind was unsettled as I lay there in the tent so I left and walked along the beach. There was no hope of finding the Southern Cross last night. A big fat coconut moon was floating across the sky, scaring away the stars. So bright and powerful was the moon's light, only darkness surrounded it. A giant circle of darkness. Yet I knew somewhere beyond all that darkness around the moon, the stars danced, in hiding, as vibrant as ever and waiting to shine again.

For some reason that gave me peace and I could sleep after that.

I've been wandering through an unfamiliar enchanted haze today, feeling misplaced, lost, not only on this island but in the world itself. This world has become so strange to me that I could almost be afraid of it. And yet, I can't help going further, deeper, and losing myself in it just a little more.

I don't know what's happening to me. I don't feel young and carefree anymore, not today. I once wanted the world but now the world is too much to have. I have to find the way back to my old self. She must still exist, buried under too many journeys. If I stop and look closely inside, I see the way back is clear. I know I can no longer linger near what is dark and what isn't good for me merely because it's exciting, or a challenge to my sense of adventure, my sense of the extreme. My heart isn't something with which to wager and play lightly. My heart has become too fragile for such folly. Maybe I shouldn't have told Genevieve my story about meeting the Devil. Look what telling the story has done to me.

Every week I say good-bye to my friends at the campground entrance. We hug and exchange addresses, tell each other we'll write and never forget this place, nor each other. I watch them walk down the road towards the little airport, or the other way, to the boat. New people show up to replace them; we talk and laugh, tell stories and exchange addresses. Then they leave too. I stay. Genevieve left yesterday. She's looking for a boat to work on to sail to North America. I miss her. Before she left, she doubled me on the back of her bike all the way to the shop. The Giant Aunts came down to watch us on the road and I've never seen them laugh so hard.

I've discovered something about the Giant Aunts. Underneath their coconut fat is a layer of compassion, or possibly the compassion is rolled into the flesh itself. They want what is best for their families. They follow the straight and tried paths they know, have always known, the paths they learned from their mothers, their aunts and grand-mothers. These paths are safe, because their flesh must also be protection, insulation from life's harsher realities. A soft warmth against the weight of the world.

I'm at loose ends. School is on break. I've read every book on the island. No new campers have shown up since Genevieve left, except for an antisocial couple from Switzerland who haven't even said hello. The beach is empty. Even Laudi and his cousins and uncles left today and won't be back until tonight. They're off to another island that's three hours away by motorboat, to some sort of turtle ceremony for men only.

This is what I always crave here: a chance to be alone. But now that I'm finally alone, I forget what to do.

I walk along the beach, pick up shells, and look out at the sea, trying to remember what lies on the other side, that other world where people move faster, think harder, where they drink cappuccino, eat lunches from delis, and absorb the daily world news—what they call keeping abreast of things. But that's just one world in a sea of millions.

How can I continue to stay in this island world? I can't. I can't because I finally understand why it's impossible for me to stay forever: geography. I feel a tremor, an upheaval, a shifting, not of land, but of something much deeper. It's a shifting in me, a tremor that says I can no longer ignore things that go on here, the deception that follows every footstep, the half-heard whispers, the doctrine of mass conformity, the terrible misunderstanding between the sexes, all the things I know I could never permanently endure. For its beauty alone I could almost stay forever, for the road and the sky and the sea. For the curvature of land.

But geography of the interior is more important to explore. I've explored it.

The sky and sea feel heavy today, thick with heat that presses down like a human hand, massive and cruel. The sun is knifing into my skin. My skin was never meant to endure the tropical sun. It was meant for the low-lying misty grey clouds of the Scottish Highlands. I close my eyes against the relentless hundred-degree temperature and imagine myself standing for five minutes in the silence of the snow-laden woods of northern Ontario, standing by the cabin I once lived in with its wood stove, its rustic grace. I know it would be cool but not cold there now, with the last of the winter snow crunching under my feet, the creaking of the young maples in the wind. It would be midnight. The snow would flash diamonds like a crystal palace from the moonlight streaming through the trees. Just to be there when I opened my eyes, just for five minutes.

My backpack sits in the tent corner waiting to be packed full again, waiting to leave, to be swung up aboard a boat, thrown on top of a train rack, waiting to move on, as it always has moved on in the past. For surely this must be the season of leaving. In this land of no seasons, what is there to mark the passage of time? A decade could go by and be called one hell of a long hot summer.

I need a swim.

I don't go for one of my marathon swims way out there,

although I'd love to. I stopped that long ago after they told me to stop. The water feels far warmer than usual. Strange, it doesn't even cool me, even when I dive deeply into it. When I do my tumbling succession of back flips in the water I can't see anything but blackness, so I swim back to shore as fast as I can. The afternoon sun filters in, ghostly and faded, through a filmy floating heat, and casts a strange haze on the beach, one I've never noticed here before. The trees stir as if a storm were coming, although there is no wind and no clouds. I turn to watch the waves smash the light out of the ocean as they arch and curl into the end of the day. The ocean's deep black heart rises up like a shy sea monster unacquainted with the world above. I usually see this blackness only from high up on the road, and never at this time of day. This is when the sea is usually pink from the sun, when I'm awash in a pink glow from the sun setting over the sea.

L A T E R

I must have been asleep for hours. I hear thunder, or maybe a crashing. It must be the throbbing of the sea. It crashed into my dreams. It's dark. A wind of unsound mind is forcing the walls of my tent to cave in. Where are Laudi and his cousins? Surely they must be back by now. Where is everybody?

I leave the tent, walk out to the shore. In all my time here I've never seen waves like these. They're like the waves in Hawaii: heaving, dangerous, violent. Rain is sweeping across the ocean, on its way here. Everything looks different.

I run along the beach that should be familiar to me, a beach filled with stories, songs, stars, and the history of ten thousand waves. I run all the way to the Beached Whales. On top of the largest whale rock, looking at the sea, I stand on the edge of two worlds. The waves splash up on my legs with surprising force, almost enough to knock me down. How tempting is this navy-colored sea, drenched in passion, begging to be plunged into. As I stand here, a different kind of wind seems to break against the night, a wind uncaged from a secret source. This wind has been around since the beginning. This is the wind that blew the earth into being. It puffed the first breath of life into the first animals. It forced intricacies of extraordinary subtlety: dancing light on water, the golden swaying of wheat in a field, clouds that swirl into creatures showing the world that we too can change and be moved by dreams that sweep through us. This wind crushed hearts into one another, when those same hearts once stood alone. It blew each of us to where we stand now. Tonight this wind will slit a chasm between beauty and fear.

I love to be dramatic. If we breathe life into the elements, they return the favor tenfold. This is a big wind.

I walk back along the shore into the woods and it feels as if I'm walking through the ruins of an ancient city that's trying to come alive again. Shadows of rubble gather, move across the sand and then disappear. The light of the moon, full tonight, is obscured behind clouds that are rampaging across the sky. Frantic air pervades the beach; it's eerie and unfamiliar. Trees are moaning, writhing, twisting, cracking. Bushes whisper at me. And the sea. The sea is pounding so loudly it's frightening. It's shouting, *I need to roar. I've been waiting far too long to roar like this.* In my mouth I taste salt that the sea is spewing ashore. Branches of the biggest trees whip down, almost touching the ground, and then fly back up just as quickly, as if they too have been waiting a long time for this.

When the moon hides behind dense fuming clouds, it gets very dark, and the darker it gets, this beach, which I thought to be so familiar, and these formations of driftwood and rock, become stranger and stranger.

I can't pretend any longer. This is a storm, the kind of storm I normally love, thrive on, the kind that charges the air with something completely new, that shakes the world awake. But tonight is different. This storm is vengeful, full of hate, reducing me to a flimsy leaf carried away by the wind. This storm doesn't want me here. I want to run inside it, feel free and wild as the unfurling sea breaking on the shore, throwing up pebbles and debris. But I'm at the mercy of its weight. It's forcing down on me like a coffin's lid. Torrential rain is rocketing down from the black sky, smacking the sea, the beach and me on it. A little harder and the downpour would be stabbing through my skin, drowning my bones. And this wind. How vicious. The wind is flinging sand, boiling up the waves, thrusting them into the sky and charging them to shore. Soon it will be uprooting trees, the *bures*, carrying all of us away. I try to stand still and listen. Through the monstrous roar, I hear a kind of song coming out of the sea, something I heard the night I returned here. It's twenty times louder tonight. I want to shout into the storm, but I'm mute against this power and rage. All the secrets the ocean hides—its underworld of colossal darkness that neither sun nor moon can penetrate, its deep black heart buried far below the sun-lit surface—all these things and more are unleashing now: the overpowering stench of rotting fish, rockweed, brackish salt, deeply buried mud. Everything screams out in revolt. The whole soul of the sea is hurling out. It's infernal.

We don't know our way around down there because it's dark and frightening and new, although it's always been there...waiting.

The waves must be at least ten feet high now; crests of foam are vomiting seaweed. Water is everywhere, pouring out of the sky and pluming across the expanding ocean. The force of the water yearns to lift up the island and carry it away. Flashes of lightning over the sea reveal the panoramic chaos of the physical world, the elements in an ecstatic state of disarray. But where are Laudi and his cousins? Oh God, please, let them be safe, not out in their boat in this madness. Unbelievably, the Swiss couple's tent hasn't collapsed yet—must be Swiss-made. They're arguing in there. Black rain beats against my cheeks, streaming down from the sky as thick as blood. Still, I can't leave this storm. I'm swept into its very body, like a nightmare you can't shake because your eyelids feel glued shut. I can feel the storm's rumbling heart in my blood.

Amidst the fury, I think I hear something new: someone is shouting. I look down the shore and see a man standing with his feet in the water, facing the sea. With both arms stretching over his head, he looks as if he's waving violently at someone out there, but there is no one, couldn't be, and it's too dark to see far anyway. He's shouting something. And laughing.

Is Vix mad?

They say his body, when possessed, crawled with evil spirits. Some say they never crawled out.

What's he doing? Have I wandered into a bad movie? Something peculiar is coming out of his unsheathed and raspy voice. As I take shelter in the kitchen and try to see him out there, a terrible understanding comes to me: he loves the storm. It shares his black heart, caring not at all for the ruin of human lives.

I don't want him to see me here. God, that's the last thing I want. Everyone needs a hiding place at certain times in her life. A child always has a hiding place, a little fort, a dark closet, a space under a bed, a secret spot where she can wedge herself away from the world and its complications. A hiding place is instinctive. When the moon flees behind the clouds, my hiding place is the darkness, the velvet darkness.

I had Fiji in the palm of my hand and the Devil could never find such an out-of-the-way place.

He's not screaming at the sea anymore; he's staggering around the beach. He must be drunk. When the lightning flashes, I can see his haggard face as he walks up here, his hair plastered against it, moist with sweat and rain, clinging like dead seaweed. Repulsive. His eyes are bloodshot and filled with a filmy liquid. Don't look my way. Does the Devil have night vision? I must be as crazy as he is for being out here. Now he's close enough that I feel hot air from the storm moving deeply inside his body, disturbing my own breathing.

I stand motionless in the dark of the kitchen, fascinated and petrified, listening to him groan and laugh as the wind blows his body around the beach. He's shouting into the clapping thunder of the rain and sea. He's enjoying this because he *is* the storm. Tonight he's on speaking terms with his demons.

Where I come from, the dark unconscious is inside the body. In Fiji, it's outside, in the bushes, trees, rocks. It even hovers over some women, or so the men believe. Tonight it's in the storm.

One of the Giant Aunts, Aunt Sala, is calling me. I see the outline of her body moving along the sand. She's almost running. I see the whites of her eyes, wild and huge. Water drips from her hair onto her gleaming face.

"Laurie, come up! Why are you down here like this? Vaneesa told me you were here. Come away from this. Come up the hill with us."

"They're all dead, you know," Vix shouts at us from the beach. "Laudi, Adi, and all of them, all gone, drowned. They won't be back."

"Stop that!" shouts Aunt Sala. Vix is her brother-in-law and I've never heard her raise her voice to him before. She's furious.

Vix stumbles up to me, thrusts his face inches from mine. I see his blood-red eyes and smell his whiskey-laden breath. Vix beats a stick to the ground and laughs. "They're all dead, you know. Leave here. Go home. They're all dead."

As he says the words, as one by one they leave his mouth and coil inside me, he is transformed before us. Suddenly in his face in this jungled darkness by the roaring sea is an evil I've known before. Nobody speaks for a time. Then a thin line of sin slides across his face.

My blood changes its tidal pull. All reason ends here…

My senses must be drenched and deranged. This can't be right. This can't be right at all because I hear these words drip quietly from Vix's mouth: *Big ta-wa building.* And this: *Move.*

Get a grip on yourself, Laurie. This is absurd. Ludicrous. My mind and the storm and my too many months on the road, all are colliding, confused, trapped in this crazy night's fractured darkness. Why would he say that?

A tremendous "NO!" rises up inside me but doesn't escape. The truth is I'm terrified of this man.

"Come up the hill," calls Aunt Sala. "He's been drinking all day. Don't listen to him. Laudi will be fine. They'll be back tomorrow. Come up the hill."

"Yes, leave here. Leave my campground. This is my place, my place." Again, Vix smashes the stick on the sand.

"You can't stay here. It's my place, all for me. They'll try and take it away from me. Tomorrow. Tomorrow they'll try. It's my place."

Okay, so he's not the sharpest knife in the drawer, I think to myself.

I look deeply into his face—something I don't often do—and notice the skin under his eyes hanging in dark, tired folds. Once more he says it, this time in a near-whisper: "It's my place."

Suddenly I feel as if I've intruded on something shameful, a family secret, something I'm not supposed to see. This is no longer scary. The Giant Aunt takes my arm to go. Vix stares almost pleadingly, as if he has somehow gauged the degree to which his beating the stick to the ground like a child has stirred me.

It's my place, whispered.

Back In My Tent

The storm has quieted. I've just been up the hill with the women for the past two hours, talking about the storm and Vix and the men who left this morning in their boat. The women fed me and I ate everything they piled on my plate. Vix has passed out at his house. We're all worried to death about the men. But what can we do?

In my fragile tent I hold my breath, listen for the sounds that rise above the wind and patter of rain, the hushed throbbing of the sea. I have a northern, winter body unsure of tropical rhythms. Even here, January flashes through my chest, making me roll over and shiver and pray for the darkness to end.

I can't sleep. The sea is slicing into my veins. At a time like this, the soul must hang there in the night sky with the stars, waiting. Oh God, please, let all of them be safe. I drift off for seconds at a time and wake up in starts, believing or half-dreaming that they've returned, that I hear Laudi's voice. Then the face of the Devil invades my thoughts, appearing unsummoned when I shut my eyes. And I thought I had laid his face to rest. Certain horrors never leave us, no matter how hard we try to rip them from our hearts.

I think I finally sleep for a while, but wake up to a stream of light glowing on my tent. When I look out the flap I see her, not Vaneesa, but the moon. She's been here all along behind the storm like something very brave and ancient and only just remembered.

The next story I've told no one until now, no campers here on the beach, no travelers, nor friends. Only the moon. Because I've come to realize the moon possesses an alarming sensitivity to all aspects of humanity.

HEIDI ON THE EDGE

Sometimes the most dreadful things happen in the most beautiful places. It's always a shock. We wonder how things could possibly go wrong amidst such godly splendor, in the incorruptible air of mountain nirvanas innocent of the fallen cities below. Later, we may realize what seemed dreadful was beautiful after all and lived up to the glory of its earthly domain because the grace of the earth itself swooped down to remind us we are not separate, like orphaned children, but a melody in this grace carrying the earth's strength inside us. Then we can walk on, protected with this primal knowledge, to face any darkness on our way.

I WAS TRAVELING NORTH through Italy after two months of swimming in waves, waitressing in tavernas, and reading books in the shade while camped on the Greek island of Naxos. At twenty-three years old, one is allowed to do that kind of thing.

Even in temperate northern Italy, I was still hot. Greek

heat, like halcyon days spent in that country, lingers deep inside of you, and I craved cool alpine breezes on my skin. Since I'm a redhead, I wilt readily.

I found myself studying a map of the Italian-Swiss Alps one morning while I sat on a bench next to Lake Como, using my stored Greek heat to melt the dark Swiss chocolate in my mouth. I hoped to eat snow later that day. As for getting up to those chilly mountains, I didn't yet have a plan.

So I was happy at first, when they came along. After only ten minutes on the bench two men in hiking boots asked to check my map for trails into the mountains. My plan had just walked up to me on four tanned and muscular northern-Italian legs. Good timing. Nice legs.

"*Ciao,*" I said to them, which pretty well covered the extent of my Italian. They both squinted their eyes in a confused kind of way as if I had just asked them to explain Fellini symbolism to me. I tried my French instead. "*Bonjour, comment ça va?*" They laughed and let loose a watershed of lexicon from one of those Romance languages. I was fairly sure it wasn't French because I didn't understand a single word of it and I *do* come from Canada. I smiled back as if I understood them completely and pointed at myself. "Laurie."

"La…urie, ah *si,* Laurie." Good, they got that.

The especially good-looking one had a Renaissance grandeur to him, with a strong and tall natural body, wavy brown hair like suede and blue-green eyes that looked ocean-fed. If he'd struck a pose of passive contemplation while someone drenched him in a bucket of white paint he could have auctioned himself off as a Michelangelo statue. He pointed at himself and said, "Chico…Chico."

Then his friend smiled, pointed at himself in exact imitation and said, "Chico…Chico."

Either they were both named Chico or the second one was really stupid.

It didn't matter much. Somehow we communicated that we all wanted to hike in the mountains that day. I discovered they were Italian but spoke a little French and a little English—and when that didn't work I spoke broken Spanish to them, which sounds rather Italian. It was good enough for me—they had a car.

Before setting off into the mountains, we stopped at a restaurant for cappuccino. I drank lots of the stuff because I figured I'd need all that caffeine to shoot itself through my leg muscles to keep pace with the Chicos. I could see they were born for the sole purpose of climbing mountains.

Then a strange thing happened. The second Chico stood up to go, leaving me and the Chico-Adonis face to face, alone. Things in the air changed then, unspoken things, things not part of any language. I wondered what to do next.

The atmosphere among the three of us had been light-hearted with the kind of laughter that accompanies foreigners who understand nothing of each other. The idea of the three of us hiking together had held a serendipitous, spontaneous bravado to it. This would be a casual jaunt, capricious, harmless. I felt this even with the language barrier, a barrier that prevented us from learning detailed, possibly mundane facts about each other's lives but didn't obstruct an unspoken camaraderie. I felt like a player in a trio of wandering misfits wondering what to do on a sunny day. With Chico #2 so quickly gone, I was at a loss. And Chico #1 across the table from me was no longer a comrade, but a stranger.

I knew as I sat talking to him, watching his face over my coffee cup, that he was the most handsome man I'd ever seen up close. His eyes were blue and watery enough to swim in. He was rugged and strong with life and he laughed hard at my botched attempts to speak languages other than English. Those libido currents of electric intrigue that pass between strangers who find each other not quite believable quietly charged themselves with intensity. We liked what we saw in each other because we saw what we wanted to see. Projection is easy: just fill in the blank spaces with your hidden dreams.

Since I watched him closely I couldn't help noticing that something almost sinister would break out of his eyes—not very often but enough for me to catch—and his handsomeness would melt into a crude brutality of bones hiding under smooth skin. But I tried to pretend I hadn't seen any private darkness escaping from his eyes and deduced the glint was some Italian male testosterone condition. I wanted to go hiking.

"Laurie, you and me. We go up in the mountains today to a different place, visit my aunt and uncle. They live up high in the mountain village, small. Beautiful, very beautiful place like you can't believe. Not far. Quiet, only the river and cowbells make the noise. People, they like you in this place."

"And snow? Will we get into the snow?" He smiled and narrowed his eyes as if ascertaining whether snow meant a good or a bad thing to me. My expression betrayed me.

"Yes, a little snow, I think. Really beautiful. You make the picture with the camera."

His eyes were aqua then and sparkled like the waves I'd watched from the beach in Greece. Any darkness stowed away in those eyes drowned in lighter shades of blue virtue.

Still I was hesitant, of course. I'd been in the Mediterranean long enough to understand the warped single-mindedness of its men. Heck, I'd been on Planet Earth long enough. The Mediterranean doesn't hold a monopoly on sexism. But I also understood this: every so often one must wave off caution and be defiant of better judgment for the sanctity of adventure, for survival of the soul. Maybe that's a symptom of age twenty-three. Maybe a definition. In this case, my desire to go hiking into the mountains with a questionable Roman god exceeded my fear of danger. I've never been big on fear. Or danger. I knew this ascent to the unknown might not be good for me but I also knew I would do it. I hung on like a cantankerous fisherman holds on to his line in the belief that this would be an innocent escapade between new friends. Because I wanted to believe it, because gypsies dance and because I was twenty-three years old, people were good and life was whimsical.

So with a sudden impulse of recklessness and something not far from wild abandon, I said to Chico, *"Andiamo!"* hoping that meant "Let's hit the road" and didn't mean "Please play your music with more animation."

Chico had to make a few stops along the way before the hike. I waited in his car for a whole half-hour outside of what I assumed to be his house. He returned carrying a backpack full of goods that he said his aunt needed in the mountains. I imagined his aunt to be a sweet woman of doughy abundance who would kiss me on both cheeks the way Europeans tend to do, stuff me with copious amounts of pasta, then ask me two hundred and forty-six questions in Italian and not hold it against me that I could only nod and smile in return. Already I could taste the pasta and feel her vivacious amplitude press itself against my body. That's what I love about Italy: zest.

We drove towards Lugano and parked the car by a raging river at a place where tall pines obscured the sunlight. I left my backpack locked in Chico's car, thinking I wouldn't need anything out of it for the afternoon hike. As we slammed the car doors and walked towards the trailhead, awkwardly smiling at each other, a thought struck me: we all live in our own heads. This person and I hardly exist to each other. We're each a living embodiment of each other's imaginations based on our separate lives up until now. Who I am in his eyes may be based on an American television show he once watched. Likewise, the Chico in my head and this real Chico don't even know each other. I followed him up the rocky path, sincerely hoping he'd never caught an episode of *I Dream of Jeannie.*

The beauty of the place nearly knocked me over. The color green relieved every part of my being after the desert and arid sparseness of Greece. The trail followed alongside a stream which ran full and noisily, crowding out our voices. Not that Chico and I had much to say to each other. We mostly smiled a lot. The sun behaved the way I like it to, warming my skin without scorching; the cool breezes and I had found each other. The world was a happy place inside my head that afternoon.

We walked for a long time without stopping. Hours passed and the sun made its way down to the gentler place in the sky where it offers the world its pink subdued time of day. Ahead of us stood nothing but mountains—massive, grey and imposing. The trail gradually disappeared the higher we climbed, although Chico seemed to know exactly where we were going as we trudged through boulder fields, thick shrubs and, at times, the stream itself. I began to wonder when we'd arrive at the village. Remote and high as we were in the wild heart of this lone-wolf place, I began to wonder if there was a village.

Darkness fell and Chico's smiles had gone the way of the

trail and the sun. It was as if his layers of charm kept shedding the higher we climbed. We'd become strangers.

I was thirsty so I cupped my hands into the stream to drink. "Here," he said, "drink this." His manner was gruff and irritable as he handed me a canteen. I took a drink of what I discovered was red wine.

Eventually he stopped in front of me and I could see a flicker of light ahead of us although I couldn't make out what it was. He shouted something, a sharp call, as if someone he knew was near. Another man answered as a door slammed. "Come," Chico said to me. Anger belted through me at his orders, and because I could do nothing but obey.

We entered a little hovel of a home containing a wooden table in the center, a single chair, a tiny bed covered with a sparse grey wool blanket, and a wooden counter cluttered with dirty cooking things. The feeble light given off by the oil lamp on the table wasn't tempting enough for moths. An odor of recently fried fish barely made its escape out of an old pan to overrule the ranker, mustier smell of the cabin itself. An oldness hung about the place, an oldness depriving and aging even the place's inhabitant. I could see the old man living there couldn't fight it, wouldn't even try, and fate would have him bound to that shack long past the time when his body began to crumple in on itself, decay and freeze. Really, he and the shack were part of the same thing.

The old man never looked me in the eyes. I wasn't a person to him. He and Chico talked in Italian, clearly about me. At one point, Chico held up a piece of my hair to show the old man, as if I were a prize horse. Then the old man poured Chico a glass of red wine which Chico guzzled as we turned to go. Even though I hated the place, and the old man, I wanted to stay there rather than continue to walk further up into the night.

Another two hours must have passed and still we walked. The cooling breezes had given way to cold breezes and I wasn't dressed for their harshness. The caffeine had long since abandoned me and my body ached with exhaustion. Caffeine still lingering in my body wouldn't have made sense anyway because I was no longer that silly person who had gulped cupfuls of cappuccino with two handsome Italians that morning. She no longer existed.

I knew I couldn't just take off somewhere and hide from him because I'd be so cold, having left my clothes and sleeping bag in his car. I'd also be lost. How could I find my way back to his car the next day when we'd come so far in the dark and had left the trail so far behind? We'd crossed over and followed so many different streams that any one stream couldn't lead me back. I had to follow him.

The night wore on endlessly as if the world had decided forever to remain dark. I was on a treadmill walking upwards into a perpetual present, with no way of knowing how long or how far we'd continue like this.

Thankfully the moon rose. She lay back half-eaten in her rocking-chair position over the mountains so I no longer stumbled over rocks in the dark as I scrambled to keep pace with the monster. The moon's light reflected off tree leaves, boulders and water shimmering in the rapids. I slowed down to watch the moon glide through the pine trees as we walked. Chico yanked my arm and yelled at me: "Go more fast!" A peculiar dark look had come out of his chest through his eyes, which were no longer aqua but black. No moonlight reflected itself in those eyes and I knew Chico no longer existed either.

The curious thing was I couldn't quite believe any of it was happening to me so I wasn't particularly scared. We were in this beautiful place lit up by the moon, so far away from where anything truly bad could ever happen; it made no sense to me that everything wouldn't be all right in a place like this, and I wouldn't let it make sense. I walked faster but continued to watch for the moon.

At last we came to a clearing. I could smell food cooking and wood smoke, and not far off I heard the familiar hollow clanging of cowbells. Lights shone behind glass windows and I could make out a cabin in front of us. More than anything, the clatter of the cowbells came as the greatest relief. Again I experienced the feeling of being safe under the reign of what is natural and innocent in this world. Big, dumb Alpine cows made me think of Swiss cheese, Swiss chocolate, Heidi and all things wholesome, and I couldn't associate that with anything sinister.

I followed Chico into the cabin. This was no inhospitable decaying shack like the old man's, but a home well cared for. Almost everything was made of pine and the place had a Swiss Alps homey freshness to it. A woman was in there, stirring something in a large pot over a wood cookstove. I wondered what she would be cooking so late in the night. She wasn't an especially old woman but she barely looked up when Chico and I arrived, as if she'd lived too many years already and life held little further interest. Her husband came in from outside and pulled back two chairs, motioning us to sit down. Although he didn't smile, it was the first act of kindness shown towards me since what felt like a distant forgotten time. I was conscious of being human again.

The woman served hot tomato vegetable soup which I devoured while the three of them sat at the far end of the table from me and spoke Italian. Again they looked me over as if all that existed of me was my extremities—my red hair, my skin, my legs and arms. My secret was that these things weren't really me at all. Somehow, I knew that in this also lay my protection.

Finally the husband spoke to me. "You Chico's wife," he said flatly, accusingly.

"No," I answered, although I don't think it had been a question. I looked to the woman for help, for some sort of universal motherly warmth, for understanding. I found none of these things. She seemed to hate me as much as the two men did.

Well, gee, thanks for the soup. Delicious. I'll be toddling off now. I'll visit again someday when another lowlife scum-sucking dirt-bag excuse for a man asks me to go on a little afternoon hike with him. Nice meeting you all. Ta ta.

If only.

The three of them didn't seem to know how to take me. Their discussion in Italian continued, even got a little heated, but they never took their eyes off me as they spoke. They didn't have to make it so obvious. Very impolite, I thought. I suspected they weren't discussing the possible ramifications of German reunification but at least they could have pretended.

I hate being excluded. This was worse than being chosen last for baseball teams. I tried staring back at them, quizzically, so they might know how it feels to be a freak on a stage or a caged animal.

Then Chico stood up. "Come."

"Where?"

"Come."

The husband walked to the door and held it open for us, stone-faced, gesturing with a sweeping motion of his arm for us to get lost. This mountain village hospitality was overwhelming. And he was my favorite of the three.

Back out in the cold night I gazed up into the sky, jealous of and dazzled by the stars I saw so distant, oblivious to the Italian Alps. I found it incredible they'd still be up there. My world was falling away, a different place entirely from what it had been that morning, and still the Big Dipper dipped along the same as ever. I had to stay strong, keep myself intact. But this was becoming difficult. Never had I been so thoroughly spent, so drained of myself.

We didn't have to walk far before reaching another cabin. This one felt empty and cold inside. Chico lit an oil lamp and started to make a fire in the wood stove. I could see a series of bunk beds, stern little hard cots covered tightly in grey wool blankets of the type I'd seen at the old man's shack. Why hadn't I demanded to stay there? Could I have? The limits, the rules, in this bizarre game weren't clear.

The sight of the tiny beds came as a relief, austere as they were; they were single. I didn't know what was happening inside Chico's head but I was so completely ready to drop, only deep sleep mattered to me. With determination, his presence could be blocked out of my awareness. A numbness throughout every part of me had frozen any lingering fear and anger. Only a vague tiredness in my leg muscles remained to faintly remind me I still existed.

I collapsed on top of the nearest bottom bunk bed, too weary to try to figure out what "good night" could be in Italian. I didn't care. I couldn't even summon the effort to take off my shoes. On top of the hard cot, I tried to pretend this was normal, not a moment to become unhinged. Everything would be fine. After making the fire, he'd fall onto his own cot and in mutual exhaustion we'd both become unconscious, slip away back into our own safe and separate worlds. I shut my eyes against the weightiness and confusion of it all. The next morning I'd get away on my own. I'd get away and reclaim myself.

The fire's warmth steadily took over the place. Chico blew out the oil lamp. My body clenched itself into an adrenaline factory of nerves as I listened in the quiet for every rustle. First his voice, angry and hard, came out of the darkness—Italian, talking to himself. Then the careless and noisy throwing off of his clothes—the heavy leather boots, kicked off in different directions, the wool coat dropping to the floor, the zipper of his jeans unzipping too close to my ears. "Move." It was almost a shout but not quite and I didn't move.

"Move," he said again. On my back, I rolled my knees up to my chest to kick. I knew he was strong with life but so am I.

So began a fight of wills that continued far too long into a night that insisted on perpetuating itself. For the first time we faced each other as the people we were. I called up every part of myself that I thought had deserted me that day. He won in the end, his body stronger than my will. A feeble winning. I didn't have anything left in me to fight with; nothing remained for him to conquer.

When it was finally over I lay on the cot staring up into the blackness with an anger inside me like I'd never known. Sleep no longer offered itself as a temporary rescue. I needed to get his car keys out of the pocket of his jeans so I could try to find my way down the mountain at the first light, get my backpack out of his car and get away, north to Switzerland. I groped around in the dark as silently as possible, only to discover his jeans were under his head, being used as a pillow. Too empty to cry and too defeated to move, I let sleep take me away from there.

The next morning I realized Chico had no intention of going back down the mountain. Not that day or any day soon to come. He had enough supplies in his backpack to last us a long time. Us. Somehow, he had the idea that he and I would stay up there together, that we'd be like husband and wife. Somehow, I would submit to this.

I'd heard of things like this happening before, maybe in the Middle Ages, maybe in the white slave trade. But not now, not to me.

If anything, Chico's demon charm had grown even more unbearable. His hatred for me seemed as entrenched as mine for him. So deep ran my loathing, I couldn't look him in the eye, nor would he look at me. Rather than try to understand it, I concentrated on getting away. Outside in the bright morning I gazed around at the snow-peaked mountains on all sides of me and knew I had no idea how to find my way back down. Somehow, the previous night's dark madness had displaced me into a snowy medieval kingdom not part of this world.

I started walking. The husband and wife who had fed me the soup in disdain would be of no help, but surely others would. A few more cabins were close by; I could smell the wood smoke. Maybe somebody could give me a map, or at least point me in the right direction. I came across an old man chopping wood in front of his house. I smiled, said "*Ciao*," but he grunted at me and continued with his chopping. What was wrong with these people? Another elderly couple tending to their goats proved to be equally enchanting. Was the word *whore* written across my forehead? Had the darkness inside Chico passed itself on to me? Had they never read *How to Win Friends and Be Kind to Strangers*?

I'd have to do this on my own. I walked along beside the stream through the valley, leaving behind the village and the cowbells in the distance. I couldn't see any way out of this. I wondered how I could have been so stupid as to get myself into such a situation. What could I have been thinking? The thought occurred to me that what is safe and nice and known in this world has never been enough for me. I always have to tread too closely to that line beyond which nothing makes sense anymore and nothing is known absolutely. I live for that line; that line gives my life substance. I have to push it out to a further edge, to the brink of myself. This time I'd pushed it too far.

I sat down on a big rock by the edge of the stream. The sun had just reached high enough in the sky to topple over the closest mountain and pour its warmth and light onto me and the rock. Nothing but excruciating beauty surrounded me. Beside cold gushing water I sat in a green mountain valley out of a picture book. Clusters of edelweiss next to my rock stretched out along a mossy green patch to the foot of mountains dripping melted snow. Just as quietly, overhead, white-feathered birds soared. Never had I been part of such a heaven. Never had I found myself in such a hell.

I didn't know what to do. Tears kept welling up in my eyes, blurring my view of the stream. It seemed I had few options. None, in fact. I'd reached a void, an alarming impasse of hope. This ordeal had eased itself upon me too calmly and I could almost have been lost in its lull, like one surrenders before drowning. The water suddenly feels good, they say, welcoming, no longer a force to fight. Just slip into the gap of passivity. Silent resignation and never heard from again.

That's when the magnitude, the majesty of the place began to overtake me. Hell could not exist amid such beauty. It wasn't welcome. This place was sacred, a watering hole for the gods, a life force. My tears stopped and a rush of happiness washed over me as if the sun, the mountains and the stream had consented to be a joint surrogate mother and assure me that everything would be all right; I was of their world. I took in their strength, as I had none left of my own.

I walked back towards the village, towards Chico. I found him chopping wood in front of the cabin. He didn't look up at me even though I stood squarely in front of the chopping block. I had my self back when I said, "Chico, I want us to go down the mountain now." He stopped chopping.

We stared into each other's eyes and saw the world: rage,

tumbling havoc, passion, shadowy understatements, and conviction. What a larger story these same oceanic eyes told than they had the morning before over my coffee cup. But he was human after all, responding to the earth's calling, and he nodded his head in resignation. "*Si,* we go down."

At the foot of the mountains that night I was too tired to set up my tent so I lay on top of it in my sleeping bag and watched the sky. I tried to figure out if Chico was another order of being altogether or just a man doing what some men do. Either way he was nothing to me now and barely existed anymore.

Still, I felt broken. Broken because a little of who I was before this happened had died. Broken because a little of the world's whimsy had died too. But then I saw a shooting star spread itself across the whole sky and I remembered the stream and the mountains and the moon and how they'd saved me, had been on my side. And I knew that nothing could ever shake my foundation or destroy me because whatever sublime wisdom lies behind the soul of the universe is also part of me. As I fell asleep, something I once read somewhere came back to me: There is always beauty at the moment when a ray from eternity strikes upon our gross natures. We should revere every illumination, every transfiguring terror. May God give each of us his criminal and his sin to awaken us. But there must be other, gentler kinds of illumination, out of which, from far purer terrors, a deed goes up like a star.

CHAPTER TWELVE

DAWN BREAKS OVER THE BODIES of the aunts. Stretched
out like stars on their backs in the water, they gaze up list-
lessly at a night that's finally dying, losing strength. All light
seems to have gone from their eyes. They're usually buoyant
and gleaming out there but not today. Today they're crushed
by a sea of hopelessness. For a weightless moment all of us
watching from the shore hang in suspension. Time ceases.
It's neither night nor day. Then, too quietly for words or
song, the world lightens, and a notion of pink sky laces itself
sensuously with soft clouds. Morning enters the world, but
enters in a kinder way with the aunts out there to receive it.

People have come down to the shore to watch for the
return of the men, but all eyes are fixed on the aunts. We
watch the aunts with a sense of awe bordering on idolatry,
mystic devotion, as if they are negotiating secret treaties with
the powers of earth, sea and sky, and if the arrangement of
their bodies on the water is in just the right formation,

aligned just so with the rising sun and stars, some divine key will unlock; the god of the underworld will open a gloriously rusted door that the men will enter through in their little boat.

We're all in this together. Each of us is deeply connected with the men out there, wherever they are. We stand waiting, not speaking, believing in our hearts they'll return any time now. We stand on the beach for a long time, looking for a change, any change at all, on the horizon. It's Kalisi who sees the change first.

"Look! I see them! Look!" She runs into the water waist-deep, soaking her *sulu* as she waves frantically at what looks to me like the sad smooth line of the sea. It's nothing, I think. I narrow my eyes, try to see what she sees. She's right. Something is out there, a little black dot. All of us run into the water for a closer look. We keep our eyes cemented on the little black dot so it doesn't disappear, as if by squinting and focusing hard enough we can break into the veiled cult of the sea. The dot gets bigger and we discern a thin line, a white crest of foam snaking behind the dot. A boat. We wait a little longer and see waving arms flying out of the vessel. We're not seeing a mirage. It's true. They're alive. Vix was wrong. Our world won't come crashing down. Waves of collective relief wash over us. We jump up and down in the water, flailing our arms, splashing and hugging each other, laughing and crying and laughing again for everything that has accumulated inside us over the past twelve hours. The men are alive and they're waving at us. We stop to catch our breath, then check again to see if we're seeing things right. We are. A ridiculously absurd understanding comes over me that, just for a moment, God is taking us backstage and giving us a sneak preview of something golden. I doubt I've ever been so moved. I'm not sure exactly what moves me most about it, whether it's Uma's face so completely prepared in its open tenderness for her husband Adi to greet her at the shore, or whether it's little Kura beside me whispering her papa's name with just the slightest expulsion of a desperate breath, or whether it's the sight of Laudi smiling at me among his cousins' and uncles' faces. Already I feel the crush of Laudi's wet salty skin against my own. A sudden and delicious fatigue surges through me from lack of sleep. Love, pleasantly mysterious, sweet and sure and thick as honey, swells up around us to fill the cracks the night left behind.

Laudi's face today is a study in contemplation. Perhaps this is what the faces of those who have brushed the belly of death look like. After the turtle ceremony, he and his cousins and two uncles left the island they were visiting to return to Taveuni in their boat before the storm began. "The sky looked darker than it should have for the time of day, but we thought it was just a rain shower coming. We were so wrong. The waves smashed us around and we thought that was it. We wouldn't make it back to the island, any island." But somehow they did. They found their way to an uninhabited island and spent the night out in the storm. Laudi has caught a chill, the Fijian version of a mild cold, but he's alive.

"I keep trying to imagine not being here, how easily that could have happened," he says as he examines his hands, turning them over and over, as we walk through the woods to the beach. "We were so close to never being in Taveuni again, never seeing any of you again. Look at my face, feel it. I'm alive, my hands too." He grabs my waist and we laugh until we fall down to the warm sand. We listen to the waves beating a rhythm that sounds sad, a rhythm of loss, a little slow and unsteady. The sun sinks through our skin. Everything smells new to the world, as if the earth has just woken from a long disturbing sleep and is yawning. The pungent smell of decayed fish wafts by, followed by the odor of an overripe fruit mingled with fresh jasmine. The jasmine sweeps sweetness into the air and our lungs. Nearby, a Giant Aunt is roasting sweet plantain over a fire. She's calling people to come eat. I'm trying to take all of this in as I lie on my back in the sand. I'm trying to feel the world. Laudi tickles my stomach without mercy—ruthless tickling is something Fijians do, perhaps in replacement of eating each other—and I laugh uncontrollably until my stomach aches. This is what being alive feels like.

A storm has passed inside me too. I can face anything now. I thank the creamy white love of the moon that blanketed me and the world to sleep last night.

★

Tonight the relatives are gathering for a big family meeting up the hill at Nana's house. They plan to discuss Papa's
will. Some sort of controversy seems to be brewing about
what Papa left each of his sons. Vix is at the center of this
controversy. Big surprise. He's at the center of all controversy
here. Laudi and Kalisi tell me he wants the whole campground for himself. The campground is supposed to be shared
equally amongst four sons, but Vix claims it is all his. They say
he wants to develop the beach, build a big resort with a
wealthy foreigner. The thought makes my blood curdle.

Laudi invites me up the hill to the meeting. My Fijian
still isn't good, but I usually understand the gist of things.
The meeting should be interesting.

"Come Laurie, come," says Aunt Uma as we enter the
house. I feel a gigantic friendly warmth radiating from her
body as I sit next to her in a circle of at least fifteen people
on the floor.

Earlier today, I asked Uma about the marble *bothi*
implants. After she finished laughing at me for five minutes,
her eyes grew to immense proportions, the way they do
when she speaks, and she told me yes, it was true. She herself, however, has never seen, nor experienced, the marbles.

"Then how can you be sure it's true?" I asked.

"You can't. You have to find out for yourself. That's how
life is."

Maybe I'll never know for sure about the marbles. On

this island, some mystery always seems to cut people loose from the truth.

It's like a steam bath in Nana's house after all the rain. In the center of the circle sits not a bowl of kava, but an oil lamp. Its flame is casting enormous shadows like grasping fingers across the walls and ceiling. Laudi ignores me the minute we arrive at the house and he sits with his male cousins. I'm so used to this segregation of the sexes I hardly notice it anymore. Most of the family is here: the uncles, Quiet Cousins, Giant Aunts, even some children. Vix sits across from Uma and me, staring sternly at the floor. This is the first I've seen of him since last night in the storm. This is the first he has seen of me. I wonder how much of last night he remembers. We've yet to make eye contact here tonight. Hopefully we won't have to.

When everyone is seated and quiet, Vaneesa walks in and gives a high-performance "*Bula*" to no one in particular. She's late; she likes to make a show of her appearances. I watch her eyeing the room, looking for someone to sit next to. None of the Giant Aunts is thrilled about Vaneesa; they're ignoring her and mumbling to each other. Bad sign. Vaneesa's face brightens when her eyes alight on me. She smiles. I smile back. She walks over and sits on the other side of me from Uma. Uma presses her knee into mine in one of those impossible-to-detect secret signals, reminding me of what we used to do as kids in school. Vaneesa puts her hand on my other knee and says, "Laurie, I haven't seen you forever," and immediately the scent of the ocean rushes out of her. I'm amazed at her hair. Her hair has grown fanatical. It seems to have grown halfway down her back since I last saw her. How could that be? It wasn't so long ago. As I look at her, I realize her hair is an intricate enchanted wilderness obeying no societal laws whatsoever. It's everything I wish Fiji were.

"Last night. You in the storm. Are you all right?" she asks. The tragic whisper of her hair brushes against my face when she comes close.

"Yeah, great. I'm fine. And you?"

"I'm out of here soon."

"Why?"

"Time to go." She doesn't elaborate. She likes to remain a mystery, which, tonight, is fine by me.

"Good thing the storm didn't kill us," laughs Uma's husband, Adi, when everyone is seated. "We don't have a will. Gotta have a will." He clears his throat in a way that makes me realize he knows the storm is nothing to joke about. People laugh nervously. An uncle from another island, one of the brothers, talks for the next half-hour in Fijian. From what I understand, the land Papa owned, which includes the campground, will be divided and shared equally among the entire family. Since Fijians live communally anyway, things will go on here as they have in the past. This is what everyone hoped for. Everyone seems to be breathing a heavy sigh of relief.

I feel tension in the air, however, as the Giant Aunts dart their eyes about the room. I look at Vix. His face is a funereal shade of grey. I can see his temples pulsing and eyelids bulging. He looks sardonic, miserable, and not as large as he usually seems. A sense of a collapsed aura surrounds him, as if he's broken on all levels. He's still staring at the floor.

"I'm the oldest son," he says slowly. "I take care of the campground. It's mine. I can do what I want with it."

Nobody says anything and I wonder why. I hate this non-confrontational dynamic that prevails here. From what I've seen, Laudi takes care of the campground, not Vix, and big deal if he is the oldest son. The room is silent. Nobody is challenging him. What are they waiting for? What are they afraid of? It isn't my place to interfere, but I have to do something. I look at everyone in the room. Most people's eyes are lost in the flame of the oil lamp on the floor. The tension is thick enough to hear. I whisper to Uma, "Tell him what you think. Why can't he share the campground?" She looks at me with her enormous eyes and I see in them what I've never seen in them before: fear. She says nothing, presses her knee deeper into mine. I turn to Vaneesa and whisper, "What's going on? How can he get away with this?" I know everyone in the room is watching us. I don't care.

"Vix, you little brainless fool. No way the campground all for you," blurts out Vaneesa.

Their faces drop like soufflés. Everyone's. I catch Laudi's eye. The look of love slides off his face. I'm in on this. It's obvious to Laudi and everyone else that I'm in on this. I've broken a sacred island rule. Vaneesa, too, has broken it. People aren't supposed to say what they think, or what they believe. Everything is supposed to be a polite and monstrous lie.

Vix finally speaks. "I want Laurie to leave Taveuni."

The weight of his remark staggers me. His words drop into the center of the room like a dead animal and lie there. Splat. This is ludicrous. Did a dreadful man just announce to everyone here that he wants me off this island? The silence in the room is heavy, hot, itchy. This is far too long and spacious a moment. I imagine being somewhere else in the world right now, a shopping mall perhaps, somewhere anonymous, anywhere but here.

"I love Laurie."

The three words are Uma's. They slip into the room as quiet as velvet but she may as well have screamed them. They're spoken in defiance of a culture. Her words set off inside me a wave of glorious appreciation, like a private, out-of-the-way miracle, a clear and rich insight into the beauty of people. I'll take her three words with me and keep them safe for my life. I press my knee back into Uma's and smile at her.

It's time for me to get out of here. I stand up and make a kind of bowing gesture to everyone in the circle that would probably go over better in Japan, and I walk out of the room, stepping carefully so as not to trip over a mat. The moon is rising above the treetops. I hear nothing, no sounds at all from inside the house. The night, too, is silent.

As I walk down the hill, I feel as if I'm in one of my bizarre dreams. Everything feels slightly off-kilter, foggy, like the night I arrived back here off the boat in the dark, months ago. What an extraordinary and incomprehensible world we live in, I think to myself. My head spins at the complexity of human existence. As a species we've racked up millions of years of evolution, have marathoned through the ages collecting countless ideologies, philosophies, space-age technologies, innumerable inventions to enhance our daily lives, advanced systems of communication and govern-ing, night school, voice mail, birthing classes, Italian ice cream, the Internet, forty-eight varieties of new tomatoes, toll-free hotlines, Gortex.... We've built vast civilizations, destroyed them and built others; we've created long-lasting beautiful things. We've studied and analyzed ourselves as a human race historically, biologically, culturally, psychologi-cally, spiritually, geographically, athletically. Dentally. We've stored a universe of knowledge in our collective uncon-scious. We've delved into the complex inner workings of our very souls, and in some countries, we've even perfected chocolate. Yet after all this, we're still cowering to the head gorilla. Still monkeys. Surely this is a primitive aberration, a systems failure, a perversity of our psyches. How long until we spit in the gorilla's face? How difficult could that be?

I hear footsteps of someone running behind me. Laudi?

Vaneesa? Uma? A voice calls out, "Laurie, Laurie, stop." The voice sounds like Laudi. I turn around to face him, but in the dark, I can't see who it is. When a fragment of moonlight hits the face, I see Vix, head gorilla, standing in front of me. I see his dark, staring, set-back eyes, the flesh on his face hanging in unhappy, neglected folds. How strange to find Vix standing here. Laudi's and Vix's voices sound identical. I never noticed before. Both voices carry the same gentle angelic lull, although in Vix's case, his voice is a cover. Soft voice, hard man. How deceptive, perplexing. I think back to the dark night on the beach when Laudi and Vaneesa were arguing and didn't know I was there, standing inches away from them. Could that have been Vix arguing with Vaneesa that night? Or that other time, much earlier, the first night I came to Taveuni, a year ago. The gentle voice that came out of the dark into the *bure*, the voice I had assumed was Laudi's—"Is someone here? Oh, it's okay. Good night."— and dissolved quietly away. Why hadn't Laudi ever mentioned that night before?

"I came to warn you that you should go home. You don't belong here," says Vix.

"You're right."

Astonishment leaps from his face. His eyebrows rise. His lips spread back to show his teeth. They're good teeth, strong and exceptionally white. His parted lips revealing the strong white teeth approximate a smile, but with Vix, this isn't a smile. However, it's something. This is the first element of light I've detected in his face, as if something lies there beyond hate. "Well, good-bye," he says as he walks toward his house.

When Vix leaves, the darkness takes only him away, not his shadow in the moonlight. That stays.

I walk down to the campground, a little unsteady, trying to shake all this off, trying to believe deeply in the moon, stars, love and goodness, and in singing Judy Garland songs.

ONE HOUR LATER,
WHEN THE MOON HANGS HIGH IN THE SKY
"How could you do that? How could you embarrass me like that?"

Laudi is furious at me. Never before have I heard him raise his voice to anyone. We're standing in the lantern-lit kitchen shack on the beach. I'm trying to boil water for tea on the little gas stove. This is the first time I've ever boiled water for tea in this country. I don't even like tea very much.

"Why is what I did so terrible? Do you really want him to ruin this campground, build a big resort? It's horrible."

"Of course it's horrible, but it's none of your business. You're an outsider."

I can't believe Laudi and I are arguing. We've never argued like this.

"I know, but why can't you say what you think? It's a family meeting, for God's sake."

Laudi doesn't answer. His face loses all expression. All I

see is a set of impassive eyes placed in a high-cheekboned casing of sun-baked skin. A gust of salty wind blows between us. He turns away and leaves me standing over a pot of steaming water. As I watch the back of his calves stride away and disappear into the dark, I feel the whole island drifting away underneath me. This is the culmination of all the months leading up to the final, inevitable separation between me and Taveuni.

My water still isn't boiling. Lousy stove.

"This place is brilliant," says a voice behind me. I turn around to see a man standing at the far end of the kitchen. He is a very tall, narrow man with a dark beard. He's wearing horn-rimmed glasses and his hands are dug into the pockets of his pants. He sounds English. I didn't know any campers were still here. He must have arrived by plane this morning. No boats would have come during the storm.

"When did you get here?" I ask.

"I've been here awhile. Marvelous people. I've taken a swim."

"A swim? Be careful of the sharks."

"Oh yes, the sharks, of course." He smiles and narrows his eyes, as if he knows it might not be true about the sharks. But how could he know that? He proceeds to tell me about his adventures on another Fijian island.

I can't put my finger on why, but this man is different from other travelers I've encountered. As he stands in half-light at the far end of the kitchen, I see he is a figure of unnatural composure, a person of some obscure and unknown derivation, perhaps visionary. I don't know why, exactly. He has a high thin voice, fragile, like a pale bamboo reed blown through by the breeze. Something unearthly about him should unnerve me. But he doesn't unnerve me. Things are falling into perspective as I listen to this stranger, this non-Fijian. A wave of relief sweeps over me. I'd forgotten; I'm a traveler, collecting and sharing impressions of the world. I feel suddenly expanded, inspired, as if I've come hurtling through the atmosphere and now have a greater understanding of people and their relationship to their world, how each of us moves through the world differently.

I can't begin to guess the man's age. He looks freshly cut for travel, anticipatory, also prepared to collect impressions of people and places. I see it in his eyes. His eyes expect great things to come.

"How long have you been here?" he asks.

"A long time. I've lost track, but I'm leaving. And you're right, this place is brilliant."

The stranger and I stay up for hours talking on the beach. He tells me he's on his way to New Zealand, Australia, and several countries in southeast Asia, a route I know well. We talk about these places until the moon drips golden into the ocean, and disappears. Talking about these places restores color to the night.

CHAPTER THIRTEEN

THE STRANGER HAS DISAPPEARED. He never did answer me when I asked where he was from, or even tell me his name. Some people like to stand outside the world of people and places. But I'm glad I met him. When we talked about traveling, faith in the Road, in people, even in Fiji, fell back into my soul. Charles Dickens wrote that one always begins to forgive a place when one is leaving it behind.

So this is it. I'm leaving it behind. I'm leaving a tropical garden island that smells good. Leaving this place is like waking slowly from a dream in the morning. The dream gradually fades as the waking world takes over. You can't quite remember the details, or remember why the place you dreamt of was so compelling. If only you could remember; if only you could grasp it and sink back inside. But trying to grasp the dream only sends it further away.

Am I crazy to walk away from this place, so close to paradise? The loss of paradise is enacted over and over again throughout history. Maybe paradise was never really here in the first place. Maybe it never was anywhere. I uproot myself from beauty, but what choice do I have? I know I don't belong on this island. I don't belong with Laudi either. If only Laudi had Vaneesa's vitality, and Uma's strength and wisdom, if only he and I could communicate better. But things have a habit of going their own way, and, as the crazy Irishman once yelled at me, "The world holds its breath for no one." He's right, of course. In my own small way, I upset the balance of life on this island by trying to change things, the balance Taveuni has set for itself over thousands of years.

I'm packing the memory of this place in my backpack, stuffing it full, with people's faces, cryptic hearts, and jungle gods all crammed in there together like a Twister game.

As I walk along the road that once felt like an earthly paradise under my feet, and now just feels like a road, mucky and long, I think about how often I've searched for paradise and never found it to lie in a place or a culture. Rather, paradise rests on the island of the human heart—in every place, in every culture, in a thousand ways. I think about people in this floating world who roll each other up in carpets, who clap and sing on buses, men who paint visions of the jungle and the moon, a man who rides his motorcycle around a continent just to get home, people who chant Hare Krishna in ecstasy, families who throw water at each other at funerals. I think of children who laugh and wave at buses in the desert, a girl who sings to sugar cane, people who dance and make music in gardens, women who float on the morning sea.

Into the blazing night sky I look up from the Taveuni road. I can't believe it. High above the branches of trees, clear as piercing winter light, falling on me like flakes of snow, there it finally flickers, the little kite, the Southern Cross. This is the first time I've found it on my own and I feel connected to it in a kindly way. The Southern Cross isn't a cross at all, like people want it to be. The Southern Cross creates its own pattern, and although small, it's so far away that it must be a fiercely tenacious constellation to shine through all that time in space, that distance of light years. "Pleased to finally meet you," I say to the stars. Under the glow of the Southern Cross, everything suddenly feels new, as if the world were just starting. Everything is right with the world, I think as I walk along the road. I'm more me than ever, just pure me.

They say if you believe the world is throbbing with wonder, then it is. They say in old stories that you can't discover new lands without losing sight of the shore for a long time. I say, if you believe in the wonder, you'll find your shore.

Stories are bigger than we know. Once unleashed, stories travel off on their own out into the world, even to the stars, joining the zillions of other stories told of life on earth over the ages. Stories don't simply vanish after we tell them or after we die. The totality of humanity's stories told from the very first campfire is imprinted deep inside each of us and continues to grow with every tale told. Everyone has a story. If stories aren't told, they're lost to the world forever. Each story is a crucial element in the mystery of life.

Who remembers what the stars left in their wake when they sailed through the night?

It's true. I've abandoned the ocean. I'm back in my safe and sterile, pine and maple, green terrain, landlocked, far away from the upside-down aquamarine world.

I see the place now when I close my eyes. Taveuni. I see a beach filled with preposterously large-leafed trees and wonder if those leaves really could have been that big. I see the kitchen shack and the place beside it where we told stories at night. I see the Giant Aunts, Kalisi, Vaneesa, the Quiet Cousins, Vix, Uma. I see the faces of the kids at the school.

One face, however, I cannot recall. Laudi's. No matter how hard I try to remember the contours of his face, the expressions, the way it collected and reflected the sunlight, his face doesn't come back to me. The photographs I have of Laudi don't seem right at all. I keep thinking if I could just smell the right combination of things again, smell the fish from the incoming tide at the same time as I smell wood smoke, passing jasmine, and coconut oil, a key in my brain would turn and I would see Laudi's face again.

As I look over the tattered pages of my journal, I return again to that strange island. But only for a few hours in my mind. This summer night at home in Canada is just as I dreamed it would be while I was away. Except I never noticed before that the sound of leaves rustling is different here from anywhere else in the world, or that the June breeze is a good temperature to put you to sleep at night.

All summer nights flow together, wading in and out of time into the stars, tropical and windless. I shake out the pages of my travel journal to gather up moments of my life. But moments may contain a lifetime and carry us into the next. All travels have secret destinations we only become aware of years later. I've been looking for a South Seas smell in these pages but instead I have found this: We must learn to be utterly ourselves, to follow our own deep dreams. We're disappointing powerful forces and ourselves if we ignore this calling. We live lies, half-truths, half-lives. Nature craves diversity, not conformity. This is how we move forward, expand with the universe, and how we find our way back home.

Life isn't a prelude to something bigger. There is no prelude. Just life itself, right here.

Life in progress. We're at its deep and solid core.

ACKNOWLEDGEMENTS

I OFFER MY DEEPEST THANKS to Joe Fisher for his friend-ship, advice and guidance; my mother, Tena Gough, for her encouragement and vigilant grammar inspections; my father, Patrick Gough, for getting me interested in traveling by telling me countless stories of his 1940s hitchhiking days; Peter Benner for showing me how to turn on a computer in a cold cabin; J.D. Shifflett, Stephan Johnson, Kevin Shortt, and Shazea Quraishi for their love and inspiration; I thank Manuela Dias and Patrick Gunter at Turnstone Press in Canada. To the wonderful people at *Travelers' Tales,* I thank you all, especially Larry Habegger, James O'Reilly, and Kathryn Heflin. Thank you to Marybeth Bond for her encouragement, and thank you to the travelers I met on the road: Ann Austin, Lawrence Jaffe, Gaylyn Aitken, Grant Knowles, Bennedict Storm, Patrick and Nancy Hiester. I thank Serena Rykert for her lovely mansion in the woods. And of course, thank you to the Fijians: Francis, Camba, Leigh, Dodo, Meme, the children, and the Quiet Cousins.